The Living God and the Modern World

Christian Theology Based on the
Thought of A. N. Whitehead

by Peter Hamilton

united church press • philadelphia • boston

To Geraldine

230.0924
H18L
93.536
June 1975

Published by the United Church Press
Philadelphia, Pennsylvania and
Boston, Massachusetts

Type set in Great Britain
Printed in the United States of America

The author wishes to thank the publishers who have graciously granted permission to quote from their copyrighted material. A list of acknowledgments begins on page 9.

Preface

ONE of my aims in writing this book has been to relate the Christian belief in a living God to our understanding of the nature of the world in the light of modern science. My experience as a priest among boys and masters in the close-knit community of a large boarding-school has convinced me that if the Christian faith is to remain meaningful for "modern man" it must say something of God's activity within, for example, the process of biological evolution; and our belief in God as Creator must take some account of the theory of relativity and the vastness of the universe on the one hand, and of the quantum theory of electron vibrations on the other. To say this is not to "confuse" religion and science, but simply to insist that all truth is interconnected. Belief in God is immensely strengthened if it can be related *to the whole natural order*.

I emphasize that last phrase because I feel that where contemporary theology has reached out towards the scientific realm it has too often concentrated almost exclusively on psychology and the allied field of sociology. I have sought to redress the balance in this respect by concentrating upon the natural order as a whole, and making only brief excursions into the psychology of the human mind: as long as God's activity is related only to man's mind there can be no satisfactory answer to Freud's charge that religion is an illusion, no firm reason for denying the view – which I find to be widely held – that it could well be man who has made God in his own image. I am seriously alarmed at the increasing number of people within the Christian camp who regard the word "God" as a symbol which may or may not continue to be of value, but has no reality behind it. There is an urgent need to reaffirm the *reality* of God by showing him to be actively at work within the natural order. There is at the same time an equal need critically to re-examine some basic aspects of traditional Christian theology.

These two needs of our time are both met within the writings

3

of the philosopher-mathematician Alfred North Whitehead and the increasing number of Christian writers who regard him as perhaps the greatest thinker of our century, and are concerned to develop the theological implications of Whitehead's "cosmological system", or "philosophy of process"; this is itself a profound meditation upon the dynamic nature of reality as revealed by the quantum theory, relativity and evolution. The most exciting aspect of this entire school of thought is that it *requires* the existence of God and sees his activity and influence as a necessary constituent in everything that is: it further seeks in some measure to *describe* God's activity in the world, which it sees primarily in terms of the persuasive influence of love. Indeed Whitehead's deepest criticism of Christian theology is that it has so emphasized the omnipotence of God as to invalidate its own primary belief that "his nature and his name is love": by contrast, Whitehead's great phrase that God is "the fellow-sufferer who understands" helps us to see how God's love and the world's suffering can coexist without contradiction.

This broad avenue of modern thought can also, as I believe, enable us to speak meaningfully to our generation of God's indwelling in man, and especially in Jesus Christ. The existentialist approach has come to see Jesus as "the man for others", but perhaps fails to state at all clearly how "God was in Christ": the line of approach taken in this book *starts* by seeing Jesus as the man for God, who became *through prayer* the man for others. The historic creeds *affirm* Jesus to be both true God and true man: process thinking enables one to say at least something in explanation of this great Christian truth, and to relate it to our own experience of God's indwelling presence.

The reality of God and his relationship to the world, the problems of suffering, of death, and of "heaven", and the person and resurrection of Jesus Christ: these are among the problems which have most worried me since I ceased earning my living as a mathematician and engineer and began first to study Christian theology and then to preach and to teach it. I found these problems to be prominent in the minds of many of those among whom I worked in two very different parishes, and when I came to work in a school I found them to be equally prominent in the minds of many of the boys, and of my fellow-teachers. There are, of course, many other fundamental problems, both ethical and doctrinal, but in this book I mainly confine myself to those I

4

have listed; this limitation enables each one to be tackled rather more adequately. I believe that a philosophy of process can make a *positive* contribution towards a Christian understanding of each of these problems.

I also believe that if the insights of this philosophy are applied to the relevant aspects of recent psychology they can greatly help our understanding of the nature and meaningfulness of prayer. This application would need a book to itself, but I hope that enough is said in outline in the final chapter to indicate that prayer can be important and meaningful for us today, as I shall suggest that it was for Jesus.

When I find a book helpful, I always like to follow up the references given in its footnotes. It was a number of such references in Dr. W. N. Pittenger's *The Word Incarnate* that first aroused my interest in process philosophy. This in turn led me to seek out Dr. Pittenger during one of his visits to England, and it was from meeting him that I learned that a number of philosophers, theologians and scientists are currently engaged — mostly in America — in applying Whitehead's "philosophy of process" in their various fields. I find this work intensely relevant to many of today's deepest problems, as I believe it to be to the one that has increasingly concerned me for some years — the problem whether the distinctive Christian beliefs about Jesus of Nazareth *can* be positively interpreted in a way that is compatible with, and not utterly separate from, the rest of our modern knowledge of the world in which we live.

I hope that the later chapters of this book may be of help in suggesting one such way, so that modern man *can* affirm that "God was in Christ", and that "Jesus is Lord", without being obliged to add under his breath "Jesus is also the great exception to all my other thinking".

As the son of an inventor who had an extremely original mind, I am well aware of the inevitable dearth of originality in the theological field: indeed it is only in respect to the problem just referred to that this book can claim any significant originality. I am therefore the more conscious of my indebtedness to many writers, and to the publishers who have so kindly permitted quotations from works for which they hold the copyright. A condensed version of some sections of chapter three was published in *Theology*, April, 1965: I am grateful to the S.P.C.K. for their permission to repeat parts of that article.

I am deeply grateful both to Dr. W. N. Pittenger and to Dr. F. W. Dillistone for their repeated kindness and encouragement during the writing of this book. I am also most grateful to Dr. F. R. McKim and Dr. M. B. V. Roberts for their advice in scientific matters. And I wish to thank Mrs. Betty Waite for her patient typing from a far from easy manuscript.

Finally, I should perhaps explain that this book was written towards the end of the period in which we in England were digesting and discussing *Honest to God* and its sequel, but had scarcely heard the phrase "death of God", except in Nietzsche: at that time I was a school chaplain at Marlborough College, a post I have since relinquished in order to do theological research at Cambridge. I suggest in chapter five that the contemporary "death of God" theology in part at least makes explicit what is implicit in the theologians that lie behind *Honest to God*. My own experience at Marlborough confirms this: the "death of God" theology as such was largely unknown to us, but many of its themes were implicit in not a little of the preaching in our chapel and in much that was said in seminars of older boys in my study; perhaps because at that time *Honest to God* and its background and sequel were the predominant influence on many of our preachers, as well as being required reading for several of our seminars. If this book owes its inspiration to Whitehead, it largely owes its stimulus to those seminars, at which I was often at full stretch in trying to commend my belief in the living God: I record my gratitude to the many boys who took part in them. The "death of God" literature now brings these same topics into still sharper focus, and makes me the more aware of the importance of the title of this book, and of the inadequacy of my – or any – treatment of so great a theme.

P.N.H.

Trinity Hall, Cambridge.

Contents

7

Acknowledgments

The Macmillan Company, New York, and the Cambridge University Press:

A. N. Whitehead, *Science and the Modern World*
Reprinted with permission of The Macmillan Co. from *Science and the Modern World* by Alfred North Whitehead. Copyright © 1925 by The Macmillan Co., renewed 1953 by Evelyn Whitehead.

A. N. Whitehead, *Religion in the Making*
Reprinted with permission of The Macmillan Co. from *Religion in the Making* by Alfred North Whitehead. Copyright © 1926 by The Macmillan Co., renewed 1954 by Evelyn Whitehead.

A. N. Whitehead, *Process and Reality*
Reprinted with permission of The Macmillan Co. from *Process and Reality* by Alfred North Whitehead. Copyright © 1929 by The Macmillan Co., renewed 1957 by Evelyn Whitehead.

A. N. Whitehead, *Adventures of Ideas*
Reprinted with permission of The Macmillan Co. from *Adventures of Ideas* by Alfred North Whitehead. Copyright © 1933 by The Macmillan Co., renewed 1961 by Evelyn Whitehead.

A. N. Whitehead, *Modes of Thought*
Reprinted with permission of The Macmillan Co. from *Modes of Thought* by Alfred North Whitehead. Copyright © 1938 by The Macmillan Co., renewed 1966 by Evelyn Whitehead.

The University of Chicago Press:
Charles Hartshorne and W. L. Reese, *Philosophers Speak of God*

The University of Chicago Press and James Nisbet and Company:
Paul Tillich, *Systematic Theology*
Vol. I—© 1951 by The University of Chicago. Vol. II—© 1957 by The University of Chicago. Vol. III—© 1963 by The University of Chicago.

Yale University Press:
Charles Hartshorne, *The Divine Relativity*
W. A. Christian, *An Interpretation of Whitehead's Metaphysics*

Footnote references to Whitehead's works

The page numbering differs as between the English and American editions of *Process and Reality, Religion in the Making* and *Science and the Modern World*. References to these works are therefore given in two parts: *firstly* the chapter and section (for *Process and Reality* the part, chapter and section, since the numbering of chapters start afresh for each part); *secondly*, in brackets, the page reference to the English edition.

The page numbering of *Adventures of Ideas* and *Modes of Thought* is the same in the standard English and American editions. (In the case of *Adventures of Ideas*, reference to the paperback edition is given in brackets after that to the standard edition.)

CHAPTER ONE

The Intellectual Crisis Facing Christianity

The charge of falsity

MANY would agree that Christianity is now facing a period of crisis, but there is far less agreement as to the fundamental causes of that crisis. Here in England, the publication of *Soundings* in 1962 has been followed in successive years by *Honest to God*, the "Paul Report",* *The New Reformation?* and *The "Death of God" Controversy*. Anglicans and Methodists are now facing the need for a firm decision as to the reunion of their two churches; and Easter Day 1980 has been set as the target date for a far wider reunion of British Christians. The Roman Catholic Church has undergone similar convulsions, less public but perhaps more deep. I welcome all this growing awareness of the need for change. What worries me is that so much of it is directed towards internal organization and inter-church relationships, and so little towards what I regard as the most serious threat of all, the increasing number of thoughtful people who regard Christianity as not only irrelevant but untrue.

The charge of irrelevance must be taken with the utmost seriousness and overcome in every aspect of modern life. The words and actions of a number of Church leaders have done something to overcome that charge in the allied fields of race relations and of the vast and increasing economic inequality between the West and most of Africa and the East. But contemporary Christianity has said and done far too little that is relevant to two of today's most critical problems, the continuing avoidance of nuclear warfare while the number of nuclear powers slowly increases, and the re-establishment, without war, of a satisfactory relationship between the birth rate and the death rate. The Pope's great speech to the Assembly of the United Nations *was* relevant to the former, in that he put the whole

* *Report on the Payment and Deployment of the Clergy*, by Leslie Paul (Church Information Office, 1964).

weight of his spiritual authority behind the United Nations and made it clear that the existence of such an international organization is in accordance with – is indeed demanded by – his understanding of the will of God. Sadly, few Church leaders have been so outspoken, and fewer still have supported any specific proposals for reducing the danger of nuclear war – except for the advocates of unilateral nuclear disarmament, which remains at best a partial solution, since few would wish to apply it to the United States. As regards the grave problem of over-population, Christendom's ability to speak with any authority has been largely inhibited by the very sincere, but as many Christians see it the very mistaken, viewpoint taken – at least up to the time of writing – by the leaders of the Roman Catholic Church.

I pray that posterity will find Christian opinion to have played a more positive part in solving these two problems than it is doing at the present time: if it does not, then the charge that Christianity is *irrelevant* could reach a crescendo that would drown the other, deeper charge that it is illusory and, in the final analysis, *false*.

It is this charge of *falsity* which is the fundamental threat to Christianity in our time: the claim that God is a figment of man's superstitious youth, which he has now outgrown; the belief that the world simply is the way it is, and evolves the way it evolves, with no need to confuse the issue by bringing in "God" or "creation" or any "ultimate purpose"; the belief – less widely held, but a source of real bitterness to some humanists – that the Christian faith does positive *harm* by encouraging people to use the prospect of future bliss in heaven as an excuse for ignoring the urgent needs of this present world. This direct intellectual challenge to belief in God is, in my view, far the greatest danger facing Christianity. In meeting this challenge Christians will find themselves led on to face up to the problems of relevance, organization and unity: unfortunately it is all too easy to concentrate on these other problems without facing the underlying charge of falsity.

If this charge is the most fundamental of the challenges confronting Christianity, it is also the most acute in terms of the time factor and of what in another context is called "escalation". There have always been some who have rejected Christianity on intellectual grounds, but in all recent centuries other

16

than the second half of this one the process has been kept in check both by social convention and by the small number of people with enough education for intellectual doubt. Where rejection of Christianity is due to sin, laziness, or superficiality, people tend to have a bad conscience, and may make some efforts to bring their children into contact with the Church. But where the parents' rejection is *intellectual,* even if only superficially so, they have no such incentive. Indeed they may wish to preserve their children from what they regard as a pernicious influence. This process can clearly "escalate".

I meet the intellectual challenge to Christianity both in myself and in the boys I teach, and I believe that this challenge derives in large measure from the fact that Christian theology at least *appears* to be in head-on conflict at several points with the vast panorama of modern science and philosophy. There are three possibilities here: this conflict may derive from a basic error and falseness in what I have called the vast panorama of science; or from the utter falsity of the entire religious premiss; or from a mixture of truth and error, a lack of internal self-consistency, *on both sides.* The first possibility can be dismissed out of hand: the present state of scientific knowledge is full of unresolved problems, but it is not utterly false. I never contradict the boy who says, "if I have to choose between religion and science, I must choose science"; I rather ask if he is sure he knows what he means by science. The second possibility certainly cannot be dismissed out of hand: the entire religious premiss *may,* as Freud put it, be an illusion. But not all scientists or philosophers would agree that one can make sense of the world without it — and some, as we shall see, advance reasons which seem to me to be cogent for regarding a God of love as a necessity. But perhaps my deepest reason for rejecting atheism is my firm faith not only in the coherence of things but in their purpose and value. J. S. Bezzant rejects atheism on these grounds, and in so doing points towards our third possibility by emphasizing science's present lack of consistency:

"Intellectual objections to Christianity nowadays, in my judgement, and the fact that there are at present no convincing answers to them, both grow out of one root. This is that there is no general or widely accepted natural theology. . . . The only possible basis for a reasonably grounded natural theology is what we call scientific. The difficulty is that there is no such actuality as "science". There are many and increasing sciences. Their deliverances are not as yet mutually consistent. This is the root difficulty in constructing a natural theology. For myself, I cling to the hope that it will, in time, become possible. Meanwhile I think there is nothing that can be called knowledge or reasonable belief that there is or can be anything in the human mind that can possibly justify the passing of such a colossal condemnation on this inconceivably vast and mysterious universe as is implied in the judgement that it has no meaning or enduring value."*

My only quarrel with this is over the time factor: If we wait for a new theology until the various sciences have achieved mutual consistency, we may wait a long time. Indeed the opening of the introduction to *Soundings* implies a long wait:

"The authors of this volume of essays cannot persuade themselves that the time is ripe for major works of theological construction or reconstruction. It is a time for ploughing, not reaping; or, to use the metaphor we have chosen for our title, it is a time for making soundings, not charts or maps. If this be so, we do not have to apologize for our inability to do what we hope will be possible in a future generation."†

The successive publication of *Soundings, Honest to God, Objections to Christian Belief* and *The New Reformation?* has done much good. It aroused much interest in circles where the deeper religious issues had not been discussed for many years. It also led to what Timothy Beaumont described in *Prism* as the "almost audible gasp of relief" of the "young in spirit" within the Church at that time. This relief was certainly shared by those of us who had come to feel that the process of radical reinterpretation and restatement of the Christian faith should no longer be confined to academic circles.

Some of the early exhilaration has since been replaced by the rather negative feeling that today's radical theologians are more ready to pull down than to build up. This feeling was already gaining ground in England when the writings of the "death of God" school were still unknown. I shall examine the doctrine of God in some detail in chapter five, where I suggest that the "philosophy of process" can lead us to a more positive doctrine

* *Objections to Christian Belief*, ed Vidler, pp. 107 and 109.
"Natural theology" includes a theological understanding of the natural world, but in its technical usage the term denotes the whole body of knowledge of both God and the universe that is obtainable by reason alone, without the aid of revelation: it is thus used in contrast to "revealed theology".
† *Soundings* (Cambridge University Press, 1962), p. ix.

18

of God than is either contained in or derivable from the "new" theology. The chapter on the living God precedes those on Jesus because, although we indeed learn of God most especially from and through Jesus Christ, I myself believe that we cannot make much progress in understanding or learning from Jesus unless we are able to share in some measure, though in the terms of our own generation, in Jesus' faithful and prayerful waiting upon God. Indeed it is in connection with prayer – by which I mean both specific acts of prayer and also a prayerful attitude to life – that I am the most worried by the growth, both inside and outside the churches, of highly negative attitudes to the concept of "God".

Such attitudes are by no means confined to disciples of the "death of God" theology, which is only beginning to become known in England. I have for some time been finding an increasing number of schoolboys – and an alarming sprinkling of priests – who now regard prayer as a sorting out of one's ideas in which the guidance or "answers" come not from God but from one's own subconscious. Freud said as much years ago, of course – but he was not a Christian bishop. Some of the older schoolboys who so regard prayer may have a knowledge of Freud, or of some of the intellectual atheists of the generation after Freud. The priests who take a similar view are perhaps more likely to have been influenced by Christian thinkers: either by those who have directly queried the meaningfulness of the word "God", or by those who have, perhaps unwittingly, achieved a similar result by basing their whole theology on an existentialist philosophy which gives such prominence to man as to leave, in the last analysis, little or no place for the objective reality of God. We are here brought back to the charge of falsity, for if God's grace and guidance are not *given* and *received* in sacrament and in prayer then there would seem to be an element of falsity in most – if not in all – interpretations of the Holy Communion, and in what I shall describe as the central and decisive activity of Jesus himself, namely his deep prayer to God the Father.

This man-centred attitude to prayer is just one example of the present tension in many areas of Christian thought and practice: this has certainly increased since *Soundings* was published in 1962. The Christian dons and undergraduates of Cambridge may or may not perhaps be able to stand this increasing tension

19

for several years; but many people are already finding it a strain. The faith of many of us would not survive for a generation with no guidance more definite than *Soundings*; we cannot afford to wait until the "many and increasing sciences" become "mutually consistent".

It is therefore fortunate that theologians outside Britain have not waited for a synthesis in scientific thought; some of them have achieved a real depth of knowledge in one branch of science, and they offer us a truly contemporary theology that takes account of this knowledge. Prominent among these, and far the best known in Britain, is Paul Tillich. He is a theologian and philosopher, not a scientist, but he has devoted much attention to the science of psychology. Very few contemporary British theologians of the top rank have achieved a comparable mastery of any branch of science; indeed some of our recent theology shows almost no awareness of scientific thought and the problems that this poses to seekers after truth both inside and outside the Church. The danger inherent in Tillich's theology does not stem from any lack of awareness of scientific thought, but from his existentialist philosophy which leads – as I shall argue – to a perhaps inevitable weakness in his doctrine of God; whereas Tillich's study of psychology and of aesthetics enables him to speak with great power on the theology of man and of man's culture. In parts of the third volume of his *Systematic Theology* he also discusses the nature of the physical universe, but this is not a major theme in most of his writing, in which his starting-point is not the cosmos but *man*.

By contrast, the thinkers to whom we now turn *start* with their understanding of the universe: they do not, so to speak, come on to this in volume three. Because they see God as necessary to the existence and evolution of our universe – the objective reality of which few of us question – these thinkers are able to help us to meet the charge that Christianity's underlying premiss, the existence of God, lacks objective reality and is, in the final analysis, false.

Some thinkers who help us to meet this charge

Pierre Teilhard de Chardin was probably the best-known thinker of recent years to have been both a distinguished scientist and a Christian theologian. This very remarkable Jesuit priest acquired a considerable reputation in the field of geology and palaeontology.* Much of his life was spent in travelling widely in pursuit of his researches into extinct forms of life. His main writings were not published until after his death because his superiors had regarded them as unorthodox; they were, however, criticized almost more strongly by scientists than by theologians. This scientific criticism of Teilhard may be largely due to the fact that, in an age of specialization, most leading scientists are concentrating on ever narrower fields of work, and so tend to mistrust the broad, intuitive approach.

Teilhard's best-known book, and the first to be published in English, is *The Phenomenon of Man*.† In an introduction to the English edition Sir Julian Huxley records how Teilhard had read the philosopher Henri Bergson's *Creative Evolution*, which had helped "to inspire in him a profound interest in the general facts and theories of evolution ... And as a dedicated Christian priest, he felt it imperative to try to reconcile Christian theology with this evolutionary philosophy, to relate the facts of religious experience to those of natural science." Earlier in his introduction Huxley gives the gist of Teilhard's thinking:

"In *The Phenomenon of Man* he has effected a threefold synthesis — of the material and physical world with the world of mind and spirit; of the past with the future; and of variety with unity, the many with the one ...

"Père Teilhard starts from the position that mankind in its totality is a phenomenon to be described and analysed like any other phenomenon: it and all its manifestations, including human history and human values, are proper objects for scientific study.

"His second and perhaps most fundamental point is the absolute necessity of adopting an evolutionary point of view. Though for certain limited purposes it may be useful to think of phenomena as isolated statically in time, they are in point of fact never static: they are always processes or parts of processes. The different branches of science combine to demonstrate that the universe in its entirety must be regarded as one gigantic process, a process of becoming, of attaining new levels of existence and organization, which can properly be called a genesis or an evolution."

Pierre Teilhard de Chardin was a Jesuit priest who devoted himself largely to the biology of the past: Professor L. Charles

* "The study of extinct organized beings, i.e. of fossil animals and plants," *Shorter Oxford Dictionary*.

† Collins, 1959. I quote from pages 21 f. and 11–13; also Fontana paperback, 1965.

Birch is a Christian layman busy with the biology of the present, and Head of the School of Biological Sciences at Sydney University. Yet he must have devoted considerable time and thought over many years to the philosophy and theology of the natural world, as is clear from his recent short but deeply thoughtful book *Nature and God*.* His conclusions are not dissimilar from Teilhard's, on whom he builds, but his book differs considerably from *The Phenomenon of Man* in being primarily concerned with the philosophy and theology of science, rather than with his own scientific researches and deductions. At one point Birch emphatically confirms Bezzant's point that there are many sciences, whose deliverances are not as yet mutually consistent: after giving a careful account of the completely "mechanistic" theory of nature, and of his own reasons for rejecting it, Birch comments that the mechanistic theory has been abandoned by most physicists whereas "biologists are about as mechanistic as they ever were" (page 60). His own alternative, to which I shall return in the next chapter, is well summarized on the preceding page:

"I shall argue for the 'both/and' position—that there is a mechanical aspect to nature which is the outer view, and that there is an inner aspect of nature less amenable to mechanical analysis. Similarly, we do not have to deny purpose when we discover that there is room in the universe for accident and chance events. I shall argue for a role of chance in a purposive universe."

Birch describes in his preface how "The most critical time in my own search for understanding was as a young research student, dissatisfied with the answers of what called itself orthodox Christianity and excited about science". He was then introduced to the realm of "liberal Christian thinking and process philosophy", and a little later "my first professor of zoology . . . advised me to read all I could of A. N. Whitehead and Charles Hartshorne, which advice I gratefully took". *Nature and God* is deeply imbued with the ideas of these two men, as is much of my own thinking. But I wonder how many professors of either zoology or theology in Britain would have given similar advice at that time: even as late as 1964 very few people in Britain had even heard of Professor Charles Hartshorne, the American philosopher-theologian to whom Birch dedicates his book, describing him as "the greatest student of A. N. Whitehead".

* S.C.M. Press, London and Westminster Press, U.S.A. 1965.

Hartshorne is a thinker of considerable importance in his own right, as well as being perhaps the leading interpreter of the theological implications of Whitehead's philosophy; but he is not himself a scientist. The extremely close relationship between process philosophy and modern science is due in large measure to A. N. Whitehead's double distinction first as mathematician and second as philosopher. Whitehead was for twenty-five years a resident fellow of Trinity College, Cambridge, and became a Senior Lecturer in mathematics. Bertrand Russell was his pupil at Trinity and later his colleague, and they combined to write their *Principia Mathematica*. In 1910 Whitehead moved to London, where he became Professor of Applied Mathematics at Imperial College, Lecturer in Applied Mathematics and Mechanics at University College, and Dean of the Faculty of Science in the University. I give these university appointments in full in order to show how closely applied mathematics and science are interlinked: in common parlance Whitehead was a scientist. During his fourteen years in London he became increasingly concerned with philosophical matters, and in 1924, at the age of sixty-three, he joined the philosophy faculty at Harvard. Whitehead's first book at Harvard was *Science and the Modern World* (1925), followed by *Religion in the Making* (1926) and *Process and Reality* (1929). As an applied mathematician Whitehead's knowledge of science was deepest in the realm of modern physics. He was, so to speak, a contemporary of relativity and the quantum theory; during his boyhood in his father's vicarage near Ramsgate he must have heard something of the religious controversy then raging so bitterly over Darwin's *Origin of Species*.

Whitehead is one of the giants of modern thought. His philosophy is based on an intuitive view of the universe in terms of dynamic process and creative synthesis. This is very similar to the thinking of Teilhard de Chardin. Both men had indeed been considerably influenced by Henri Bergson's *Creative Evolution*. The detailed contrasts between Whitehead and Teilhard are as interesting as the underlying parallels. Teilhard, the palaeontologist, emphasizes the fact that higher forms of life, including human life, are *potentially* present in the lower forms, as they were in the gases which cooled down to form our planet. Whitehead's concern is with the present and the future, and only incidentally with the past. He describes the universe as "an ocean of feeling" – even electrons "feel", though not of course in any conscious sense. Both men are, in effect, saying that "mind" is one of the primary grounds of reality, not simply a latecomer in the course of evolution: Birch explains all this with admirable clarity.

The considerable contrast of content and format between the later writings of Whitehead and those of Teilhard – so considerable that it tends to mask the underlying similarity of many of their ideas – is due, of course, to the different purposes of the two men, and also to a basic difference in their careers. As we have seen, Whitehead had two successive academic careers. In one sense there is no clear demarcation line between the two, for his interest in philosophy dates back to his undergraduate days, and he wrote several explicitly philosophical papers during his time as Professor of Applied Mathematics in London. But in the other direction the line is clear cut: during his academic career as a philosopher he was interpreting science, but he no longer carried out new work on explicitly mathematical or scientific subjects. Teilhard's career, on the other hand, was in no sense consecutive: his double vocation as priest and scientist began when a young man and continued until his death in 1955. Thus there is some science as such, as well as much interpretation of science, in *The Phenomenon of Man.**

For myself, I feel a very great respect for Teilhard but a far greater homage, and affinity, to Whitehead. I sense three reasons for this, of which two are personal: first, I am myself a mathematician, and know far less of biology than of physics; second, again like Whitehead, my career has been in two successive parts – I have moved from mathematician and engineer to priest, and although I now teach some mathematics my basic concern is theological. This brings me to my third and deepest reason for emphasizing Whitehead: in order to validate Christian theism it is vitally necessary to consider it against the broad panorama of modern thought, and thus to see all experience, and all reality, as *one whole*. Whitehead's canvas is broad enough for this – indeed, as we shall see, this is precisely the task he sets himself in the opening sentences of *Process and Reality*.

As Teilhard's writings encountered appreciable opposition

* For this reason the general reader is well advised to begin with Teilhard's *The Future of Man*, which is less explicitly scientific.

from his fellow-scientists, so have Whitehead's philosophical writings from his fellow-philosophers. V. C. Chappell, an American philosopher who is in part an interpreter of Whitehead, suggests that this opposition may partly be due to fundamental differences of method and outlook. "Whitehead's philosophical position is not so much the *conclusion* of a philosophical *argument* as an *imaginative construction*." Chappell suggests that this "makes Whitehead's later work uninteresting at best to many contemporary philosophers", for whom philosophy is basically argumentative. "For not only do I think that Whitehead's use of philosophical arguments is different from the use these philosophers would make of them and that such arguments are of less importance to him than to them, I also think that their conception of philosophy, as argument and little else, is unwarrantedly narrow. Philosophy also, to my mind, comprehends the sort of imaginative construction that was Whitehead's forte and that he practised better, as I believe, than anyone else has done in the present century."*

Whilst Chappell describes Whitehead's position as an "imaginative construction", others have called it an "intuition", the word used by the earlier philosopher Bergson to describe his own vision of the universe as "creative evolution". Intuition may be mistrusted by philosophers, but it has a clear affinity to theology; the receiving of revelation is a form of intuition, even if it would not normally be described as an "imaginative construction". Whitehead was no orthodox Christian, and it is not surprising that he has been opposed by a number of theologians. Others, however, are now trying to learn from him. The increasing volume of constructive work on the theological development of Whitehead's ideas is being done mainly in America: it is sad that all this should be so little known in Britain.

In seeking to commend the ideas of A. N. Whitehead and Pierre Teilhard de Chardin I have deliberately drawn attention to the degree of opposition to these ideas and suggested one or two specific reasons for it. But I would claim that the root cause of this opposition may well be the relative *novelty* of the ideas, their general nature, and the extent to which they conflict with established modes of thought. I say relative novelty, for Henri Bergson's *Creative Evolution* is dated 1906, Whitehead's *Process and Reality* 1929, and Hartshorne's *The Divine Relativity* 1948.

* *Alfred North Whitehead: Essays on his Philosophy*, ed. G. L. Kline, p. 79.

Whitehead did not anticipate quick results: "Profound flashes of insight remain ineffective for centuries, not because they are unknown, but by reason of dominant interests which inhibit . . . The history of religion is the history of countless generations required for interest to attach itself to profound ideas . . . if you want to make a new start in religion, based upon ideas of profound generality, you must be content to wait a thousand years."*

The elements of permanence and change in the world

Things certainly appear to possess both an element of permanence and an element of change. Some things change more obviously and more rapidly than others: few things seem more permanent than a mountain peak, but even this would be seen to change if viewed over a long enough period of time. "The planets, the stones, the living things all witness to the wide preservation of identity. But equally they witness to the partiality of such preservation. Nothing . . . retains complete identity with its antecedent self." (Whitehead, *Modes of Thought*, p. 129). We shall see in the next two chapters how in recent years modern physics, astronomy and biology have all been placing increasing emphasis on the dynamic element of change: so has "process thinking", which itself derives from these scientific discoveries. This will become clearer as we proceed: it is desirable at this point simply to state some of the presuppositions of process philosophy in order to give some indication of the extent to which these conflict with other more familiar ways of thinking.

Much of Sir Julian Huxley's introduction to the English edition of *The Phenomenon of Man* can be applied to process thinking as a whole, and especially the last paragraph of our quotation from that introduction.† Whitehead and Hartshorne emphasize just as strongly as Teilhard "the absolute necessity of adopting an evolutionary point of view": everything is in the process of evolving (or "becoming") and, in Whitehead's phrase, "the process *is* the reality". At the same time this thinking does not deny, although it is sometimes assumed to deny, the element of permanence in the world. "The essence of the

* *Adventures of Ideas*, p. 220 (175).
† See p. 21 above.

universe is more than process. The alternative metaphysical doctrine, of reality devoid of process, would never have held the belief of great men, unless it expressed some fundamental aspect of our experience".* Indeed this element is vital to process thinking, for without some degree of permanence and continuity the universe and its contents would be chaos. But process thinking *starts* from and builds upon the element of change, not that of permanence; process, not substance; becoming, not being; the latter half of each of these pairs is seen as a special case of the former half, and not the other way round.

It will already be clear that the underlying issue is whether the nature of reality is to be seen primarily in terms of *being* or of *becoming*. Process philosophy believes becoming to be the more inclusive category. The majority of philosophers and theologians have taken the opposite view — among them Paul Tillich, who speaks of God as "the Ground of Being". Tillich has written critically of process philosophy;† Hartshorne here comments on these criticisms: "when he [Tillich] says that being comprises movement and rest, process philosophy can only reply: 'Movement itself (process, actualization) comprises elements of rest, and this is all the rest we have reason to talk about. Motion is never a mere aspect or constituent of rest, but rest is always a mere aspect or constituent of motion'."‡

An important instance is the question of personal identity. In this connection Charles Hartshorne summarizes what he terms "the classical metaphysics of being at the expense of becoming" in a single sentence: "The world is many things, I am one, you are another: this is the basic assumption."§ On this assumption, "I" possess a fundamental self-identity which persists from birth, or from the womb, through all the vicissitudes of life up to death, and perhaps for all eternity: of course "I" shall change enormously during my life, but it is generally assumed that I both possess and retain the numerical oneness of self-identity. I am greatly influenced, indeed changed, by my experiences but I am logically prior to my experiences, since "I" experience them.

* Whitehead, *Modes of Thought*, p. 137.
† Notably in his *Systematic Theology*, vol. 1, p. 200 (but see the whole section, 197–201) and vol. III, pp. 430–3.
‡ Taken from Hartshorne's essay "Tillich's Doctrine of God" in *The Theology of Paul Tillich*, ed. C. W. Kegley and R. W. Bretall, p. 169.
§ *The Logic of Perfection*, p. 16.

Process philosophy takes a different view. It sees the fundamental entity not as the persisting "self" of personal identity but as each successive "self-now". "The only strict concrete identity is seen as belonging to the momentary self, the true unit of personal existence ... Each momentary self is a new actuality, however intimately related to its predecessors".* This difference is so important that I must anticipate a little in order to explain it. We shall find in chapters two and three that, influenced here by quantum mechanics, process philosophy sees the world as consisting ultimately not of things but of *events,* each event having the microscopically short duration of a single pulse or "quantum" of energy radiated by an electron. These events do not follow each other haphazardly. Each one is very greatly influenced by its immediate predecessors and also by the other events which make up its environment and thus, in some measure, by all other events, for in this philosophy all events are interdependent and, as we shall see, inter-penetrating. Thus a person consists of a whole series of momentary selves, each intimately related to its predecessors: the series contains a great element of change from youth to old age, but it also contains an element of permanence normally called personality or personal identity. "The planets, the stones, the living things all witness to the wide preservation of identity" – without which the universe would be a meaningless chaos. So far from minimizing this element of permanence, Whitehead identifies it with the emergence of *value* in the "world of passing fact". "Personality is the extreme example of the sustained realization of a type of value ... Apart from some mode of personality there is trivialization of value."†

Thus permanence and value go together. But this is no reason for allowing our own self-interest and desire for security to make us exaggerate the degree of permanence in our world and in ourselves. Personality both persists and changes throughout life. There is no absolute self-identity between myself now and the baby I once was. Process philosophy sees "personal identity" as an abstraction: it is the element of permanence in the series of momentary selves which together constitute a "person" – *but it*

* C. Hartshorne, *The Logic of Perfection,* p. 18.
† These two sentences are taken from his lecture on "Immortality", which is printed in *The Philosophy of Alfred North Whitehead,* ed. P. A. Schilpp, pp. 690, 693.

has no existence apart from that series. Since human "personal identity" or "personality" are widely regarded as modern equivalents to the word "soul", this last statement strikes at the very roots of the idea of the immortality of the human soul – an idea that by no means coincides with the biblical doctrine of resurrection, but is none the less one of the most cherished beliefs of many Christians, whilst also acting as a major stumbling-block to the faith of many "modern men". I shall suggest in chapter four that process thinking leads to a positive re-interpretation of both resurrection and immortality: this may be the greatest service, as well as the greatest shock, that this philosophy can render to contemporary Christianity.

But the insistence that the only strict concrete identity belongs to the momentary self, that this is indeed the true unit of personal existence, also has a direct bearing on day-to-day ethics. If I am a linked series of momentary selves, then my attitude to other people need not differ fundamentally from my attitude to myself-past and to myself-future. But if I possess a fundamental self-identity, then I am likely to look upon myself and other people in two quite different lights. Thus Whitehead is recorded as having once remarked with a quizzical smile "I sometimes think that all modern immorality is due to the Aristotelian notion of individual substances".* This may sound far-fetched, for substance philosophy is what most of us have always taken for granted; let us look a little further at the implications for both ethics and theology of the great emphasis which substance philosophy places upon the element of permanence in our world and in ourselves.

If "I" am a single entity throughout my life, then knowing *myself* must be an absolutely different thing from knowing other people or other things: self-knowledge becomes self-identity, and all relationships with another become absolutely different from the same relationship with oneself. This makes it impossible, as Hartshorne points out, to "love thy neighbour as thyself". That this is no mere quibble over the word "as" becomes clear if we bring in the dimension of eternity. If my self-identity is to persist beyond death, then in loving myself I am loving and doing my best to "save" my own soul: in traditional Christian teaching there is a sense in which *this* is one's *primary* task in life.

* See C. Hartshorne's essay in *Alfred North Whitehead: Essays on his Philosophy,* ed. G. L. Kline, p. 25.

On this view, one is inevitably loving or caring for oneself in a sense *different* from one's love of others. One may indeed devote one's life to trying to help others to save their souls, but one's actions are *directly* related to the saving of one's own soul. "I am one, you are another: this is the basic assumption."*

This assumption is equally destructive of the first Great Commandment, to "love the Lord thy God with all thy heart, and with all thy soul, and with all thy mind, and with all thy strength". If my own self-identity is such as to distinguish and separate "me" from the rest of reality, then it distinguishes and separates me from God: knowing or loving God is a different thing from knowing or loving myself. Furthermore, my neighbour possesses a self-identity which distinguishes and separates him from God. Thus in so far as I either love myself, as I am permitted to do, or love my neighbour, as I am commanded to do, *I cannot* to that extent be loving God with my entire heart and mind.

This is again no mere quibble over words. Indeed it has brought us to the very heart of Christian belief, and of the destructive effect upon it of the classical philosophy of being. One of the most distinctive features of the New Testament, and especially of the two great theologians St. John and St. Paul, is the doctrine of mutual indwelling and mutual interpenetration. "We are members one of another"; "there can be neither Jew nor Greek . . . for ye all are one in Christ Jesus"; this teaching runs all through the Fourth Gospel, and reaches a climax in the great prayer of Christ "that they may all be one; even as thou Father art in me and I am in thee, that they also may be in us". All of this is rendered far more difficult by the idea of absolute self-identity and its corollary of an absolute distinction between the person and experiences of X and those of Y. Conversely, all these biblical ideas are made *easier* by Whitehead's "imaginative construction", according to which all entities are interdependent and interpenetrating. In particular, I shall attempt to show that Whitehead's system of thought makes a profoundly meaningful contribution to the central problem of describing God's indwelling in the person of Jesus.

From a theological standpoint, process philosophy perhaps differs most strikingly from the main stream of Christian orthodoxy in its concept of God. It is generally assumed that

* *The Logic of Perfection*, ch. 3.

whilst God is near to us, and indeed immanent, he is also utterly distinct and absolutely different from us, both in his nature or being and in the ways in which he acts: he loves us, cares for us and helps us, but is not himself *affected* by our behaviour in the sense of being in any way *altered* by it. Indeed it is orthodox Christian teaching to affirm that God's own being was not affected by the creation of the universe, and would not be affected if it ceased to exist. Thus Dr. E. L. Mascall, an Anglican who is a modern disciple of St. Thomas Aquinas, quotes with approval two modern theologians:

"The relation between God and his creatures is a wholly one-sided relation, in that while the creation depends absolutely upon God, God in no sense depends upon his creation. God would be neither more nor less perfect if the creation dissolved into utter nothingness. The absolute perfection of perfect being would still exist."

"God added nothing to himself by the creation of the world, nor would anything be taken away from him by its annihilation."*

Dr. Mascall's own position is clearly stated on the same page:

"In view of the widespread tendency even among theologians today to be satisfied with a doctrine of God as in one way or another conditioned by or dependent on his creation, it is important to stress the absolute necessity of the conception of the entire independence of God . . . Unless we are prepared to accept the God of classical theism, we may as well be content to do without a God at all."

When we have studied Whitehead's philosophy we shall see that it is scarcely surprising that Mascall should find this philosophy "inadequate", although he also says that it "remains as one of the most impressive and massive cosmological constructions that have been produced". (See chapter 11 of *He Who Is*, which bears the title "The Cosmology of Whitehead".)

But let us return to God's relationship of love: it is not clear how one being can love another and remain fundamentally unaffected by that other's weal or woe – but it is often assumed that God does so love, and that the divine love is infinitely deeper or "higher" than ours. By contrast, process philosophy sees God and the world as mutually inter-related, each both affecting the other and affected by the other. Thus, as we shall see, Whitehead speaks of the "consequent nature" of God,

* *He Who Is*. p. 95 f; cited from Richard Hanson in *Dogma in History and Thought*, p. 105, and from Etienne Gilson's *Spirit of Medieval Philosophy*, p. 96.

whilst Hartshorne describes God as "supremely related", and gave one of his books the title *The Divine Relativity*. Such ideas seem strange at first to Christians, as they did to me when I began to read Whitehead and Hartshorne. But the more I ponder the great New Testament truth that God is love the more I am convinced that this *must* imply that God is affected by, and in a sense consequent upon, his creatures.

We have seen that process philosophy finds elements of both permanence and change in our world: it also attributes *both* these elements to God himself.* This parallelism between God and the world is in line with Whitehead's statement that "God is not to be treated as an exception to all metaphysical principles, invoked to save their collapse. He is their chief exemplification".† It would be hard to exaggerate the theological importance of this statement. We so frequently assume its exact converse and think of God as the great exception: he loves his world, yet remains unaffected by it: he has given us free will, yet remains more truly responsible than we ourselves for any good that is in us; he is omnipotent, yet cannot be held directly responsible for suffering. We shall return to these contrasts, or contradictions, in due course: we must now consider something else which is frequently regarded as "an exception to all metaphysical principles": the Bible.

The Bible

In earlier days the Bible would have been turned to as the first answer to the charge that the Christian faith is false, but today the Bible itself is under question as regards both its status and its relevance. Anyone seriously affected by the unbeliever's charge of falsity is unlikely to be won back by the Bible alone. He will want to find some contemporary reasons or arguments for refuting the charge, and will be likely to look at the world (as depicted by both science and the arts), at the lives of individual Christians, at the life of the Church as a whole, and perhaps at some recent theology, before he makes a study of the Bible. He may be reluctant to turn to the Bible because he sees

* We have so far only considered the element of change in God. As we shall see in chapter three Whitehead describes God as both "primordial and consequent": the element of change lies in the consequent aspect, and the element of permanence in the primordial aspect, of God's nature.

† *Process and Reality*, V.2.2 (p. 486).

32

it as the product of an ancient world which he regards as unfamiliar and remote; and he may not be prepared to offset its superficial remoteness by the assumption that the Bible is "inspired".

Let us tackle the question of "inspiration" at once. Dr. Alan Richardson, the notable (if somewhat conservative) biblical scholar who is now Dean of York, has pointed out: "Like so many other words which have figured largely in theological controversy, the word 'inspiration' is hardly a biblical word at all... The conception of 'inspiration' entered Christian thought in post-biblical times from Greek sources; it originally belonged to pagan ways of conceiving of the divine *afflatus* which took possession of a prophet or sibyl, who then uttered the communication of the God in a prophetic frenzy."* In "liberal" theological circles the idea of verbal inspiration began to give way during the nineteenth century to the idea that it is the *writers* of the scriptural books who were inspired, rather than the actual words they wrote. This is certainly nearer to the thinking of the New Testament, in which men and women are often described as being "filled with the Holy Spirit"; but not even this view of "inspiration" has been able to withstand the rigorous application to the Bible of the normal methods of modern historical criticism. "Most theologians today seem to agree that the non-biblical category of 'inspiration' is not adequate to the elucidation of the doctrine of biblical revelation. Whether in its conservative form of 'inspired words' or in its liberal form of 'inspired men', it cannot adequately express the full biblical truth of God's self-communication to mankind."†

Apart from the fundamentalists, most people fall into one of two clearly defined groups as regards their attitude to the Bible. The first group regard both Old and New Testaments as intrinsically unreliable, products of a nation of the ancient world in which religion played so dominant a role as to preclude objective assessment of the events that are recorded. I suspect that this group includes a higher proportion of their congregations than the clergy perhaps imagine: I am certain that it contains a number of very reluctant sceptics, who would dearly love to place greater reliance on the Bible, at any rate on the

* In his essay in *The Cambridge History of the Bible*, ed. S. L. Greenslade, (1963), p. 313.
† From the same essay by Alan Richardson (on p. 316).

33

gospels, but feel unable to do so. Most of the second group accept the fact that there are errors and inconsistencies in all parts of the Bible – some indeed regard *most* of it as thoroughly unreliable – but they feel that at least the overall picture given by the main books of the New Testament *must* be reliable, and they therefore *assume* this. In using the verb "assume" I am thinking primarily of those with no time to make their own critical assessment of the New Testament. But Dr. Leonard Hodgson used even stronger language when lecturing to theological students:

"Without realizing what we are doing we are trying to put the Bible in the place of God. This is one form of what comes from demanding the kind of revelation we think we ought to have been given. There are others . . . [two others are cited, the doctrine of papal infallibility and the suggestions sometimes made that God's grace given in the eucharist has an independent existence, rather like a medicine]. What links together the various forms of this error is the delusion that if we are to have a revelation worth having we must be able to find an ultimate source of authority somewhere within creation. In whatever form it appears it must be resisted: it is idolatry to credit any creature with what belongs to God alone."*

This means, as Dr. Hodgson emphasized in his lecture, that there is bound to be a "subjective element in our receiving of revelation". If the biblical authors were not irresistibly inspired, then the outlook and background of each of them must have influenced his writing, just as our outlook and background must influence our interpretation of it. We must try to assess their "subjective element", and to minimize our own. But we cannot escape from either: to attempt to do so would be "idolatry".

Once we abandon the concept of inspiration we can begin to distinguish God's activity in biblical times (including his activity in and through Jesus) from the written record of it, and to regard all the biblical writers as men of their time, deeply influenced *at every point* (and not only at such obvious points as the "upness" of heaven or the existence of evil spirits) by the knowledge, thought-forms and presuppositions of their contemporaries and forebears. As Dr. Hodgson explained with great force in his Gifford Lectures, our assessment of the scriptures requires two stages:

* *On the Authority of the Bible*, an S.P.C.K. collection of recent studies (1960), p. 5, first published in *Church Quarterly Review*, October 1958.

"Careful exegesis of the text, seeking to understand what it meant in the minds of its original writers and readers, must be the basis of all attempts at exposition or the formulation of doctrine. But then the further question has to be asked 'What must the truth have been if it appeared like this to men who thought like that?' St. Peter saw it with the eyes of a Palestinian Jew. . . . St. Paul, a Pharisee who had been born a Roman citizen, after his schooling by Gamaliel had had a university education at Tarsus; St. John had a mind at home in the Hellenistic culture of Ephesus. If truth about God's revelation be such that those men saw it and wrote of it like that, what must it be for us?"*

There is one other related question about which we need to think very clearly. As we begin to distinguish God's activity in biblical times from the written record of it, we must ask ourselves in what sense that divine activity was "unique". The biblical writers themselves undoubtedly so regarded it. They believed that out of all the nations upon earth God had chosen Israel to be his special people, and had made a quite unique covenant with her, repeating this to successive patriarchs, fulfilling it by many unique acts and above all by leading Israel out of Egypt, and adhering to it despite all Israel's vicissitudes and infidelities. By the time the New Testament came to be written the Christian Church was rapidly becoming more and more Gentile, and some of its authors had one foot firmly placed in the Hellenistic world. But Jesus' own ministry was almost entirely confined to his fellow Jews, and his disciples came to believe in him as saviour of the world only *after* they had seen him as their Messiah – a unique role within their own, as they believed, unique national history. The idea of a unique relationship with God, accompanied by unique acts and activity of God, is thus common to both Testaments, and is an important element in the world of thought in which they were written.

This idea of a unique relationship with God is not an element in most contemporary thinking. The claim that "only Christians can be saved" is heard less often today: indeed recent papal references to non-Christians have shown a notable charity and humility which all of us would do well to copy. Outside the religious field we try to think of the brotherhood and unity of mankind, not of the uniqueness of our own particular group or nation. Few scientists today think it likely that ours is the only

* *For Faith and Freedom*, vol. II, p. 227 f. (Blackwell, 1957); he cited this passage in the lecture from which I have quoted.

planet in the universe on which life has evolved, and our know-ledge of biological evolution at least reduces the abruptness of the gulf between human and non-human, and indeed between living and non-living matter. All this is not irrelevant to the attitude of "modern man" to the biblical claim to uniqueness. I meet a number of intelligent people, both boys and adults, who can see no possible relevance to themselves in the life of a God-man who belonged to a nation of the ancient world which regarded itself as God's chosen people. The entire Christian tradition, with its Jewish antecedents, helps those within it to accept *both* the uniqueness of Jesus' relationship to God *and* his relevance to themselves, so that they easily fail to appreciate that claims to uniqueness are for many people an inevitable barrier to relevance.

The belief that both God's guidance of Israel and his in-dwelling in Jesus were unique is often called "the scandal of particularity", and is defended on the grounds that if God desired to reveal himself within human history he was bound to do so at particular times and to (or in) particular people. I agree, but I feel obliged to ask a further question: does the uniqueness of the biblical revelation derive from a divine activity at particular times which was different in kind from all the rest of God's activity in history, or does it rather derive from the fact that God used to the full the religious sensitivity, the openness to God, and the high degree of moral commitment of particular people, above all of Jesus? There is a fundamental difference between these two alternatives. The first rests on the belief that God has most clearly revealed himself by certain unique events and features in the history of Israel and her prophets, and most clearly of all by his unique presence in Jesus. But on the second view these events, and in particular the life of Jesus, are to be seen as the clearest illustrations and demon-strations of the *universal* facts of God's love for mankind and of the availability of God's loving guidance for those who seek it and turn to him in selfless prayer.

I suspect that many "modern men" would find – indeed that quite a number *do* find – the second alternative more meaning-ful and simpler to accept. But simplicity need not be a good guide to truth. Whitehead warned "Seek simplicity – and mistrust it"; he also warned "So far as concerns religious problems, simple solutions are bogus solutions". The real value of the second alternative is that it rests upon important instances of general truths, rather than on exceptional occurrences. This again links up with Whitehead's statement that "God is not to be treated as an exception to all metaphysical principles . . . He is their chief exemplification". The lecture given by Dr. Hodgson, to which I referred earlier, contains a similar emphasis. He urges that we can best minimize the danger of subjectivity in our religion by a deeper faith "in the living God, the faithful and true, the same yesterday, today, and for ever, who wills us to grow in knowledge of himself and of his will for us . . . For if God is one and is faithful and true there will be a self-consistency in his self-revelation."*

In seeking this self-consistency we shall now turn to examine some of the findings of modern science, and then the cosmological system of A. N. Whitehead which is based on these findings. In chapter four we shall consider the problems of suffering and death, which may appear to challenge Jesus' central teaching that God is love. We shall then be in a position to examine the doctrines of God and of Christ in greater detail. Some of the brief references to these doctrines in this chapter have inevitably been rather negative: our search for self-consistency in God's revelation of himself must begin by questioning those traditional religious ideas that appear inconsistent with other aspects of modern knowledge, all of which forms part of God's self-consistent self-revelation to mankind. But I would end this chapter by repeating that my main reason for writing this book is my firm conviction that "process" thinking can lead us to a more positive doctrine of God than is either contained in or derivable from the other strands of the "new" theology.

* *On the Authority of the Bible*, p. 9.

CHAPTER TWO

The Modern World

Our survey of some of the findings of modern science will proceed from the general to the particular. The ideal sequence would be to consider first the universe as a whole, then the evolution of life on this planet, and finally certain questions as to the nature of man. It is, however, necessary to say something of both relativity and quantum mechanics before one can consider the various theories as to the origin and extent of the universe; it is also convenient to consider the theological implications of these theories after our analysis of biological evolution, rather than before it. So I shall not discuss the rival cosmological theories in any detail at this stage, but rather state one basic assumption which is common to most of these theories. The assumption is simple but fundamental: that we must not in any way regard our own planet and solar system, or even our own galaxy, as occupying a privileged position; thus we are in no sense at the "centre"; indeed the universe would look much the same in its general appearance if our planet were located in some other galaxy. This assumption reached its logical conclusion in the theory of continuous creation, according to which the universe is infinite in both space and time, with no centre, no boundary, and no beginning. How utterly different from the earth-centred cosmology of the Bible!

Cosmology is a scientific field in which general agreement is not yet in sight, but many astronomers and biologists are of the opinion that the universe is likely to contain a large number of planets on which life comparable to that on earth could evolve. All this at least offers speculative guidance to the Christian who gazes thoughtfully into the night sky and ponders the meaning of his own life, and of his religious beliefs, in the setting of this unimaginably vast and possibly infinite universe. I have always been sensitive to the awe and mystery of the sky at night, and I vividly remember my boyhood excitement on first reading Sir James Jeans's *The Mysterious Universe*: this book was also my first introduction to the theory of relativity. Both relativity and the quantum theory are now provided with an ample non-specialist literature. Without attempting to duplicate this, we must briefly remind ourselves of the salient features of these two great theories, whose combined effect is to indicate that the nature of the physical world differs considerably — indeed drastically — from the way we normally conceive it as we go about our daily lives: our everyday ideas of things are in fact no more than convenient abstractions of reality.

Physical reality consists of events

A primary consequence of the theory of relativity, as its name implies, is that things that had been assumed to be independent are found to be related. Newtonian physics envisaged a spatial world in a progression of time. "It was the distinction of Albert Einstein to succeed in showing, by means of an extremely minute and subtle analysis of the manner in which the physicist is led by his measuring operations to constitute his own scheme of space and time, that the co-ordinates of space and time are really interlocked."* Einstein himself describes how physical reality consists of *events* in a four-dimensional continuum:

"In the pre-relativity physics space and time were separate entities. Specifications of time were independent of the choice of the frame of reference . . . One spoke of points of space as of instants of time, as if they were absolute realities. It was not observed that the true element of the space-time specification was the event specified by the four numbers (i.e. by four dimensions, three of space and one of time) . . . It is neither the point in space, nor the instant in time, at which something happens that has physical reality, but only the event itself."†

The relatedness of space and time is paralleled by the relatedness of mass and energy, and so of mass and velocity: thus the two principles known as the conservation of mass and the conservation of energy combine into the single principle of the conservation of mass-energy, a principle which the theory of continuous creation has to modify. Lastly, gravitation is shown to be in some sense relative to the disposition of matter, and to be expressible by the analogy of a curvature of space-time.

* From the article by the French physicist Louis de Broglie in *Albert Einstein: Philosopher-Scientist*, ed. P. A. Schilpp, p. 113.
† A. Einstein, *The Meaning of Relativity*, p. 30.

Much of this is beyond our powers either to visualize or to describe in words, and is only fully expressible in mathematical terms; we find the same, to an even greater extent, when we turn to the quantum theory and to the realm of sub-atomic particles. The quantum theory of radiation states that radiant energy ultimately consists of finite amounts, or *quanta,* of electromagnetic wave-energy. The size of these quanta depends on the frequency of the electromagnetic wave. Radiation is thus periodic—finite amounts at finite intervals of time—and not a continuous process. Analogies can be made between the photon or quantum of energy in optics and the electron in dynamics. It is well known that light appears to have a "dual nature", in that its photons behave in some ways like corpuscles and in other ways like waves of energy: it is perhaps less widely known that the electron is also in some ways particle-like and in others wave-like. The solution to this dilemma lies not in trying to combine these two concepts, but in abandoning both. We must be cautious in drawing analogies between things we can see, like billiard balls and water waves, and these minute units of mass-energy which we can neither see nor visualize. I have been much helped here by the comment of a scientist colleague: "An electron is an electron, and we make a mistake in thinking of it as being 'like' anything of the size-range of our everyday experience: it is an electron, and we can only know it mathematically." What goes for the electron goes for all the elementary particles, of which a large number have so far been discovered, none of them apparently a compound of the others.

Our powers of describing an electron or other elementary particle are further limited, for we cannot isolate an electron from the effect of our observations of it: in measuring its position by such means as a high-frequency radiation microscope we involve an exchange of momentum between the electron and the microscope's beam, and thereby alter the electron's velocity. So we can determine *either* its position *or* its velocity, but not both of these simultaneously. There is a further inherent indeterminacy about our knowledge at the atomic level: we can accurately predict the rate of decay of a radioactive substance, for example plutonium, but we cannot say *which* atoms will radiate and decay at any given moment. Our knowledge applies statistically to the aggregate of atoms, but not individually to any one particular atom. We are indeed both limited in our knowledge of, and utterly unable to visualize, the ultimate constituents of matter and of radiation. The discoveries I have so briefly outlined form the very foundation of Whitehead's philosophical system. Einstein saw how both quantum mechanics and his own theory of relativity depict reality as *events*. The quanta of energy are four-dimensional events, and occupy an irreducible quantity of time. Whitehead's philosophy of process is based on these *events*. Perhaps our chief difficulty with process philosophy is that we are so very used to thinking in terms of being and substance, and to assuming that things and persons are more fundamental than events. It may therefore be helpful briefly to consider the nature of our experience, perception and recognition – all of which become a great deal more complicated when we reduce our environment to its basic constituents. We have seen that it is impossible to isolate an electron. Whitehead expresses this by saying that "electrons do not satisfy the complete condition for recognizability". We can, however, recognize molecules:

"Recognition in perception requires the recurrence of the ways in which events pass. This involves the rhythmic repetition of the characters of events. This permanence of rhythmic repetition is the essential character of molecules, which are complex scientific objects. There is no such thing as a molecule at an instant. A molecule requires a minimum of duration in which to display its character. Similarly physical objects are steady complexes of molecules with an average permanence of character throughout certain minimum durations."*

Whitehead also envisaged that all events are interconnected – thus the field of an electron is the whole universe:

"At the present epoch the ultimate scientific objects are electrons. Each such scientific object has its special relation to each event in nature. Events as thus related to a definite electron are called the 'field' of that object . . . As here defined the field of an electron extends through all time and all space, each event bearing a certain character expressed by its relation to the electron . . . the character of any event is modified (to however slight a degree) by any other electron, however separated by intervening events."

Philosophers of science have given much thought to the relationship between physics and perception. I have already quoted Einstein's comment "the conception of something

* This and the following quotation are from Sections 25 and 26 of Whitehead's *The Principles of Natural Knowledge* (1919).

happening was always that of a *four-dimensional* continuum; but the recognition of this was obscured by the absolute character of pre-relativity time" [my italics]. Bertrand Russell was in close agreement with Einstein's comment when he wrote that what we perceive "occupies a volume of space-time which is small in all four dimensions . . . and what we can primarily infer from percepts, assuming the validity of physics, are groups of events, again not substance". The theory of relativity interprets space and time very differently from the way in which we perceive them, or imagine that we perceive them. To quote Russell again: "If physics is correct, the relation of a percept to a physical object is very remote and mysterious".* Such comments may make us the more inclined to ponder and reflect upon Whitehead's system, and not to dismiss it out of hand as either "artificial" or "contrary to experience".

Is there an element of purpose in biological evolution?

In turning, slightly less briefly, to biology we shall link the nineteenth century discoveries and theories of Charles Darwin† with two fields of research which are still young and far from complete: the problem of how organic life first emerged from inorganic compounds, and the researches of the science of genetics into mutations. Darwin's theory had two parts: that all life is linked together in a process of evolution, and that changes occur through *natural selection*. Research as to how organic life first emerged from inorganic compounds already enables us to extend Darwin's concept of evolution back beyond the first organic life, and the young science of genetics, unknown in Darwin's day, can tell us a good deal as to the genetical mutations from which nature selects. The fact of biological evolution need not detain us: the evidence for it is overwhelming; each new discovery of pre-man or proto-man gets wide publicity. Less publicity attaches to the laboratory research into how the first living organism emerged on the primitive earth.

It is still widely assumed by non-scientists that there is a sharp discontinuity between living and non-living material. And yet it

---

* Both quotations are from *The Analysis of Matter*, pp. 284 and 338 f. Part II of this book is entitled "Physics and Perception".

† His *Origin of Species* was published in 1859; for comparison, Planck began quantum mechanics in 1901, and Einstein's relativity physics began with his "special" theory in 1913.

was as long ago as 1935 that this discontinuity was severely questioned by the isolation of a virus in crystalline form which further research has shown to consist of a single molecule of DNA (the short term for deoxyribonucleic acid) surrounded by a coat of protein. "Here was something that exhibited properties of the living and the non-living . . . On infecting an organism the virus casts off its coat and is simply a naked nucleic acid molecule. We can call it a living molecule as it has the capacity to reproduce when in the cell of a living organism. Yet in a test tube it has the appearance of a crystalline powder . . . Life may have originated from one such molecule in a shallow sea of some 2,000 million years or more ago. If we could synthesize the DNA molecule in the laboratory then we would probably be well on the way to knowing something about how life first arose."*

It seems likely that in due course scientists will be able to synthesize this molecule from purely inorganic materials, and thus establish as proven what they already regard as virtually certain: that life emerged or evolved from non-life without the addition of "something extra" from "outside".† Repetition of this emergence in a laboratory would doubtless attract much publicity, for it would close one of the gaps in our knowledge in which divine intervention is still widely assumed. The Christian will be protected against this "shock" if he has come to think of the entire history of this planet as one continuous process of evolution from the time it spun off from the sun to the present day (and beyond), and to see God's love as operative throughout this entire process, not concentrated at certain key points. Teilhard de Chardin offers us a vision of this in *The Phenomenon of Man*, and A. N. Whitehead and Charles Hartshorne attempt an analysis as to *how* God's love is operative.

We now turn to the second part of Darwin's theory, *the natural selection of chance variations,* better known as "the survival of the

* L. C. Birch, *Nature and God*, p. 38.
† In the early nineteen-fifties Stanley L. Miller succeeded in synthesizing amino acids from simple inorganic materials. Even nucleic acids have now been synthesized in the laboratory, but not, as yet, directly from the simple inorganic materials which are thought to have been the constituents of the primitive atmosphere. See A. I. Oparin, *Life: its Nature, Origin and Development* (Eng. edition, Oliver and Boyd, 1961). (Miller's experiments are described in detail in his article "The formation of organic compounds on the primitive earth" in *Annals of the New York Academy of Science*, 1957, *69*: 260–75.)

fittest". I prefer the former phrase, since the second – borrowed by Darwin from Herbert Spencer – includes no specific reference to the element of chance in evolutionary change. I shall examine this element of chance with some care, both in Darwin and in modern genetics, because I believe it to be one of the more important intellectual causes of contemporary atheism. It was certainly the cause of controversy, both scientific and theological, in Darwin's day: the element of chance was just as opposed to the prevailing mechanistic theory of nature, and its accompanying deism, as the concept of evolution was opposed to a literal interpretation of Genesis. There were those who were ready to accept evolution, but sought to interpret it as proceeding according to a definite plan. Darwin's great supporter T. H. Huxley called this last view "teleology", and contrasted it vividly with Darwinism:

> "According to Teleology, each organism is like a rifle bullet fired straight at a mark; according to Darwin, organisms are like grapeshot of which one hits something and the rest fall wide.
> For the teleologist an organism exists because it was made for the conditions in which it is found; for the Darwinian an organism exists because, out of many of its kind, it is the only one which has been able to persist in the conditions in which it is found ... Cats catch mice ... Teleology tells us that they do so because they were expressly constructed for so doing—that they are perfect mousing apparatuses ... Darwinism affirms, on the contrary, that there was no express construction concerned in the matter; but that among the multitudinous variations of the Feline stock, many of which died out from want of power to resist opposing influences, some, the cats, were better fitted to catch mice than others, whence they throve and persisted, in proportion to the advantage over their fellows thus offered to them.
> Far from imagining that cats exist *in order* to catch mice well, Darwinism supposed that cats exist *because* they catch mice well— mousing being not the end, but the condition, of their existence."*

"Teleology" is less prevalent today, but it is still sometimes assumed that evolutionary change is primarily *adaptive* – cats so adapting themselves as to be better mousers and passing on this ability to their offspring by heredity, rather than a *chance* variation of inherited mousing ability, with only the abler varieties catching enough mice to survive, breed, and pass on this ability by heredity.

* T. H. Huxley, *Lay Sermons, Essays and Reviews;* cited in Birch, *Nature and God,* p. 30.

In the last thirty years the young science of genetics has revealed a good deal as to the manner in which variation occurs between successive generations. An individual's hereditary characteristics are determined at the moment of fertilization by his particular complement of the hereditary determinants known as genes. Each of our cells probably contains thousands of genes, and each gene or small group of genes controls a different characteristic. For a variety of reasons changes sometimes occur in the genetical constitution of organisms, and when these occur in the reproductive cells they may have profound effects on the characteristics of the offspring. These changes, known as mutations, play a vital role in biological evolution: they provide the genetical variation in populations upon which natural selection can operate. The total number of possible mutations of genes is astronomically large, because of the way the genes are attached to each other within the large and highly complex DNA molecule – for genes are made of DNA, which we earlier described as probably the first living molecule. The history of evolution of species is, in effect, the history of the mutation of genes, and of the survival of organisms containing certain mutations and the extinction of others.

A Polish geneticist, Dr. A. Bajer, has made some most remarkable films of cell division. He put a smear of endosperm tissue under a powerful microscope and filmed a considerable number of cases of cell division, both cases in which a cell divides normally and cases in which visible abnormalities occur in the behaviour of the chromosomes. The magnification is high enough to show the movement of the individual chromosomes both before and during cell division, and the events are speeded up considerably by the use of time-lapse photography. Each individual cell contained, in this case, some two dozen chromosomes: these are flexible thread-like objects, each of which contains a different set of genes. As each new cell grows and matures, its chromosomes prepare for subsequent cell division. Each one produces a duplicate alongside itself, and thus becomes, so to speak, a pair of "Siamese-twins": the pair are so closely linked or bound together as to look, under the microscope, like a singleton rather than a pair; the fact that each chromosome has become a pair – known technically as a pair of chromatids – only becomes apparent just before the cell divides.

45

Cell division is not possible until the chromosomes have completed this "Operation Siamese-twins".

When watching Bajer's film of the movements of chromosomes within a cell, I was so struck with the resemblance to a rugger scrum that I can best describe it in football language, freely adapting the rules of Rugby Football to suit my purpose. To start with, the chromosomes appear to be swirling around within the cell, not unlike a loose scrum on a muddy day. But as the moment of cell division approaches the chromosomes – each now in fact a pair of chromatids – form a "line-out" across the equator of the cell. Just before the cell divides the pairs of Siamese-twins separate, and there is then a great swirling and scrummaging movement in which all the "North" twins charge towards one side of the cell – one "goal mouth", so to speak – and all the "South" twins towards the other, while the entire cell splits in two along its equator. Normally the entire "North" scrum ends up in one "goal-mouth" and the entire "South" scrum in the other: the result is then two new daughter cells, each containing the same number and types of chromosomes as the original parent cell, and therefore exactly reproducing the parent cell.

But one pair of chromatids may have been wrongly placed or wrongly orientated in the "line-out", with the result that both its chromatids end up in the same "goal-mouth". Or again, in the general scrummage and numerous collisions during the process of cell division, one of the chromatids sometimes appears to get pulled into the wrong "goal-mouth" by a member of the other "team", with the result that there will be one chromosome too many in one daughter cell, and one too few in the other. Sometimes, again, a chromatid breaks and one of the pieces is dragged into the wrong goal. In all these cases the daughter cells finish up with an abnormal set of chromosomes, and we can say that a mutation has occurred.

Dr. Bajer's film offers neither proof nor explanation, but in watching it I was very forcibly struck by two things: first, the *orderliness* of this sequence of events, particularly the "line-out" and the subsequent separation of the "twins" to opposite "goals"; second, the apparently *chance* nature of the abnormalities which can lead to the type of mutation I have described. I believe that there *is* an irreducible element of chance in the occurrence or non-occurrence of mutations, and that in watching this film I was privileged to observe at the cellular level the kind of *chance variations* assumed, but not directly observed, by Charles Darwin.

Two comments need to be made here. A number of mechanisms occur which cause changes in the combinations of genes: Bajer's film only illustrates the sort of way in which *some* mutations are known to occur. Furthermore, the effect of such mutations depends on where they occur. If they occur during the renewal of normal body cells—the cells of my little finger, for example—it may be of little or no consequence. But when such a mutation occurs in the reproduction cells its effect on the subsequent child and its progress to adulthood can be calamitous. Mongolism, for example, is caused by the presence in the cells of one extra chromosome: and this is known to arise from abnormal cell division in the formation of the mother's egg.

Those of us who are not biologists need to grasp the fact that most mutations are deleterious and only a tiny minority are beneficial. In *Nature and God* Professor Birch cites a recent paper on genetics which lists five pages of human diseases that are known to be due to gene mutation in man.* The advance of evolution is due to the astronomical variety of possible gene mutations, and the fact that the relatively few organisms in which beneficial mutations have occurred are the ones that continue to survive in the face of adverse changes, or increasing "competition", in their environment: since the complement of genes is repeated at replication or reproduction (save for the possibility of further mutation), the added survival potential of these few organisms or animals is inherited by their offspring, with the cumulative effect of a geometric series.

A process in which most changes are harmful is evidently "wasteful", but this is precisely the adjective which an economist would be likely to apply to the manner in which life on our planet is known to have evolved. Birch describes this as "a continuity of transformation of first life over some 2,000 millions of years into some 500 million or more species, most of them now extinct".† Cuenot's famous diagram "The Tree of Life" vividly illustrates the colossal profusion of the evolutionary process. Teilhard reproduces this in *The Phenomenon of Man* (page 135), and comments that the quantitative insignificance of

* For details see *Nature and God*, p. 120, ref. 10.
† *Nature and God*, p. 39.

mammals (let alone man) in this Tree is comparable to that of our solar system in all the galaxies of the universe. The concept of "wastefulness" implies a value-judgement that may well be erroneous or invalid: I use it merely to emphasize that the statistics of mutations as revealed at microscopic level by the study of genetics run parallel to the global findings of geology and palaeontology. The fact that most mutations are deleterious may be said to corroborate the claim that there is here a real element of chance, since neither theist nor atheist can be anxious to regard an effect which is usually harmful as having been deliberately contrived in each and every case.

I hope that what has been said sufficiently stresses the fact that the phrase "element of chance" is *not* being used – as the word "God" is sometimes, unfortunately, used – to cover up a gap in our knowledge. Birch states that the "sorts of mutations that occur are completely unrelated to the need of the organisms at the time they occur", and illustrates this by a fascinating piece of biological history. It is well known that some insects are now resistant to D.D.T. "In some cases the resistance is conferred by the mutation of a single gene which alters the insect's capacity to deal chemically with the poison. Now the amazing thing is that all the evidence points to the view that mutation for D.D.T. resistance has been going on before D.D.T. was ever invented."† There can have been no purpose or advantage in this mutation before the advent of D.D.T., and if it then occurred it *must* have been a chance occurrence – an interesting confirmation of my own impression, from watching Bajer's film, that environmental requirements and pressures simply *cannot* direct the movements of individual chromosomes during the "scrummage" of replication.

This irreducible element of chance rules out the completely mechanistic theory of nature which was prevalent in Darwin's day, as it had been in the preceding centuries. Professor Birch describes the history of this theory and its accompanying deism, "the compromise which religion made with mechanism",* and explains both Darwin's and his own rejection of it with great care: indeed a considerable part of *Nature and God* is concerned with the history and refutation of this theory – perhaps because, as Birch says, most of his fellow-biologists are still "about as

* *Nature and God*, p. 41–42.
† *Nature and God*, p. 31.

mechanistic as they ever were". He then moves on to his own constructive solution: instead of purpose *or* chance he argues "for the 'both/and' position . . . we do not have to deny purpose when we discover that there is room in the universe for accident and chance events. I shall argue for a role of chance in a purposive universe. The alternative is virtually complete mechanical determinism, for which I find no evidence."*

The alternative could perhaps be defined rather more precisely before it is rejected. Mechanical determinism can be modified to allow for an element of chance, and I know a number of people who would argue that they see a good deal of evidence for a *combination* of mechanical determinism and sheer chance that owes nothing whatever to any cosmic purpose. They will admit the chance nature of genetical mutations, perhaps suggesting that Darwin had foreseen some such state of affairs. They will then stand firm on the rest of Darwin's theory: first, chance variations occur: then the environment effects a natural selection from these variations, and does so in a purely mechanistic or mechanical manner. The discussion so far is incomplete in that it ignores the question of choice. Most people would argue that man – and perhaps the higher animals – exercises at least some degree of choice; the philosophy of science I seek to commend sees at least a rudimentary element of choice, perhaps at the sub-atomic level, throughout the material world. (Choice and indeterminacy need not be different: choice may perhaps be indeterminacy as seen from the "inside".)

We shall consider both choice and individual freedom later; for the moment we will confine ourselves to the broad sweep of the evolutionary process, in the earlier stages of which the element of choice is less apparent. Familiarity with the concept of evolution can blind us to the truly remarkable nature of the process by which single-celled organisms have evolved over vast stretches of time into mammals, primates and now man. We must ask ourselves whether this can best be explained by a combination of chance and determinism without cosmic purpose, or by "a role of chance in a purposive universe". Those who adhere to the first view regard the natural selection of chance variations as a sufficient explanation: chance variation, plus selective survival of the "best", plus a reproductive process

*Nature and God, p. 59.

49

in which variations are the exception rather than the rule, means that the "best" – however defined – must inevitably get "better". But Darwin himself was not entirely satisfied. He wrote this in 1860, a year after the publication of his *Origin of Species*:

> "I cannot anyhow be contented to view this wonderful universe, and especially the nature of man, and to conclude that everything is the result of brute force . . .
> "I cannot think that the world as we see it is the result of chance; and yet I cannot look at each separate thing as the result of design . . . I am, and shall ever remain, in a hopeless muddle.
> "But I know that I am in the same sort of muddle . . . as all the world seems to be in with respect to free will, yet with everything supposed to have been foreseen or pre-ordained."*

Darwin's comparison with free will was shrewd and apposite, and much of the world is still in that particular muddle. In thinking about Darwin's "natural selection" we need to remember that it is the environment, the totality of organisms, which causes the selection to occur. Thus the statement "the evolution of higher forms of life from lower forms is the result of natural selection" is equivalent to saying "the evolution of higher forms of life is the result of the effect organisms have upon each other". Hartshorne takes this a stage further back to the interadjustment of atoms and particles, and correctly points out that Darwinism *assumes* such interadjustment.

> "The idea that adjustments are the result of natural selection among unpurposed or blind variations is not incompatible with that of cosmic purpose. For the maintenance of the general conditions under which chance and competition will produce evolution *may itself be purposive*. Darwinism derives generally higher forms of inter-adjusted species from lower; but interadjustment itself and as such is *assumed*, not explained. Interadjusted atoms or particles involve the same essential problem. Theism can explain order as a general character of existence; can any other doctrine?"†

Darwin's natural selection of chance variations implies and assumes the interadjustment of which Hartshorne speaks. This, in turn, implies some universal limitation on the element of chance in the world. Process thinkers regard this limitation as an aspect of the *purposive* element in the universe – an element which, in their view, can only derive from God. In Hartshorne's

* Written in letters to the American botanist Asa Gray; See F. Darwin, *Life and Letters of Charles Darwin*, vol. 11.
† Hartshorne, *The Logic of Perfection*, p. 206 (my italics).

words "There must be cosmically pervasive limitations upon chance, since unlimited chance is chaos; supreme purpose or providence is the sole positive conception we can form of this chance-limiting factor."* "Theism can explain order as a general character of existence; can any other doctrine?" Those who believe that the world is governed by a non-purposive combination of chance and mechanistic determinism still need a "chance-limiting factor": for this they assume precisely that interadjustment of things which underlies Darwin's concept of natural selection; this property of interadjustment is assumed to have existed throughout time. The atheist or agnostic often accuses the theist of making an arbitrary assumption as to the creation of the universe, oblivious of the assumption he is himself making as to the nature of things. (We shall see that the theistic doctrine of creation relates to the present and the future as much as to the past.) The theist and the atheist in fact make the *same* assumption as to the interadjustment of things, or organisms, in our evolving universe – but the theist believes this interadjustment to be purposive.

I do not expect to be able to *prove* that the universe, and in particular the evolution of species, possesses this purposive element, any more than I expect to be able to prove the existence of God. Indeed, the two propositions are interlinked. I doubt whether proof of the former can go beyond Harthorne's claim that "supreme purpose or providence is the sole positive conception we can form of this chance-limiting factor". But the concept does not necessarily possess any positive interpretation. The chance-limiting interadjustment of things may just happen to be a part of the natural order: "things just are like that", as boys so often say to me. But in that case the evolutionary process is highly remarkable. Granted all the wastage in terms of extinct species and harmful mutations, granted also the vast periods of time that are involved, the evolution of *homo sapiens* from the bacterium (and indeed from the incandescent gases that first erupted from the sun) must remain an exceedingly remarkable sequence of events, unless there be some cosmic purpose and influence to guide it.

There are two aspects of the living world which it is hard – perhaps impossible – to explain on the basis of mechanical determinism, even if this be modified by a limited element of

* *The Logic of Perfection,* p. 207.

chance: the real and creative freedom of at least the higher creatures, and the emergence of mind. To these we now turn.

The element of creative freedom

A. N. Whitehead expresses the coexistence of chance and purpose in terms of creativity: the individual organisms are self-creative. This is a deeper analysis of the concept of freedom in a context of evolution. Not only is an organism free to make certain choices, it is itself affected by these choices, which help to determine, and therefore to create, its own future. We are familiar with this in human terms: each of us is the sort of person he is partly because of the past choices and decisions made by himself and others: these past choices have helped to create the present person. Whitehead applies this to all organisms and not only to man. Every entity* is self-creating and as such "co-creator of the transcendent world: the world is self-creative".† What Whitehead calls "the neglected side" of "the evolutionary machinery" "is expressed by the word *creativeness*. The organisms can create their own environment. For this purpose, the single organism is almost helpless. The adequate forces require societies of co-operating organisms. But with such co-operation . . . the environment has a plasticity . . . "‡ We shall see later how God's influence is the necessary co-ordinating factor in Whitehead's interpretation of this evolutionary process.

Hartshorne suggests that Darwin's "hopeless muddle" can only be solved by this concept of universal self-creativity:

"As Darwin repeatedly declared, chance cannot explain the world as an ordered whole of mutually-adapted parts. It was because of this dilemma that Darwin gave up the theistic problem: purpose could not explain details, and nothing else could explain order as a general fact . . . Darwin, like so many others, tended to think of science as committed to determinism. 'What we call chance,' he explains elsewhere, 'is not properly that at all, but causes unknown to us.' Moreover, it was probably not apparent to Darwin why cosmic purpose should leave anything to chance, at least apart from human free will. Only a philosophy of universal creativity can untie this knot. The 'metaphysics' of his day . . . did not present him with a clearly-conceived creationist philosophy."§

* This term is defined in the next chapter.
† *Process and Reality*, II.3.1 (p. 118).
‡ *Science and the Modern World*, ch. 3, p. 140 (italics in the original!).
§ *The Logic of Perfection*, p. 207.

This philosophy of universal creativity regards the divine purpose as the most important factor, but not the over-riding factor, in the universe. Whitehead and his interpreters speak of God and the world as interacting upon each other. God's influence upon the world is immense, but he does not have an absolute world-plan: "even a world-purpose must be indeterminate as to details. For one thing, an absolute and inexorable purpose, supposing this meant anything, would deny individuality, self-activity, hence reality, to the lesser individuals, the creatures."* This philosophy thus maintains the reality of human free will as one instance of the creatures' self-creativity: we shall later see how this is accompanied by a denial of some traditional interpretations of God's omnipotence.

The element of mind

"If the non-living world is completely devoid of mind, and if, as it seems necessary to believe, there was a time when no life could exist, how did mind appear? Lloyd Morgan† treated the emergence of mind as a phenomenon of the same sort as the emergence of a new organ, or physiological capacity, in evolution. A new organ, however, involves nothing more mysterious than differential growth, leading for example to an outpocketing from a flat surface, that turns out to be useful and may be elaborated by further differential growth . . . Emergence of mind from no mind at all is sheer magic."

This passage is taken from a recent essay "Biology and the Philosophy of Science"‡ by the distinguished American biologist Dr. Sewall Wright, who has written a large number of articles on both genetics and evolution. He goes on to point out that the problem posed by the emergence of mind is not confined to the remote past; a similar problem arises in each generation:

"The fertilized egg, while a living cell, behaves in a way that suggests a purely physico-chemical interpretation rather than one involving mind. If the human mind is not to appear by magic, it must be a development from the mind of the egg and back of this, apparently, of the D N A molecules of the egg and sperm nuclei that constitute its heredity."

* *The Logic of Perfection*, p. 206.
† *The Emergence of Novelty* (London, 1933).
‡ In *Process and Divinity*, the Hartshorne Festschrift, philosophical essays presented to Charles Hartshorne and edited by W. L. Reese and E. Freeman. I quote from p. 113–14.

At this juncture we must pause to consider the nature of the picture of things that is offered to us by science. Professor Birch sees this as, inevitably, an abstraction:

"The supporters of the mechanistic theory of nature fail to understand the nature of science, which is to abstract from nature. The abstractions of science are pictures of reality and not reality."*

Forty years earlier, A. N. Whitehead had said the same of physics:

"The laws of physics are the laws declaring how the entities mutually react among themselves. For physics these laws are arbitrary, because that science has abstracted from what the entities are in themselves."†

Process philosophy seeks to analyse "what the entities are in themselves", which Teilhard de Chardin calls "the within of things", whereas science is primarily concerned with their outward aspect. Sewall Wright, Birch, Teilhard, Whitehead and Hartshorne all believe that there is an element of "mind" in everything: molecules, electrons, individual cells may appear mindless from the outside, but they would all be found to possess at least some element of mind if only we could know them from the inside. Teilhard de Chardin describes consciousness, spontaneity, and his term "the within" as "three expressions for the same thing", adding in a footnote that "the term 'consciousness' is taken in its widest sense to indicate every kind of psychicism, from the most rudimentary forms of interior perception imaginable to the human phenomenon of reflective thought".‡ Whitehead similarly uses the word "feeling" to include non-conscious feelings, and insists that it can even be applied to electrons; Birch points out that our thoughts affect the movements of electrons within the brain. In a second footnote on the same page, Teilhard quotes J. B. S. Haldane; "We do not find obvious evidence of life or mind in so-called inert matter, and we naturally study them most easily where they are most completely manifested; but if the scientific point of view is correct, we shall ultimately find them, at least in rudimentary forms, all through the universe." (*The Inequality of Man*, p. 113).

Sewall Wright describes his own viewpoint as "that of dual-aspect or monistic panpsychism"; mind is universal, present not

* *Nature and God*, p. 57 f.
† *Science and the Modern World* (1925), ch. 6, p. 133.
‡ *The Phenomenon of Man*, p. 57.

only in all organisms and in their cells but in molecules, atoms and elementary particles. Furthermore:

"If mind and matter are coexistensive, they may be looked upon as two aspects of the same reality. They do not, however, stand on an equal footing. All that any of us can know directly is our own memories, emotions, thoughts and volitions. Matter (or physical action) is always a deduction from regularities that we find in our experience. In general, mind may be considered the inner aspect of the reality of the observer, matter the external aspect of a reality in the inner aspect of which the observer does not partake, except in so far as perception implies interaction."*

Mind and matter, organic cells and inorganic molecules, indeed *everything* on this planet, is ultimately composed of the *same* elementary particles, in an almost infinite variety of combinations. And everything has come to its present form by an evolutionary process which almost certainly contains no discontinuity from man right back to the origin of our planet, whether this was an incandescent eruption from the sun or a cold condensation of a dust-nebula that then surrounded it. In the human realm, physiology and psychology point to the interdependence of body and mind, and embryology reminds us that body and mind both evolve from the cells of ovum and sperm. All these insights of modern science imply that *one single reality* underlies the entire material universe.

The abrupt conflict between the theory of evolution and the literal meaning of Genesis had a major influence upon Christian understanding of the Bible. This conflict was, of course, quite incidental to the scientific and philosophical importance of the theory itself, but the ensuing battle over biblical status and "inspiration" so distracted the theologians that it was not them but the philosophers of science who first faced up to the deep significance of evolution. A good deal of Christian theology has not yet faced up to that significance, but still assumes the threefold nature of reality – matter, mind and spirit – and tries to draw an abrupt distinction between *homo sapiens* and all other forms of life. One of the great merits of process thinking is that it joins with modern science in insisting that reality is *one*: there is an element of chance, an element of mind, an element of creative freedom, and an element of cosmic purpose within this one reality. As we shall see, God himself is to be found

* Dr. Sewall Wright in *Process and Divinity*, p. 117.

55

within this one reality and not beyond it – so that *all* reality is one.

Some recent cosmologies and the belief in God as Creator

There is reason to believe that the universe is itself evolving, so that much that has been said about the evolution of life on this planet can be applied to the universe as a whole. Process thinking sees an important sense in which the entire universe is one single organism. Whitehead frequently insists that the environment of each entity is nothing less than the entire universe and all its past history; only a tiny part of this will have any appreciable effect on the particular entity, but the entire universe is inter-connected. Teilhard de Chardin also emphasizes the unity of the universe; he is primarily concerned with the unity of what he calls the *biosphere* enveloping the surface of our planet, within which our biological evolution occurs; but he traces this back to its origin as part of the sun, and shows its continuity to be an instance of what he calls the "fundamental unity" of all matter.

The astronomers' theories as to the nature of the universe similarly emphasize its fundamental unity. These theories are concerned with the physical nature of the universe and its development or evolution, whereas the theological doctrine of creation primarily expresses the belief that the material universe is in an ultimate sense dependent upon God, and would not exist at all without God. Thus the scientific theories and the theological doctrine are complementary, and indeed fundamentally independent: they are, however, closely linked in our thinking. Much misunderstanding is still caused by the widespread idea that the doctrine of creation is mainly concerned with God's initial act. I suspect that this lies behind the sense of unreality with which many churchgoers approach the festival of Harvest Thanksgiving. They enjoy the hymns, the decorated church, and the harvest supper afterwards; they believe that God created the world, but they cannot help wondering whether he really had much to do with this year's harvest. This present tense of creation is clear enough in the Old and New Testaments; it is seldom mentioned in some Christian teaching today, perhaps because the lack of a theology of the natural world puts many Christians on the defensive wherever their faith impinges on the realm of science. Paul Tillich carefully distinguishes three tenses, or aspects, of the doctrine of creation:

> "Since the divine life is essentially creative, all three modes of time must be used in symbolizing it. God *has* created the world, he *is* creative in the present moment, and he *will* creatively fulfil his *telos*. Therefore, we must speak of originating creation, sustaining creation, and directing creation."*

It is important to distinguish these three aspects because we so often think only of the first; but it is also important to be clear that they are three aspects of a single process. In discussing the evolution of life we were mainly concerned with sustaining and directing creation, but there is an element of origination whenever new combinations emerge: life from non-life, or rational beings from those in which the element of mind was less developed. There is also a real sense in which a new life originates each time an ovum is fertilized. In that sense, there is originating creation throughout the evolutionary process. In the sense of "creation out of nothing" there can be no origination during an evolutionary process: for example, everything on this planet can be traced back to the sun. If we wish to single out originating creation in that sense we must go back to the origin of our sun, and perhaps of the universe; indeed we shall find that the concept of "creation out of nothing" is explicitly denied in some modern cosmologies.

The over-emphasis on an initial act which characterizes much Christian thinking about the doctrine of creation is no doubt partly due to the emphatic opening of the book Genesis "In the beginning God created...", to which the opening of the Fourth Gospel—"In the beginning was the Word"—is a deliberate parallel. Both the Hebrew of Genesis and the Greek of St. John can mean "in principle" as well as "in the beginning". Commenting on the opening words of St. John's Gospel, William Temple pointed out that "when a word in one language is represented by two or more in another, it is always necessary to choose one or other of these; very often a word covers several meanings because the meanings really are connected together, and the mind easily passes from one to the other without consciousness of movement. So the word really means both things; and here the expression used means both

* *Systematic Theology*, vol. I, p. 281.

'in the beginning of history' and 'at the root of the universe'."*
In the case of the opening of Genesis, this implies that God's
creativity is to be seen both in the beginning of the universe
(if it had a beginning) and as its root principle. It is this second
aspect which process philosophy affirms.

I began this chapter with a very brief reference to some of the
theories as to the nature and origin of our universe. I shall now
examine these in slightly greater detail, without attempting a
full analysis of the various theories. I assume that both our own
galaxy and the universe are at present expanding, that is to say
that the other visible galaxies are receding from each other and
from us. (The evidence for this is the reddening, or "red shift",
of the light from these galaxies, as observed from the earth.
Relativity theory predicts such a shift in the light spectrum
from a rapidly receding source, and enables the velocity of
recession to be deduced from the amount of this shift. Analysis
of the light from the farthest visible galaxies suggests that these
are receding at speeds comparable to that of light. There are
other possible explanations of this red shift, but most astronomers take the view I have outlined.)* The cosmological theory
which offers the most obvious, and in the view of many the most
likely, explanation of this expansion is the "big bang" theory,
according to which all the mass-energy of the universe was
initially highly concentrated, was scattered by a vast nuclear
explosion, and has been expanding ever since. It is not difficult
to conceive that if there was this initial concentration of incandescent matter it could well have proved unstable, and been
rent asunder by a vast nuclear explosion. The weakness, if it is
a weakness, of this theory is that it offers no explanation as to
the origin of this great concentration of mass-energy; it further
assumes that we are in a privileged position in the time-scale of
the cosmos in that we happen to be living "soon" enough
after the cosmic explosion still to have other galaxies within
sight — whereas if the universe had been expanding for sufficient
aeons of time no galaxy not tied to our own would now be
visible from earth.

Both these points are overcome by the theory of infinite
oscillation. On this view, the universe is of infinite age — that is,

* *Readings in St. John's Gospel*, p. 3.
† See for example F. Hoyle, *The Nature of the Universe*, ch. 6: "The
Expanding Universe".

it has always existed throughout an infinity of time – and goes through successive phases of expansion and contraction: we happen to be living during an expansion-phase. This phase began with a "big bang", which caused galaxies of stars to shoot out at vast speeds. Throughout this phase the forces of gravitational attraction which exist between any two masses have been gradually slowing down the expansion of the universe, and will eventually overcome this expansion and begin to pull the galaxies inwards towards the centre of gravity of the universe. The change over from expansion to contraction will be gradual, but eventually all the galaxies will be rushing towards each other until their density becomes so great that there is another "big bang", and the cycle repeats itself. The time period for a complete cycle has been estimated at 8,400,000,000 years. This theory of infinite oscillation has relatively few advocates. It is an elaboration or refinement of the once-for-all "big bang" theory, which has a great many advocates. For myself, I cannot help suspecting that one of the attractions of this theory over the once-for-all "big bang" is that it postulates an infinity of time and thus avoids the necessity for an initial act of creation. If this be so, then atheistic assumptions have been allowed to influence cosmological ideas in precisely the same sort of way as that for which traditional religion is often attacked!

I again emphasize that belief in God as Creator is in no way dependent upon there having been a cosmic beginning-point to the universe. Indeed I myself find it *easier* to think that the material creation of the eternal God may itself be of infinite age. Love and creativity would seem to be among the most basic characteristics of God; so it is hard to imagine how God can ever have existed without a universe in which to exercise his creativity, and with nothing to love other than himself.

Christian theology has attempted to overcome this last difficulty by thinking of God as a Trinity of Persons, so that in the absence of a universe God's love can still be expressed through the mutual relationships between the three Persons. There seems to be an element of artificiality here, for the three Persons form one God, who must therefore be loving himself.

St. Augustine's great insight that the world was created not *in* time (i.e. during time) but *with* time does not overcome the difficulty: it rather places it outside the realm of time. (It also superbly anticipates relativity physics by its inter-relation of time and matter.) Traditional Christianity has also supposed that "before" the creation of our universe there were (and still are) myriads of angels as objects of God's love and creativity: it will, however, be suggested in chapter four that the creation of angels – if these exist – must have followed, and not preceded, that of the material universe.*

Whether it be thought of as "in" time or "beyond" time, I regard the concept of God without a material universe as a difficulty – but not an insuperable difficulty – confronting belief in God as Creator. Thus my own religious faith is *helped* by the suggestion of some modern cosmologists that the universe may be of infinite age – but my faith is certainly not dependent upon that suggestion.

The concept of an infinity of time, indeed of space-time, is fundamental to the theory of the continuous creation of matter, which Professor Fred Hoyle has explained to the general public through his writing and broadcasting. This theory has recently been under heavy fire; it may even have been abandoned by the time this book is published. I shall, however, give a brief outline of this theory, both because it is of considerable interest in itself and because its existence among recent cosmologies should make Christians all the more careful to ensure that their doctrine of creation includes a present tense, and is not confined to giving a theistic interpretation to an initial act of creation. The novel element in the theory of continuous creation is the hypothesis that matter gives rise to a creation field and generates new matter. "Matter that already exists causes new matter to appear. Matter chases its own tail."† (By "matter" Hoyle means nuclear mass-energy: he is *not* just saying that out in space radiant energy converts part of itself into matter.) This new matter is created at such a rate as to maintain the density of matter in the universe – otherwise the density of an expanding universe would get lower and lower, and infinitely low after an infinite time. Hoyle originally assumed that this new matter would be created uniformly throughout space, but in 1964 he suggested that this creation of new matter might alternatively be concentrated in certain regions, and might be

* See below, p. 120.
† F. Hoyle, *The Nature of the Universe* (1950), quoting from p. 110 of the Pelican edition.

the explanation of the extremely high energy-density of the "quasi-stellar objects".

Recent observations of the radiation from these "quasi-stellar objects", or "quasars", have in fact thrown considerable doubt on the whole concept of continuous creation. Cosmologists have suggested:

(a) that these "quasars" are among the farthest known objects – in which case the radiation we are now receiving from them will have been emitted an extremely long time ago.

(b) that when this radiation was emitted these "quasars" consisted of extremely dense concentrations of galaxies.

If both these suggestions are correct, it follows that there was an extremely high density of matter in the oldest known region of the universe. This appears to support either the "big bang"or the continuous oscillation theories – and to oppose the theory of continuous creation of matter, which is also known as the "steady state" theory because it envisages that the broad pattern and average density of the universe have remained steady throughout all space-time. It is precisely this steadiness which appears to be called in question by these observations of the radiation from the "quasars".

Any cosmological theory which assumes some or all of the universe to be of infinite age – whether it be the theory of continuous creation or that of continuous oscillation – must part company with the traditional Christian doctrine of *creatio ex nihilo*, creation out of nothing. This doctrine was intended both to express the doctrine underlying Genesis I and to deny dualistic ideas of God moulding an evil, pre-existent matter as a potter moulds his clay: it affirms that the divine potter created the clay, out of nothing. We have today got right away from the old pagan idea that matter is inherently evil, though traces of this remain in some attitudes to sex. A theistic interpretation of continuous creation or the oscillation theory replaces the concept of pre-existent matter with the concept that matter and energy have co-existed with God throughout an infinity of time; there is no place either for the dualistic idea of a godless unformed world awaiting its creator or for the idea of a solo God existing without a world. This runs parallel to the insistence of process philosophy that both God and the world are creative and that each affects, and is affected by, the other. It is no surprise to find Professor Hartshorne simultaneously condemning worship of "the absolute" and "creation *ex nihilo*", and commenting:

"This last phase adds scarcely any spiritual insight to the idea of creative fiat, but dangerously hampers its generalization into the idea of a creation of creators. For if we too in our humble way create, then God's action in the world now does have 'materials', for we have partly made them. 'But, at the beginning . . . '? Ah, is it the idea of a beginning which you worship? Do you exalt God's power by deciding that he has created only a finitude of past time? Whence this passion for limiting God by explicit negations?"*

The vastness of the universe

The vast size of the known universe cannot but prompt the question "are we alone – are we its only rational inhabitants?" Here we can only talk in terms of probability. Most scientists accept the possibility, or probability, of rational beings on planets of other stars simply because the exceedingly small mathematical probability that any given planet will possess conditions suitable for any imaginable form of life is far surpassed by the incredibly large number of stars that could possess planets. Sir Bernard Lovell has said that he thinks it highly likely that there are civilized beings elsewhere, but unlikely that there will ever be any form of communication between them and us, due to the vast distances involved.† If there are other civilizations and other rational beings, some may be more advanced than us and capable of a deeper understanding of God's love. This is a humbling thought, but not a discouraging one. God's love for every creature is maximal, according to its nature: he does not love the sparrows any less because his love for us contains aspects that cannot be present in his love for them. We know in ourselves, and see in Jesus, how much God loves *us*: "people" in space – even "people" more advanced than ourselves – in no way affect or reduce God's love for us. Two theologians with very different outlooks, E. L. Mascall and Paul Tillich, have concluded that the possibility of rational life on distant planets presents no essential difficulty to Christian

* *The Logic of Perfection*, p. 123.
† This was said with particular reference to the reports (later denied) that a Russian scientist had suggested civilized beings as a possible cause of the cyclical variation in the radio waves from a very distant quasi-stellar object.

belief. Indeed Frank Weston, Bishop of Zanzibar, wrote this as long ago as 1920:

"I do not know if other planets support rational life. If they do, I am quite certain that Christianity is revealed to them in some way corresponding with its revelation to us. Our Christianity is the self-unveiling of eternal Love in terms and forms intelligible to us. If, therefore, other planets support rational life, their Christianity will be the self-unveiling of eternal Love in terms and forms intelligible to them . . . It is only those who erect a false barrier between the universal activity of the Word and his incarnate life as man who will boggle at the possibility of his self-revelation in a created form on another planet."*

Paul Tillich has pointed out that if there are rational beings elsewhere we cannot continue to regard the life, death and resurrection of Jesus as of literally cosmic significance. However we interpret these events so crucial to our race we cannot suppose they relate in themselves, and in their Palestinian setting, to beings who may inhabit a planet some thousands of light years distant from Jerusalem. To do so, in the light of modern knowledge, is surely to succumb to a conceit parallel to that involved in assuming our planet to be the "centre" of the universe. When St. Paul attributed cosmic significance to the Atonement he was thinking in terms of angels and arch-angels, not physical beings at vast distances. This does not in any way reduce the significance of Jesus Christ for us who in-habit this planet:

"God may have other Words for other worlds,
But for this world the Word of God is Christ."†

The main difficulty that modern cosmology presents to religious belief is in the realm not of the intellect but of the emotions. Our intellect tells us that if there is a God he must be the God of all the stars and of all the generations of mankind, the number of each being quite irrelevant. But we know that our telescopes have penetrated to distances of 5,000,000,000 light years,‡ and that our sun is simply rather a small star in a

* In his book *The Revelation of Eternal Love*. This passage is quoted in W. N. Pittenger's *The Word Incarnate*, p. 251. He describes Bishop Weston as a "rigidly orthodox theologian".

† Written by Mrs. Hamilton King, and also quoted on p. 251 of *The Word Incarnate*.

‡ Some scientists believe the "quasars" to be at twice this distance.

typical galaxy. All this can have a considerable effect on our emotional attitude to religious belief. We easily feel utterly insignificant against so vast a backcloth, our short life-span utterly dwarfed by the age of the universe: how can God even notice our actions, let alone mind about them?

We must let intellect and not emotion be our guide. With his limited horizon and short span of life man has always tended to feel insignificant as compared with his environment; yet Jesus believed and taught that even the sparrows are of value in God's sight, even the hairs of our head are numbered. The vast age and size of the known universe is only significant if our idea of God is too small to match it. We need to follow Dr. Tillich in thinking of God as the source and ground of all existence, and also to remember what Jesus said about the sparrows.

"And God saw everything that he had made, and, behold, it was very good."* This great verse is saying not only that there was no evil before the "Fall", but also that everything has intrinsic worth and value in God's sight. The vast dimensions of space and time must make us the keener to avoid those over-simplifications which find ultimate value within the material universe *only* in the moral choices of rational beings, thus making God ultimately indifferent to the whole created order other than *homo sapiens* and such "people" as may exist elsewhere. Process thinking helps us to see value in creative freedom, God's greatest gift not only to man but to the universe. There are many different levels of creative freedom. One could substitute "freedom" for "flesh" in this verse from St. Paul: "All flesh is not the same flesh: but there is one flesh of men, and another flesh of beasts, and another flesh of birds, and another of fishes".† There is indeed one freedom of men, another of fish, another of single cells, and another of electrons.‡

Our moral choices involve the use of creative freedom, and Jesus is the supreme example of creative freedom in complete yet voluntary dependence upon the will of the Creator. But there is an element of freedom in everything: the whole of this vast and perhaps infinite universe is of value in God's sight; in the matter of value we must neither attempt to dwarf, nor

* Genesis 1: 31.
† 1 Corinthians 15: 39.
‡ Human free will is discussed in the appended note that follows.

allow our emotions to be dwarfed by, the vast universe in which we live.

APPENDED NOTE

Free will or computer control?

The reality of human free will is crucial to Christian theology, for without it we are reduced to puppets. Quite apart from the theological problems associated with it, the very existence of human free will is now called in question, though not as yet directly challenged, on scientific grounds. Are human beings free agents, influenced by a whole complex of factors but making their own decisions, or are these "decisions" completely determined by the totality of factors, from the past as well as the present, that exert influence upon them — factors that could be roughly classified under heredity, training, experience, and present situation? When the workings of the human brain are fully understood, will the entire process now called "decision" be explainable without remainder as an automatic computation of information fed in from sense stimuli, from memory cells, and from other parts of the brain — or will there be a remainder, a personal element which either influences this computation or accepts it and decides how to use it, or both? These questions are raised by the relatively new branch of science known as cybernetics, which examines the working of the brain and makes use of analogies with the working of electronic computers.

In a recent lecture under the title "The Brain" given to the upper school of Marlborough College, Professor J. Z. Young gave a fascinating description of the series of experiments he and others have carried out on a breed of octopus found in the Bay of Naples. This octopus was chosen because its senses are few and its brain simple. It depends almost exclusively on the sense of sight, has only two pleasures, food and sex, and only one fear, attack. It is taught by repetition that if it sees a vertical sheet of metal in its tank it is safe to advance towards this and grab food, but that if it advances when the same sheet is held horizontally it will get an electric shock. Having got these facts implanted in its memory cells, the octopus's reactions are on each occasion entirely predictable, even including its degree of hesitation if it is presented with the puzzling situation in which the metal sheet is inclined at an angle between vertical and horizontal. After a number of experiments the signals are switched: what used to indicate food now produces shock, and vice versa. The octopus takes a definite number of experiments, and receives several shocks, before it erases the old information and reacts correctly to the new.

The brain of this type of octopus has been dissected, and its millions of memory cells located. There are no other factors, or more complex parts of the brain, to complicate the issue. The choice or assessment between weal and woe is therefore shown to be an *automatic* reaction to vision plus memory. The memory cells function in a manner analogous to an electronic computer. The eye supplies present vision experience. The memory cells are searched, working backwards from the most recently activated cells, for similar past vision experience and what it entailed. This search is automatic, as in a computer, and the resulting impulses coming out from the memory cells cause the animal to advance or retreat. That Professor Young sees this as a completely automatic, computer-like process was brought home to me by his reaction to a question at the end of the lecture. A boy asked whether, if the signals for food and shock were switched often enough, the octopus would have a nervous breakdown. The question was humorous, but also perhaps reasonable and even clever – but the lecturer clearly regarded it as frivolous: a computer does not have nervous breakdowns, and neither does an octopus.

So brief a summary does scant justice to the care with which the series of experiments was conducted. The lecturer confined himself to these, and declined to extrapolate for the human brain. Plenty of amateurs were prepared to do this for themselves afterwards, and to argue that science might one day be able to draw similar conclusions about human decisions, however different and more complex the human brain may be.

Let us leave the octopus to his food or his shocks, and consider the author writing this book. It happens to be late, and well past supper-time. The decision to put down my pen in a moment is dictated by hunger plus some faint consideration for my wife. What of the decision to continue after supper, or to knock off? Will this be equally determined by an automatic balancing of factors such as repleteness, tiredness, and tele-

66

vision programme versus the degree of importance or urgency I attach to the task; this in its turn being determined by a string of factors which could, at least in theory, be evaluated? Or will these factors influence my decision without determining it? Am I a free agent who, in the last resort, balances all the information and makes a decision which, unlike that of the octopus, is not entirely predictable? Am I a deciding agent, or a calculating machine? It may be many years or decades before the scientist has mastered the entire mechanics of the human brain, so that the questions I have just raised are not ones upon which scientists are ready to pronounce even a tentative judgement. They are, however, beginning to ask them, and theologians and philosophers must do the same.

That these are questions which the Christian should take seriously is firmly maintained by Dr. I. T. Ramsey in his paperback *Religion and Science,* subtitled *Conflict and Synthesis: some Philosophical Reflections.** This includes, as a lengthy supplementary note, the record of a discussion on the challenge of cybernetics to Christian beliefs between Dr. Ramsey, Professor of the Philosophy of the Christian Religion at Oxford, and Mr. J. Dorling, a student of psychology and philosophy. I quote part of Mr. Dorling's summary of the problem:

"There are two related assumptions which the majority, or at any rate a very powerful minority, of workers in this field make, and which certainly seem to run counter to traditional Christian views.

(a) That if we knew enough about the brain we would, in principle, be able to explain completely human behaviour and human experience.

(b) That in principle there is no aspect of human behaviour that could not be duplicated by an appropriately designed machine."†

Mr. Dorling then asks six questions, which the Professor answers. As the note is entitled "men and machines" it is hardly surprising that the questions deal mainly with *(b)*, and with the moral implications of the analogy between man and machine. The whole discussion deserves study, but we must here confine ourselves to assumption *(a)*, which is the more fundamental of the two: *(b)* would appear to depend upon *(a)*. If scientists learn enough about the human brain, as they already have in the simple case of the octopus, may it be possible completely to

* S.P.C.K., 1964. Dr. Ramsey has since become Bishop of Durham.
† Page 50.

explain human behaviour? I want to outline three attitudes to this question:

1. Dr. Ramsey's approach is to explain the philosophical distinction between subject and object, and between first-person and third-person accounts. He considers the difference between a man recently recovered from polio exclaiming "I'm dancing" and a friend remarking "he's dancing". He suggests that we become aware of ourselves, of "I", when a disclosure situation occurs, as it does when a man who has once been paralysed is suddenly aware of himself as dancing. Ramsey says that in the end all the arguments "appeal to a first-person *subjectivity* of which each of us is aware in himself and which, as subjectivity, is irreducible to third-person objects, which indeed all presuppose it".* The synopsis at the beginning of the book summarizes this point by saying that "each of us has a first-person subjectivity which is never – logically never – exhausted by any or all third-person accounts, of which cybernetics is one".† Dr. Ramsey makes the point again in answer to Mr. Dorling's question on free will:

"To believe in 'free will' is to believe that in certain cases of decision—whose ancestry may be more and more revealed, at least once the decision is 'taken', by scientific inquiry—in certain cases of decision, at the moment of decision, we know ourselves active in a way which transcends all that a scientific story, however complex, might talk of. On what ground do we make this claim? Well, consider the alternative. On the alternative, our behaviour is wholly a matter of 'objects' and thus we have committed the *logical blunder* of objectifying the subject. Or—another point—look at those who have tried to account for what each of us knows himself to be in terms of 'objects'. What then becomes of self-identity? It was in relation to this question, we may remember, that Hume had to confess that his effort to account for the self in terms of objects was a failure."‡

This statement is in two parts. The first sentence defines belief in free will as belief that sometimes, at the moment of decision, we know ourselves active in a way that transcends all possible scientific accounts. This is then supported by the argument that the alternative includes the logical blunder of objectifying the subject. Now free will and awareness of self

* Page 36.
† Page xi.
‡ Page 57 f.

are not the same. Young's octopus may possess neither. I believe that we possess both. But just suppose it to be conceivable that a scientist might have proved human free will to be an illusion, but that our self-awareness remained unaffected, since the discovery had not yet been published. At a moment of decision we would mistakenly imagine ourselves active as free agents. In fact, we would not differ greatly from Young's octopus, except that we would possess self-consciousness. Each person would be aware of himself as the subject of his own actions, which he would wrongly regard as decisions. (The mechanism supposedly determining our actions must of course be below the level of consciousness – otherwise intelligent men would never have imagined themselves to possess free will in the first place.)

This, surely, is the practical alternative to the reality of human free will. Does this also contain the logical blunder of objectifying the subject? If so, Dr. Ramsey would seem to have proved the reality of free will. If not, he has assumed it. Ramsey does not, I think, use the verb "prove" in this connection. For myself, I do not believe it can be used. There is an interesting parallel between Ramsey's approach and Whitehead's philosophy of process, which *assumes*, and makes no attempt to prove, the existence in our universe of a multiplicity of free agents.

2. I will be more brief in discussing a second approach to the possible challenge of cybernetics to the belief in human free will: this approach suggests that the theologian and the hypothetical scientist of the future would be giving two different but *complementary* views. This approach is an example of what is often called "the principle of complementarity". Thus a primrose can be described botanically, or the poet can call it God's promise of spring. These descriptions are complementary. I imagine that most modern sermons on the subject of creation involve this principle, explicitly and implicitly. Thus the "Big Bang" theory, and the theological statement that God created and is creating the universe, may each either be true or false. Neither disproves the other. Neither is incompatible with the other. They are complementary, and may both be true. Unfortunately the same cannot be said of the hypothetical situation that would indeed arise if cybernetics were to describe the working of the human brain as a response, without remainder, to past and present influences. This claim and the claim that God has given man free will would not be complementary,

but mutually exclusive. If the former were true, the latter would be false. The believer can regard scientific descriptions of any part of our world as descriptions of how that part of God's creation works, but a determinist description of human behaviour would be a description of God's puppet called man, not a description of a being with free will.

3. In considering how far man may resemble a machine we must accept the finding of cybernetics that there is a pretty close analogy between the electronic computer and the memory cells of, say, an octopus. On this analogy the entire octopus resembles a machine operated by a computer: its body is the machine, its memory the computer; its senses, notably its eyes, supply the input signals to the computer; the rest of its brain corresponds, on the electronic analogy, to the electric circuits and electrically operated mechanisms by which the computer output signals automatically drive and control the machine. I suggest that this analogy will need one vital modification before it can be applied to man, or perhaps to some other animals. The revised analogy will be to a more complicated machine, coupled to a large computer: for some of the simpler operations the computer output signals drive and control the machine, as before; but for the rest the brain-computer works in the other way in which computers are used – not to drive a machine directly, but to carry out an analysis which will supply information, very rapidly, to its operator. He will be guided by the information supplied by the computer, and in many cases this guidance may virtually determine his actions. In others the guidance will take the form of a recommendation, an assessment of pros and cons; the operator, whilst enormously assisted by his computer, must still decide for himself what action to take. Thus the analogy is now to machine, computer and operator rather than to machine entirely controlled by computer. The range over which the operator has to take any action may be narrower than some had imagined – but I suggest that it will not prove to be zero.

The term "operator" in this analogy may not correspond to any one particular section of the brain, nor is "he" an immaterial inhabitant resembling some uses of the word "soul". The term rather denotes a dimension of life which the lowest animals do not possess, and for which the simpler form of computer analogy can find no place. Because parts of the brain resemble a computer it does not follow that the *whole* mind and brain functions automatically. The fact that A resembles B in a number of ways in no way necessitates that it should resemble B in all ways. Those who predict that a complete analysis of the brain will totally disprove free will perhaps overlook this basic logical truth. Whatever the mathematical similarity, why should the operating methods of a mass of nerve cells resemble in every way those of an assembly of electronic valves? There is the further point that a computer has to be set up before it can work; the fact that it needs to be programmed precludes any element of real *novelty* in its working.

Novelty and freedom go together: they bring us back to the question of decisions. Here I must speak personally. I certainly feel myself to be, apparently, making decisions – both small and great – all the time. I also deduce that other people are free agents from observing their varied and often erratic behaviour, which certainly appears to introduce a strong element of novelty into human affairs. I make this assumption both from my observation of my contemporaries and from my reading of history. Other people also have this feeling, and make this deduction: to take but one example, our legal system is based on the assumption that a normal man is capable of making decisions, for which he must accept responsibility.

Our experience also suggests that human beings are not the only free agents. Some pairs of birds will guard their young with great parental concern even in face of danger, while other pairs of the same species abandon their nest with no apparent cause. (I have tried to use words with as little moral overtone as possible, to avoid bringing ethics into this.) But is each case entirely determined by heredity and environment? Granted that each bird inherits a certain bias towards steadfastness or bolting, does this bias influence, or does it determine, an individual decision to stay or to bolt? There seem to be good reasons for supposing that the class of free agents is not limited to humans, and I strongly support the assumption – fundamental to process philosophy – that there is an element of freedom in everything, even in the elementary particles of which matter is constituted. But we are at present concerned with the question whether human free will is real or illusory. It may not be possible to *prove* that there is even a limited field within which we humans possess genuine freedom of choice. But it seems to

71

me that much can be said in favour of this assumption, whilst I can find no valid argument against it: I have attempted to show that the computer analogy cannot be pressed so far as to invalidate it. I therefore assume the *reality* of human free will. I recognize that this is an assumption: indeed it is one of the fundamental assumptions upon which all my thinking is founded.

CHAPTER THREE

A Philosophy of Process

(a) A. N. WHITEHEAD'S INTERPRETATION OF THE UNIVERSE

"Actual entities"

A. N. WHITEHEAD's method as philosopher is to consider our universe and attempt to describe its ultimate nature in terms capable of a maximum degree of generality. Such terms involve great abstraction, which makes his writings distinctly heavy going. At the heart of the universe Whitehead sees dynamic process. Existence cannot be abstracted from process: the two notions presuppose each other. Whitehead does not talk in terms of how things are, or what they are made of, but of how they *become*. Whitehead bases his descriptive system not on substance but on the *events* of which the universe is made up; he calls these "actual entities". The scope of this term is remarkable. It applies to all forms of matter or life, and even to God. It is the basic fact, the building brick, of a universe of process. This process is the becoming of actual entities:

"*How* an actual entity *becomes* constitutes *what* that actual entity *is:* so that the two descriptions of an actual entity are not independent. Its 'being' is constituted by its 'becoming'. This is the 'principle of process'."*

As we shall see, actual entities are also described as self-creative.

Whitehead's next underlying assumption is that our universe and everything in it is *interdependent:* everything affects or depends upon everything else: the past affects the present, and the present depends upon the past. The actual entity "becomes" as it absorbs influences from all other entities in its environment, including God. The absorbing of any such influence is called a

---

* *Process and Reality*, I.2.2 (p. 31): Note the parallel between "becomes" and "is"; the italics are Whitehead's.

73

"prehension". This term is of great importance. The word means literally a grasping or seizing. Whitehead chose it as being a lower form of "apprehension", which carries the meaning of "thorough understanding", even perhaps "grasping with the intellect", and therefore implies consciousness. In Whitehead's usage "prehensions", like feelings, need not be conscious: as we have seen, he denies the concept of "mere matter" and insists that there is at least a rudimentary element of mind in everything. Thus a stone has feelings, and prehends its surroundings:

"Every prehension consists of three factors: *(a)* the 'subject' which is prehending, namely, the actual entity in which that prehension is a concrete element; *(b)* the 'datum' (or object), which is prehended: *(c)* the 'subjective form' which is *how* that subject prehends that datum."*

Notice that the prehension is described as a concrete element in the subject entity: A's prehension of B is what B is for A, and as such a constituent in A's own process of becoming. Notice also that the subject entity prehends the other entities in its world, including God, by grasping at and seizing influence from these others, as distinct from being influenced by them. This is active, not passive. Because it matters which way round prehensions work, Whitehead described them as having a "vector character".† In everyday speech we might say of a man "he is dominated by his wife". In Whitehead's term one would have to say "he prehends his wife excessively": this form of words implies that in some sense he brings it upon himself.

At this stage the distinction may appear mere juggling with words. We cannot assess its importance until we have delved deeper into Whitehead's system. But the reader may perhaps welcome a short digression to show the relevance of this to one of the central problems of theology, that of God's grace and our free will: how does the infinite God influence a mere man without, in influencing him, also compelling him? On Whitehead's terms this gets put round the other way: not God influencing me, but me accepting, grasping, prehending God. The new form of words implies, as with the hen-pecked husband, that I retain the initiative even in prehending God. I grasp

* *Process and Reality*, I.2.2 (p. 31).
† *Process and Reality* I.2.1 (p. 25). A vector is a quantity having direction as well as magnitude; it is a common term in applied mathematics.

his grace, but retain my free will. In this digression the issues are simplified, for we have not yet discussed the third factor in prehension, the "subjective form". We shall find that Whitehead's system does preserve our free will as compared with God, but that it modifies the concept of God in ways which some may, at least initially, feel bound to resist.

Whitehead calls the becoming of an actual entity a "concrescence" because it is the growing together of all its prehensions. This growing together is self-creative: each entity concresces in accordance with its own "subjective aim". An actual entity is also an occasion: it occupies a brief, indivisible epoch of time. Its process of concrescence is known as "microscopic process": it reaches the fulfilment or "satisfaction" at which it has aimed, and then "perishes" as a subject, although continuing to be available as an object which succeeding entities prehend in the wider process which Whitehead calls "macroscopic". The quantity of space-time occupied by a single occasion or entity is of the sub-atomic or electronic order of smallness, so that it is the "macroscopic" processes of which we are aware in everyday life. We shall shortly consider what Whitehead has to say about the objects, the living things, and the human persons of everyday life, but it is convenient to defer this until we have looked further at the nature of the individual entities of which these are composed.

Whitehead describes the process of becoming of an actual entity as "dipolar", with its physical and mental poles. The two poles are "a twofold aspect of the creative urge . . . No actual entity is devoid of either pole; though their relative importance differs in different actual entities."* The two poles are indissoluble;† they correspond closely to "the without" and "the within" of Teilhard de Chardin, and to what a number of writers call outwardness and inwardness.‡ As Whitehead describes it, this dipolar character of "growing together" provides in the physical pole for the objective side of experience, derived from the surrounding world, and provides in the mental pole for the subjective side of experience. The inwardness of the process of becoming is governed by the entity's "subjective

---

* *Process and Reality.* III.2.2 (p. 339).
† *Process and Reality,* III.3.1 (p. 346).
‡ For example the Anglican theologian O. C. Quick in *The Christian Sacraments* (1927), chapter one.

aim": it is self-creative in that it shapes and alters its aim, which it gets in the first place from God. "It derives from God its basic conceptual aim, relevant to its actual world, yet with indeterminations awaiting its own decisions."*

Whitehead also expresses the dual or dipolar nature of inwardness and outwardness by saying that "an actual entity is at once the subject experiencing and the superject of its experiences. It is subject-superject, and neither half of this description can for a moment be lost sight of."† (The word superject means a throwing-above, or throwing-outwards, and thus an outward movement beyond oneself.) As subject an entity presides (inwardly) over its own process of becoming; as superject it exercises its (outward) function of being an object which influences other subjects. Whitehead illustrates this in our human realm by our notion of moral responsibility. As subject a man is responsible for being what he is in virtue of his feelings; he is also a superject, held responsible in some measure for the consequences to others of his being what he is, because these consequences derive from his feelings.

We have so far said nothing as to how an individual actual entity terminates. In the concrescence or process of growing together of its prehensions there is a succession of phases in which new prehensions arise. The final phase in this process "is one complex, fully determinate feeling. This final phase is termed the 'satisfaction'." Until this final phase has been achieved an entity cannot act as an object affecting other entities – cannot, in fact, act as a "superject" at all. Once an entity has achieved its satisfaction it then perishes as a subject, but continues as an object which is prehended by subsequent entities. Whitehead describes this as "objective immortality": when applied to God's prehensions of persons, we shall find this concept highly relevant to the question "what happens when we die?" (The statement at the beginning of this chapter that Whitehead saw everything in the universe as *interdependent* was a deliberate over-simplification, and needs to be modified at the level of individual entities: two exactly contemporary entities or occasions are, in Whitehead's view, strictly independent; neither can be an object for the other.)

* *Process and Reality*, III.1.5 (p. 317).
† *Process and Reality*, I.2.4 (p. 39).

Whitehead's "actual entities" or "occasions" are at two removes from our everyday experience of the physical world. Even in the physics laboratory the "things" we encounter occupy some extension in time, if not in space, whereas an individual entity occupies no extension in either: it perishes, but is so strongly prehended by its successor that the latter may be virtually a replica of its immediate predecessor; this repeated inheritance from former entities is termed "serial ordering", and such an ordered series of entities is termed an "enduring object". Whitehead applies this last term to both an individual electron and a molecule (although the latter is not strictly a single object).

Enduring objects are still at one remove from our everyday experience of sticks and stones. A stone comprises a vast number of closely inter-related molecules; Whitehead calls such an object a "corpuscular society". A stone persists through vast periods of time: it is wholly analysable into a very large number of enduring objects, each of which is an ordered series, with massive inheritance and absolutely minimal novelty as between each entity and its successors.

An understanding of the universe that is based upon "entities" or "occasions" which are thus at two removes from our normal thinking may appear artificial. But we have already seen that physical reality does in fact consist of sub-microscopic *events*, and that it possesses both an element of permanence and an element of change. Both elements find their place in Whitehead's view of the universe, but he differs from most philosophers in seeing change as the more fundamental of the two. We shall return to this question when we consider personal identity, but we must first turn from stones to living things. In Whitehead's terms both a stone and a jellyfish is a "corpuscular society": he sees the difference between the two primarily in terms of *novelty*, for " 'life' means novelty . . . Life is a bid for freedom".* The massive inheritance and minimal novelty as between the successive entities comprising a molecule of a stone arise from the fact that the element of "mind" is minimal and each entity's prehensions of its predecessor are virtually confined to the physical pole.

* *Process and Reality*, II.3.9 (p. 145).

We have not yet considered Whitehead's "eternal objects or pure potentials". These supply the element of novelty to the world, and to its individual entities. An entity prehends an eternal object through its mental pole, and in so doing grasps at the potentiality of novelty, the possibility that the becoming occasion will differ from its predecessors in acquiring a quality which they did not possess. The eternal objects themselves derive from God, who is thus the originator or creator of novelty; but entities possess at least some freedom of choice as to whether they do or do not prehend each of the "eternal objects" available to them. Brief discussion of Whitehead's eternal objects is not possible as this must raise the difficult philosophical problems of potentiality and actuality and of particulars and universals. The predominant trend in contemporary philosophy would be utterly opposed to the granting of any sort of individual existence to the members of an infinite set of "eternal objects or pure potentials". Commentators on Whitehead have, however, suggested that the concept of eternal objects is not integral to his philosophical system, and can in fact be omitted from it without damage. The concept that God in his primordial aspect is the ultimate source of potentiality and of novelty would appear to be self-sufficient, without the further concept that this aspect of God contains or initiates an infinite set of eternal objects.*

No stone, and no single enduring object, remains unchanged for ever: the question of life or non-life is the question of the degree of novelty. There is a parallel here with the refusal of modern science to draw an abrupt distinction between the living and the non-living.† Whitehead sees "life" as a quality which cannot be wholly abstracted from its surroundings: thus the individual living cell largely – indeed mainly – consists of enduring objects such as molecules. But it also contains other entities whose mental pole predominates: it is these entities that prehend the "eternal objects" which are potentials for novelty. The primarily mental and the primarily physical entities are intimately interrelated, so that the cell combines

* For an extended discussion see Everett W. Hall's essay "Of what use are Whitehead's eternal objects?", *Journal of Philosophy*, 27 (1930), reprinted in *Alfred North Whitehead: Essays on His Philosophy*, ed. Kline, p. 102 ff.

† "It is obvious that a structured society may have more or less 'life', and that there is no absolute gap between living and non-living societies." *Process and Reality*, II.3.7 (p. 142).

the stability of its molecular enduring objects with the novelty which *is* its life. If the term "empty space" be used for those regions of the cell that are not occupied by enduring objects such as molecules, then "life is a characteristic of 'empty space'."* This would seem to be saying indirectly not so much that this space is not in fact empty as that a living cell is not wholly reducible into molecules and electrons, but rather consists of a fundamental interrelationship between these chains of primarily physical entities and the chains of primarily mental entities through which come novelty and life.

Just as there is no absolute distinction between living and non-living, so there is none between the various forms of life, including the human. Anyone who has examined the pools on a rocky beach or indulged in underwater swimming off such a beach will be well aware of the difficulty of distinguishing "animal" forms of marine life from "vegetable". There may be no absolute division between the two, but Whitehead does make a distinction in terms of authority. The individual cells that comprise a vegetable work together as a "democracy", whereas an animal possesses one or more ruling members, which he calls "dominant" or "presiding" occasions.† At any given moment of time the presiding occasion exerts central direction over both the brain and the body of the animal – and it is a feature of the higher animals that when awake and in good mental health they possess just one presiding occasion. Whitehead uses the phrase "living person" to describe the ordered series of these presiding occasions. "Our own self-consciousness is direct awareness of ourselves as such persons."‡

Whitehead describes the defining characteristic of a "living person" in terms of the complex, or "hybrid", prehensions transmitted from occasion to occasion of its existence. Each such occasion or entity is the living person at a moment of time, and its "hybrid" prehensions are the prehensions by one subject, namely the living-person-now, of the conceptual prehensions belonging to the mental pole of another subject, namely that-person-earlier. These conceptual prehensions will have included the earlier subject's grasping at and incorporating certain

* *Process and Reality,* II.3.10 (p. 147).
† *Adventures of Ideas,* p. 264 (207).
‡ This and the following quotations are from *Process and Reality,* II.3.11 (pp. 149–53).

eternal objects or forms of novelty. Thus the later subject's hybrid prehensions of its predecessors make available for itself all the novelty inherent in former occasions, and give a very high degree of novelty and originality to the series which constitutes a living person. "By this transmission the mental originality of the living occasions receives a character and a depth."

The "living person" inhabiting an animal or human being is located in the brain. Whitehead himself described these "presiding occasions" as located in the "empty space" within the brain, just as he described the "life" of a living cell as located in the "empty space" not occupied by its molecules. He did not suggest a permanent location in any one particular interstice of the brain, since he recognized that different senses and mental activities – and therefore different regions of the brain – predominate at different times. "The route of presiding occasions probably wanders from part to part of the brain, dissociated from the physical material atoms." This wandering about does not seem very satisfactory, and Whitehead's followers and interpreters have suggested alternatives. Thus John B. Cobb, who follows Whitehead's later practice in using "soul" instead of "living person".*

"In opposition to Whitehead's view, I suggest that the soul may occupy a considerable region of the brain including both empty space and the regions occupied by many societies. This proposal assumes that it is possible for the region that constitutes the standpoint (or locus) of one occasion to include the regions that constitute the standpoints of other occasions."

Dr. Cobb advances three supporting arguments;

"First, the inheritance along the route of presiding or dominant occasions is more intelligible if there is continuity in the regions occupied by these occasions. If the dominant occasion is now here and now there, the degree of continuity and identity actually experienced is surprising. . . .
"Second, Whitehead's view seems difficult to reconcile with the apparent joint immediacy of inheritance from many parts of the brain. Hearing, seeing, remembering, and calculating seem to occur concurrently in one dominant occasion. If these functions are most intimately related with diverse portions of the brain, then it seems necessary to suppose that the dominant occasion is present at the same time at all these diverse places."

* *A Christian Natural Theology* (Westminster Press, Philadelphia, 1965), p. 83 ff.

The nub of his third argument is concerned with the perspective from which projections of direction are taken in the successive dominant occasions which comprise one's own "living person" or self. For "we can detect no shifting from one part of the head to another in the center from which projections of direction take place, whereas if the dominant occasion does move from place to place such a shift must, in fact, occur".

(The present work does not attempt to provide a detailed critique of possible variations and interpretations of Whitehead's philosophical system, and I shall not here pursue the merits or demerits of Cobb's underlying assumption that the locus of one primarily mental occasion can include the locus of other occasions. Whitehead himself never made such an assumption, and as I interpret him he probably conceived of all actual occasions – that is, all entities other than God – as microscopic in size. On the other hand, Charles Hartshorne would appear to make precisely this assumption as regards the relationship between human consciousness and brain-cell events: he certainly makes a similar assumption as regards God.)*

In *Process and Reality* Whitehead always used the term "living person" for the seat of central direction and self-consciousness; in his later, less formal writings he more often used instead the single word "soul". He never attempted to analyse either term physiologically or psychologically; this perhaps explains why he never entered into any detailed discussion of the location of the dominant occasion, or of its relationship to the various parts of the brain. Whitehead did emphasize that the word "soul", as he used it, can equally be applied to the non-human animal as to the human. I have, however, preferred the term "living-person", precisely because "soul" is so widely assumed to have a solely human connotation.

Whitehead saw the difference between the human and the non-human as immense, but not absolute. Thus, at a practical level, this difference is closely inter-related with the development of language – a rudimentary form of which may be used by some animals. "Apart from language, the retention of thought, the easy recall of thought, the interweaving of thought into higher complexity, the communication of thought, all are gravely limited ... It is no accident that the Athenians

* See Hartshorne's essay in *The Philosophy of Alfred North Whitehead*, ed. Schilpp, p. 545; see also ch. 5 below.

from whom we derive our Western notions of freedom enjoyed the use of a language supreme for its delicate variety."*

Whitehead also saw the difference between the human and the non-human in terms of degrees of novelty. "The conceptual entertainment of unrealized possibility becomes a major factor in human mentality. In this way outrageous novelty is introduced, sometimes beatified, sometimes damned, and sometimes literally patented or protected by copyright." Significant novelty is introduced for a purpose, and it is in terms of purpose, ideals and values that Whitehead saw the most basic difference between man and other animals. For a man may pursue ideals which greatly affect his life, yet appear to be only loosely connected, if at all, with his own well-being. Whitehead here expresses this in terms of importance:

"For animal life the concept of importance, in some of its many differentiations, has a real relevance. The human grade of animal life immensely extends this concept, and thereby introduces novelty of functioning as essential for varieties of importance. Thus morals and religion arise as aspects of this human impetus towards the best in each occasion. Morals can be discerned in the higher animals; but not religion. Morality emphasizes the detailed occasion; while religion emphasizes the unity of ideal inherent in the universe.

"There is, however, every gradation of transition between animals and men. In animals we can see emotional feeling, dominantly derived from bodily functions, and yet tinged with purposes, hopes, and expression derived from conceptual functioning. In mankind, the dominant dependence on bodily functioning seems still there. And yet the life of a human being receives its worth, its importance, from the way in which unrealized ideals shape its purposes and tinge its actions. The distinction between men and animals is in one sense only a difference in degree. But the extent of the degree makes all the difference. The Rubicon has been crossed."†

Personal identity

To conclude this discussion of living persons and enduring objects, I would refer back to the discussion in chapter one sub-titled "The elements of permanence and change in the world." This is largely concerned with the question of *personal identity*. Whitehead did not minimize the importance of personal identity. "It is dominant in human experience: the notions of

* *Modes of Thought*, p. 49 f.
† *Modes of Thought*, pp. 36, 37 f, and 39.

civil law are based upon it. The same man is sent to prison who committed the robbery; and the same materials survive for centuries, and for millions of years." But he and Hartshorne are completely agreed in denying that there can be any absolute self-identity throughout any series of occasions, including the type of series constituting a living person: "The only strict concrete identity is seen as belonging to the momentary self" (Hartshorne).

A philosophy that envisages the universe in terms of transient occasions might be expected to encounter some difficulty in describing the thread of personal identity that runs through those chains of occasions that comprise an enduring object or living person. Whitehead's philosophy has been so criticized: I believe that it presents a better balance as between permanence and change than does much of our everyday thinking. There is food for thought in this passage from Whitehead. Having emphasized the wide preservation of identity in "the planets, the stones, the living things", he turns to the partiality of this preservation:

"Nothing in realized matter-of-fact retains complete identity with its antecedent self. This self-identity in the sphere of realized fact is only partial. It holds for certain purposes. It dominates certain kinds of process. But in other sorts of process, the differences are important, and the self-identity is an interesting fable. For the purpose of inheriting real estate, the identity of the man of thirty years of age with the former baby of ten months is dominant. For the purpose of navigating a yacht, the differences between the man and the child are essential; the identity then sinks into a metaphysical irrelevancy."*

We have seen how Whitehead distinguishes living persons from other enduring objects by the "hybrid" prehensions which predominate in the former. He similarly distinguishes our own personal identity in terms of a special mode of prehending, or inheriting, from the previous occasions that comprise our own "living person" or self:

"We—as enduring objects with personal order—objectify the occasions of our own past with peculiar completeness in our immediate present."

"An enduring personality in the temporal world is a route of occasions in which the successors with some peculiar completeness sum up their predecessors."†

* *Modes of Thought*, p. 129.
† *Process and Reality*, II.7.2 (p. 225), and final section.

Whitehead never explained what he meant by "peculiar completeness". Before we can even speculate about this we first need to examine his general analysis of experience. We must be clear that he saw *all* actuality – everything, in common parlance – as "experiencing activity"; most entities in our universe are far below the level of conscious mentality or feeling, but they all possess a "within" as well as a "without"; to say that all actuality is experiencing activity is another way of saying that every entity has a "mental" as well as a physical aspect or "pole". Whitehead's insight as to the immanence of entities actually "present in" other entities follows from this: as one entity grasps at another it includes that other, objectively, in its own experience, which *is* itself. Thus the object-entity is *included in* the "becoming" subject-entity. We shall make use of this insight when we come on to consider the Christian belief that "God was in Christ".

In considering the concept of experience we normally think first of our own sense-experience of colour, sound, taste, and so on. Whitehead repeatedly denies that this form of experience is fundamental:* such sense-experience – which he terms "presentational immediacy" – is based upon and derived from a *more fundamental* type of experience, which Whitehead terms "causal efficacy". He demonstrates the necessity for this type of experience by considering the lower levels in the evolutionary scale. At these levels there is no sense-perception yet there is reaction to environment, which is a type of "perception".

We can confirm the existence of this more fundamental type of experience by reflecting upon the derivation of our own conscious sense-experience. We see *with* our eyes and hear *with* our ears. Thus "sense-perception of the contemporary world is accompanied by perception of the 'withness' of the body. It is this withness that makes the body the starting-point for our knowledge of the (surrounding) world. We find here our direct knowledge of 'causal efficacy'."† We see *with* our eyes; we do not *see* our eyes: our conscious perception itself derives unconsciously from the operation of our sense organs, whose transient occasions inherit from their predecessors by what Whitehead terms "causal efficacy". Thus even our conscious

* See, for example, *Modes of Thought*, chapter 6.
† *Process and Reality*, II.2.6 (p. 112).

sense-experience itself depends massively upon this other more fundamental type of experience.

If asked to describe the thread of personal identity running through my life, I could do so in terms of a certain identity that persists throughout the enormous changes in my body. Individual cells are replaced over the years, and none – except in the central nervous system – persists throughout life. And yet my body, even my recently dead body, could probably be identified by a once-close friend who had not seen me for twenty years. This persisting bodily identity must be a function of the way in which, in the aggregate, cells inherit from their predecessors.

I could also describe the thread of personal identity in terms of memory. Indeed my conscious memory of past occasions *is* my own *awareness* of self-identity: but it is only a small part of that identity. Modern psychology has revealed the immense influence of the unconscious mind. The psychiatrist can help us to bring long-buried fears and cravings above the level of consciousness, so that their power may be diminished. Skilled questioning combined with the drug LSD can bring to light the unsatisfied cravings of earliest infancy, perhaps for mother's milk or mother's love: it is claimed that a patient can re-live the extreme pressure endured in a painful birth, or even, perhaps, maternal tension or neglect experienced by the foetus in her womb. Such experiences normally remain wholly buried; yet they can have a lasting effect throughout life, and must therefore contribute to the person's persisting self-identity.

We can now return to Whitehead's statement that "We ... objectify the occasions of our own past with peculiar completeness in our immediate present". His theory of "prehensions" states that in the case of a sequence of physical prehensions an entity or occasion can only prehend, and so objectify, its immediate predecessor: there must be a direct succession from entity to entity, with no gaps or jumps. But Whitehead states equally clearly that this does not apply to "hybrid" prehensions, which transmit mental feeling. This is because mental feelings are not anchored to one particular spot in space-time in the same way as physical ones. "Thus the doctrine of immediate objectification (or prehension) for the mental poles and of mediate objectification (i.e. mediated from one entity to another in a continuous succession) for the physical poles seems most consonant to the philosophy of organism ... This conclusion has some empirical support, both from the evidence for peculiar instances of telepathy, and from the instinctive apprehension of a tone of feeling in ordinary social intercourse."*

This has led John B. Cobb to make the suggestion that:

"There may be immediate objectification of many, perhaps of all, of the past occasions in the living person. In this way, a peculiar completeness of summing up would be accounted for . . . Also, my own experience of personal identity . . . would be explained. I do experience immediate prehensions of former mental experiences, sometimes with considerable vividness. This experience does assure me of my personal identity, not of course of numerical identity, with that earlier occasion of experience.

"We need not make personal identity in this view dependent upon the unmediated prehension of *all* past occasions in the person in question. So long as all those past occasions of experience are potentially available for such recall, whether spontaneously or under hypnosis, the peculiarity of the sense of identity can be explained. Whether or not in the unconscious dimensions of our experience they are continuously effective is a factual question best left to the depth psychologists."†

Dr. Cobb sums up his proposal in a single sentence. "It is that personal identity obtains whenever there is a serially ordered society of primarily mental occasions (a soul) in which each occasion actually or potentially prehends unmediatedly the mental poles of all its predecessors." Cobb freely acknowledges that this goes beyond anything actually stated by Whitehead, but it would seem to me that his suggestion is fascinatingly in accord both with Whitehead's philosophy and with the general lines of depth psychology. There is a need for a detailed study of man and of the human mind and personality in the light of process philosophy, relating this both to psychology and to Christian thinking about what theologians call the doctrine of man. But in this book we must confine ourselves to seeking first a general picture of process philosophy and then a more detailed understanding of the relationship of that picture to the doctrines of God and of Christ. To complete our general picture we need to consider God's place and role in this philosophy. We return to this in greater detail in chapter five, but a brief consideration is necessary at this point.‡

* *Process and Reality*, IV.3.4 (p. 436).
† *A Christian Natural Theology*, p. 77.
‡ My reason for this two-stage exposition of process thinking about God is that it contains two elements that may be novel, and perhaps uncongenial,

"God is an actual entity, and so is the most trivial puff of existence in far-off empty space." For Whitehead, God is an actual entity but not an occasion. Occasions perish, but God is everlasting: he "exists through time without loss of immediacy". God is unique in that he supplies each entity with its initial aim: but he resembles other entities in being "dipolar". Corresponding to an entity's inwardness or "mental pole" is God's primordial nature, which is the primordial fact in the universe;* it is from this that each entity derives its subjective aim. Corresponding to an entity's outwardness or "physical pole" is God's consequent nature: as with the physical pole of any entity, this grasps, takes into itself, and is in turn affected by all other entities. This is of momentous importance. God and the world affect, and depend upon, each other: his primordial nature is unchanging, but his consequent nature is related to the world's happenings. God grasps at or prehends all other entities, takes them into his own consequent nature as objects, and in so doing *is affected by them:*

"God, as well as being primordial, is also consequent. He is the beginning and the end . . . Thus, by reason of the relativity of all things, there is a reaction of the world on God. The completion of God's nature into a fullness of physical feeling is derived from the objectification of the world in God. He shares with every new creation its actual world; and the concrescent creature is objectified in God as a novel element in God's objectification of that actual world . . . God's conceptual nature is unchanged, by reason of its final completeness. But his derivative nature is consequent upon the creative advance of the world."†

The phrase "the objectification of the world in God" is another way of referring to the process of becoming in which

* Primordial: "constituting the beginning or starting-point; original, not derivative" *(Shorter Oxford Dictionary)*. It need not refer to God. Disraeli used the phrase "the primordial tenets of the Tory Party".

† *Process and Reality*, V.2.3 (p. 488).

to readers unfamiliar with Whitehead and Hartshorne; a major modification, if not denial, of the concept of divine omnipotence; and a highly God-centred concept of heaven. I deem it more helpful to examine these two issues with some care (in chapter four) before considering the doctrine of God in any detail. But this examination itself requires some knowledge of process thinking about God. All doctrines are indeed interdependent in what Tillich aptly called the "theological circle".

God "prehends" all other entities: he takes them into himself as objects, and in so doing he is affected by them. This forms a novel element in God's nature.

"The image—and it is but an image—the image under which this operative growth of God's nature is best conceived, is that of a tender care that nothing be lost.

"The consequent nature of God is his judgement on the world. He saves the world as it passes into the immediacy of his own life. It is the judgement . . . of a wisdom which uses what in the temporal world is mere wreckage.

"Another image which is also required to understand his consequent nature, is that of his infinite patience . . . tenderly saving the turmoil of the intermediate world by the completion of his own nature . . . He is the poet of the world, with tender patience leading it by his vision of truth, beauty and goodness."*

Prehensions are mutual and interdependent. The development in God's consequent nature is reflected back into the temporal world, "and qualifies this world so that each temporal actuality includes it as an immediate fact of relevant experience. For the kingdom of heaven is with us today. (This) action . . . is the love of God for the world. It is the particular providence for particular occasions. What is done in the world is transformed into a reality in heaven, and the reality in heaven passes back into the world. By reason of this reciprocal relation, the love in the world passes into the love in heaven, and floods back again into the world. In this sense, God is the great companion — the fellow-sufferer who understands."†

In Whitehead's categories God is an actual entity, whereas a person is a sequence of entities unified by a persisting, but not absolute, personal identity. As we shall see in chapter five, Hartshorne has modified Whitehead's concept and suggested that God is rather a succession of entities — a concept which more closely resembles that of a "living person". We now confine ourselves to Whitehead's own concept of God as an actual entity, and attempt briefly to answer the question "can we derive a *personal* God from Whitehead's philosophy?"

Whitehead, like Trinitarian theology, avoids describing God as "a Person". But his idea of God certainly possesses, in supreme form, what we associate with personality. I shall not attempt a detailed analysis of "personality", but its ingredients

* *Process and Reality*, V.2.4 (p. 490).
† *Process and Reality*, final section (p. 497).

surely include (1) unity and self-identity; (2) consciousness or awareness; (3) freedom to choose ends, and capacity to act according to aim; (4) capacity to communicate. For Whitehead, God has all of these. The unity of one single, everlasting entity is greater than that of a person. "The consequent nature of God is conscious." God's aim, which is the purpose behind the universe, is for maximum intensity of experience for the totality of all entities, including God himself. He freely chooses this aim, acts accordingly, and communicates his aim to everything without resorting to absolute compulsion. Whitehead would not need to follow Tillich, who spends some time in justifying the statement that God is both individual and participant. Both facts follow immediately in Whitehead's system. As the quotations have shown, Whitehead describes God's activity in terms of the *personal* images of tender care, judgement, wisdom, patience and – above all – love. Indeed the deepest way in which his philosophy can help Christian belief may well be its meaningful interpretation of *how* God loves the world.

(b) SOME WAYS IN WHICH PROCESS PHILOSOPHY HELPS CHRISTIAN BELIEF

"A most ingenious paradox"

One of the great advantages of applying process thinking to Christian theology is that it both demands and helps to achieve a removal of internal contradictions. The scientist of today has learned to live with a question-mark at the heart of his subject, but he will not live with a contradiction. As we have seen, the fact that electrons appear in some experiments to behave like particles and in others like waves of energy is not dealt with by trying to reconcile these two sets of properties, which often directly contradict each other; but by accepting that "an electron is an electron", and cannot adequately be described in terms that apply to objects of visible size. There is therefore a considerable question-mark, or impossibility of visualization, at the heart of physics – but no contradiction. There is also deep mystery, but no contradiction, at the heart of God: while seeking some partial understanding of the mystery, the theologians ought to be as careful as the scientists to avoid contradictory ways of thought – and yet:

89

"Theologians have rather generally admitted that the idea of God, as formulated by them, involves insuperable paradoxes. We are even told that a God conceivable without paradox would not be God. Admittedly a being conceivable through and through without mystery, in the sense of aspects inaccessible to our knowledge, would not be God. But what, in this connection, is meant by paradox? A theological paradox, it appears, is what a contradiction becomes when it is about God rather than something else, or indulged in by a theologian or a church rather than an unbeliever or a heretic."*

Paul Tillich distinguishes between paradox and contradiction. He gives a careful definition of paradox and goes back to its Greek derivation:

"Paradoxical means 'against the opinion', namely, the opinion of finite reason. Paradox points to the fact that in God's acting finite reason is superseded but not annihilated; it expresses this fact in terms which are not logically contradictory but which are supposed to point beyond the realm in which finite reason is applicable . . . There is, in the last analysis, only *one* genuine paradox in the Christian message—the appearance of that which conquers existence under the conditions of existence. Incarnation, redemption, justification, etc., are implied in this paradoxical event. It is not a logical contradiction which makes it a paradox but the fact that it transcends all human expectations and possibilities."†

Thus Tillich accepts an element of paradox, whilst Hartshorne rejects the term completely. All the same, I suggest that it is the degree of agreement between these two thinkers which is significant: both agree that there are aspects of God and his activity which are beyond our knowledge or powers of reason, and both deny that contradictions have any legitimate place in theological thinking. We now consider an instance in which paradox is often invoked, but condemned as a meaningless contradiction by Professor Hartshorne.

God's grace and human free will

"By the grace of God I am what I am . . . I laboured more abundantly than they all: yet not I, but the grace of God which was with me." (1 Corinthians 15: 10).

The bearing of the young science of cybernetics upon human free will has been briefly discussed.‡ We are here concerned

* C. Hartshorne, *The Divine Relativity* (1948), p. 1.
† *Systematic Theology*, vol. 1, p. 64.
‡ In the Appended Note at the end of ch. 2.

with the relationship between God's grace and human free will. This is one of the central problems of Christian theology. In his book *God was in Christ* D. M. Baillie called it "the central paradox":

"When I make the wrong choice, I am entirely responsible, and my conscience condemns me. And yet (here is the paradox) when I make the right choice, my conscience does not applaud or congratulate me. I do not feel meritorious or glow with self-esteem—if and in so far as I am a Christian. Instead of that I say: 'Not I, but the grace of God'. Thus while there is a human side to every good action, so that it is genuinely the free choice of a person with a will, yet somehow the Christian feels that the other side of it, the divine side, is logically prior. The grace of God is prevenient. The good was His before it was ours."

Baillie went on to suggest "that this paradox in its fragmentary form in our own Christian lives is a reflection of that perfect union of God and man in the Incarnation . . . and may therefore be our best clue . . . to the mystery of the Incarnation itself".* Indeed this relation of "the paradox of the Incarnation" to our individual experience of "the paradox of grace" is one of the main themes of this beautifully written and much loved book. And yet I feel bound to question whether it is possible to say that our actions have both a human and a divine "side", of which the latter is "prevenient" (going before), and at the same time to preserve our free will. The concept of God's prevenience runs through many of our collects and prayers, and much Christian writing from St. Paul and St. Augustine down to D. M. Baillie and many others. But I fear that an increasing number of people find this whole concept incomprehensible, and would agree with Hartshorne:

"For God to do what I do when I decide my own act, determine my own concrete being, is mere nonsense, words without meaning. It is not my act if anyone else decides or performs it."†

I cannot share with Baillie "the conviction which a Christian man possesses, that every good thing in him, every good thing he does, is somehow not wrought by himself but by God". I appreciate that in some ways he and I are trying to say the same thing, for Baillie immediately describes this as "a highly paradoxical conviction, for in ascribing all to God it does not

* *God was in Christ* (Faber, 1948—now a paperback) p. 116–17.
† *The Divine Relativity*, p. 134.

abrogate human personality nor disclaim personal responsibility". But I suggest that where Christians do possess this conviction it results from the way they have been taught to think, and does not arise from their experience. If I perform some good and unselfish action, the *experience* that I feel is that God has helped and guided me, *not* that God has wrought the action: God influences me – very greatly, perhaps – but the decision is neither God's nor God's-and-mine, but mine alone. The problem remains: God's greatness stands in such sharp contrast to us that his influence must, seemingly, swamp and coerce the individual: if God "puts into our mind good desires", how can we fail to perform these?

That we are not swamped by God's influence follows immediately from one of the basic definitions in Whitehead's philosophical system, that of "prehensions": each entity "prehends" or grasps at the influence of all other entities; we have seen that the verb is active and not passive. Thus every entity has at least a rudimentary element of freedom in its response to all other entities, including God. Where the subject-entity who is prehending is far more significant than the object he is prehending, his freedom will be great and the effect of the prehension will be small. Thus God is influenced and affected by us, but only in small degree; whereas he has great freedom in his response to us. Conversely, God's influence upon us is very great, and we have only a narrow freedom in our attitude and response to his influence – but this narrow freedom is real and inviolable.*

Thus process philosophy sees the inviolability of human free will as an example of the real, though limited, freedom of *all* entities in our universe. The tension between God's grace and our free will is replaced by that between the freedom and the order in the universe. The tension remains, but in its proper place: contradiction is avoided.

A theology of the inorganic

"The universe is not a museum with its specimens in glass cases. Nor is the universe a perfectly drilled regiment with its ranks in step, marching forward with undisturbed poise . . . The essence of life is to be found in the frustrations of established order. The universe

* We shall consider this further in the next chapter, where we discuss the concept of God's omnipotence in connection with the question of pain and suffering.

refuses the deadening influence of complete conformity. And yet in its refusal, it passes towards novel order as a primary requisite for important experience. We have to explain the aim at forms of order, and the aim at novelty of order . . . Apart from some understanding, however dim, of these characteristics of the historic process, we enjoy no rationality of experience."*

The coexistence of freedom and order may be a truth too deep for our finite minds fully to grasp or our language to express: neither Whitehead's language nor his cosmological system is faultless. But I deem it a great advantage that his system *starts* with the fact of this coexistence, from which beginning he attempts to describe the reality of the universe. The importance of freedom is something about which most men would agree. We may feel glad that the last hours of a friend's painful illness should pass in a coma; but, when a road accident results in a victim living for years in a permanent state of coma, we are inclined to question whether surgical skill and devoted nursing are in fact achieving anything of value. We so question because we instinctively attach value to freedom, and great value to conscious human life. In discussing the vastness of the universe in relation to our own *biosphere* I suggested that process thinking helps us to see value in *all* matter by its insistence that every entity possesses some measure of freedom: if there is value in freedom there is, therefore, value in everything that exists. There are differing degrees of value, just as there are differing degrees of freedom: we matter greatly to God, but he is not indifferent to the death of a sparrow. The series of gradations of value contains no absolute discontinuity as between man and other forms of life.

Paul Tillich expresses a similar thought with his phrase "the multidimensional unity of life"; this forms the title of the first chapter in volume three of his *Systematic Theology*, which contains this passage:

"The religious significance of the inorganic is immense, but is rarely considered by theology . . . the quantitatively overwhelming realm of the inorganic has had . . . a strong antireligious impact on many people in the ancient and the modern worlds. A 'theology of the inorganic' is lacking."†

This lack cannot but be a serious barrier to Christian belief,

* A. N. Whitehead, *Modes of Thought,* pp. 123 and 119.
† Page 19.

particularly in the modern world. By its insistence that there is an element of "mind" and of freedom in everything, process philosophy does offer a "theology of the inorganic".

God "keeps the rules"

"Philosophy frees itself from the taint of ineffectiveness by its close relations with religion and with science, natural and sociological. It attains its chief importance by fusing the two, namely, religion and science, into one rational scheme of thought . . . Religion is the translation of general ideas into particular thoughts, particular emotions, and particular purposes . . . Philosophy finds religion, and modifies it; and conversely religion is among the data of experience which philosophy must weave into its own scheme."*

This quotation from the opening chapter of Whitehead's *Process and Reality* needs to be read in conjunction with his earlier book *Religion in the Making*, in which he describes religious experience. He insists that "This is a revelation of character, apprehended as we apprehend the characters of our friends. But in this case it is an apprehension of character permanently inherent in the nature of things. There is a large concurrence in the negative doctrine that this religious experience does not include any direct intuition of a definite person, or individual." He cites Confucian, Buddhist, and Hindu philosophy in support of this "negative doctrine". "Christian theology has also, in the main, adopted the position that there is no direct intuition of such an ultimate personal substratum for the world. It maintains the doctrine of the existence of a personal God as a truth, but holds that our belief in it is based upon inference. Most theologians hold that this inference is sufficiently obvious to be made by all men upon the basis of their individual personal experience. But, be this as it may, it is an inference and not a direct intuition."†

I am not at present concerned with the negative aspects of this. I should myself agree that belief in a personal God is an inference rather than a direct intuition, but I would add that the inference follows very directly from the nature of religious experience. Whitehead's positive statements are of great help to Christian belief. Having earlier defined religious experience as an apprehension of character inherent in the nature of things,

* *Process and Reality*, I.1.6 (p. 21).
† *Religion in the Making* (1926), 2.2 (p. 61–3).

Whitehead says explicitly in *Process and Reality* both that religion is among the data of experience of which philosophy must take note and that religion and science must be fused into one rational scheme of thought. Such a fusing remains impossible as long as religious thought is wedded to a use of paradox tantamount to contradiction. It is rendered possible by Whitehead's insistence that "God is not to be treated as an exception to all metaphysical principles, invoked to save their collapse. He is their chief exemplification."* I would like to paraphrase this by saying that God "keeps the rules", and does so over a wider field than is usually recognized.

That God supplies the element of order in the universe may indeed be a helpful idea, but it is far from new: it is found in one sense in Genesis 1 and in another in the Christian belief that in Christ we receive a newness of life which is the direct gift of God. But traditional teaching perhaps attaches too much emphasis to the other side of the coin when it continually underlines the fact that "His ways are not our ways". Whether or not we call ourselves scientists or technicians, we live in an age which expects things, and even in some measure people, to behave and react according to definite laws or rules. We would feel less hazy about God if we could demarcate certain areas or aspects of life in which God also "keeps the rules". Whitehead's system helps us to do this; as we have seen, one of its basic assumptions is the interdependence of things — everything affects all subsequent things, and is affected by all that came before. Whitehead would include God in this: God is neither remote nor unaffected; he receives influence from us as he "prehends" us; we influence him just as he, and everything, influences us. It is indeed partly true that God moves in a mysterious way, but it is also true that God is one of the objects we prehend. As has been said, by no means all "prehensions" are conscious feelings. We receive some influence or guidance from God at the level of consciousness, and some below this level — just as we do from other people, or from society as a whole. In all this God keeps the rules — he does not make a new set of rules especially for himself.

The second aspect I would stress, which is closely allied to what has just been said, is the great emphasis Whitehead places on the *love* of God. It is because God loves that he extends his

* *Process and Reality*, V.2.2 (p. 486).

gift of creative novelty to all his creatures. It is equally because he loves that he works to bring all things together into greater unity. The unity or order in the universe, which is so basic to Whitehead's entire philosophy, quite simply *is* the love of God. To adapt Bonhoeffer's phrase, the love of God is to be found not at the edge of Whitehead's philosophy, but at its centre. That God is *actus purus* – pure activity unsullied, and in the last resort unaffected, by the world's sufferings – is an ancient and apparently venerable idea, but it surely stands contradicted by the great truth that God is love. In daily life, in literature, and in the life of Christ we assess the depth of someone's love by the extent to which he is utterly at one with the object of his love, and utterly affected by the other's fortunes and concerns. If God's nature is too remote or too unsullied for this, then can we properly apply the word love to him at all? To love is to be affected, to love deeply is to be deeply affected, to love as Christ loved is to be utterly affected. Can God the Father be the one exception? If the depth of God's love for us far surpasses the deepest human love, ought we not to assume that he will be more deeply affected by our sorrows and sufferings than we humans can ever be by the sufferings of those we love? Here especially we can see the wisdom of Whitehead's insistence that God is not an exception to the principles we find elsewhere, but is in fact their deepest exemplification. God keeps the rules, and above all the rules of love.

CHAPTER FOUR

Suffering, Death and Heaven in the Light of Process Thinking

(a) CAN WE RECONCILE SUFFERING WITH A GOD OF LOVE?

THE existence of widespread suffering, animal as well as human, is one of the great difficulties, some would say the greatest difficulty, in the path of belief in the God of love on whom the Christian gospel rests: an intellectual difficulty for those who try to think out their belief and relate it to the world around them; and also a practical difficulty with deep emotional overtones for those who have known great suffering in themselves or those nearest to them. For purposes of thought we can divide the problem into two. We will consider first the general problem of why God allows pain and suffering to exist, and then come on to the deeper problem of particular cases.

1. The general problem of pain is epitomized by the title of Austin Farrer's essay on providence and evil: *Love Almighty and Ills Unlimited*.* Any scientist or doctor would, I think, agree with Dr. Farrer's conclusion that pain and suffering are necessary and inevitable in the physical world in which we live. It is also arguable that they are preferable to the alternative of a monochrome uniformity without either sorrow or joy, but the main point is that pain and suffering are inevitable. Competition is basic to life, and this competition includes both sudden murder as the early bird eats its worm and slow strangulation as the dense foliage of forest trees deprives the undergrowth of the benefit it would otherwise derive from the rays of the sun. When reading to a three year old I often felt that some of the superbly told and illustrated Beatrix Potter stories ought to be classified as horror comics. If Mr. Macgregor catches Peter Rabbit he will not smack his backside and let him go, but eat him as rabbit-pie – indeed we are told that this happened to Peter's

* Collins, 1962. (Also recently published as a Fontana paperback).

father. In her stories – indeed in many children's stories – all the characters are animals, and the entire excitement is supplied by the question of who eats whom first. Surprisingly, this seldom seems to worry the very young: I write as the father of three daughters. Perhaps children accept the unbridled competition of who eats whom more readily than even the most capitalist parents. Perhaps it is only the adults who need Dr. Farrer's reminders that even the molecules in a gas are constantly knocking each other around, that the world is not one harmonious system but the interaction of systems innumerable, and that the mutual interference of these systems is the cause of all physical evil. Farrer thus sums up this part of his argument:

"When we lament the mutual destructiveness of physical things, of what do we complain? Is it that unintelligent creatures are not like virtuous men, or indeed, better? Good men consider one another and, in Kant's pedantic phrase, never treat their fellows as mere means to the furtherance of their own purposes, but always at the same time as ends-in-themselves. Yet the best of men cannot extend such benevolence to all sorts of creatures with which they share the field of space. Our stomachs ruthlessly destroy what they consume, and if we spare animals, we shall still butcher vegetables. Only pure spirits could be wholly non-destructive."*

Pain also, of course, has its uses. The fact that he felt acutely ill and feeble when he had a high fever doubtless made a cave man lie down and cover himself with skins, which may have saved his life. Acute pain in the stomach sends us to the doctor, and our appendix is removed before it bursts. The happily rare case of a child born with no sense of pain is treated as extremely serious: he may walk into the fire, and every effort must be made to cure him of this dangerous lack of a sense of what we normally regard as evil. Pain, both human and animal, is a necessary ingredient in our universe. To say this does not, however, absolve us from asking why a loving God created a physical universe, and thus in a sense created pain: could he not have created only spiritual beings? This is a proper question to ask, and we shall attempt to answer it in the next section, to which it more naturally belongs.

2. We now come to the more acute question of particular suffering, the problem why some people – and indeed some animals – should suffer an enormous and apparently quite excessive amount of pain. Let us consider the alternative. The

* *Love Almighty and Ills Unlimited*, p. 57 f.

idea that no one should suffer more than a total *quantity* of pain is untenable: quantity equals intensity multiplied by duration; all uncured illness would have to prove fairly rapidly fatal if a certain relatively low total quantity of pain was never to be excelled: thus Paul's "thorn in the flesh" would have killed him long before he got to Rome. On such a basis, life would have become extinct. The only possible form of this alternative is a lowering of the cut-off point at which pain's intensity kills. This also would jeopardize the survival of the species. To take one example, in earlier centuries people frequently survived a burst appendix and made a full recovery — yet they must have suffered a high intensity of pain when it burst. I do not see how mammals could survive with too low a limit to the intensity of pain they could endure. At a certain level of pain an animal does in fact lie down to die; by comparison, we humans often increase our resistance to pain with an added will to live composed of sense of duty, responsibility for others, and fear of death.

If a brief analysis of the circumstances of human and animal life has shown both pain and the capacity to withstand a good deal of pain to be necessary ingredients, a moment's reflection on the nature and movement of microbes, bacteria, malarial mosquitoes and the like will show that there is — at least to all appearances — an element of chance in the incidence and causation of some forms of illness. In my view it is as impossible to believe that the movement of these organisms is precisely determined, either by God or by any external control, as it is impossible to deny a real element of chance in the movement of individual chromosomes during the replication of a cell. Man can, of course, do a great deal to cure and to prevent some forms of illness, but a random element in their incidence remains.

There is a long list of illnesses which are caused in whole or in part by human agency. Road accidents, venereal disease, and the effects of smoking, alcohol and drugs are at the head of the list, which also includes those illnesses which arise from overwork, over-eating, too little exercise, and so forth: in such cases the sufferer can be said to have brought it upon himself. In general, however, there is no evidence whatever to support the view that illness is a punishment for wickedness. In so far as one can assess the moral status of others, one can scarcely fail to observe that most forms of illness fall indiscriminately upon the just and the unjust.

It is remarkable that the opposite view should still persist in this scientific age, but anyone with experience of visiting homes afflicted by serious illness or death will know that there is still a widely held feeling – not always strong enough to be called a belief – that major illness is a divine visitation. Many people who have little explicit religious belief are still superstitious enough to attribute to God those things whose causation they cannot understand. Others, whose religious belief is more definite, still adopt the assumption of much of the ancient world, and many of the Jewish psalmists, that God's sense of justice must predominate over his love. Needless to say, Christian theology does not take that view and certainly does not regard illness as God's punishment for sin. On the other hand, I wonder whether Christian preaching should not do more to emphasize that venereal disease and alcoholism are not the only illnesses mankind inflicts upon itself, and that there is an element of sin both in carelessness on the roads and also, perhaps, in heavy smoking.

Much of this may seem too obvious to be worth saying. Most thoughtful people accept in principle both the necessity of pain and a certain randomness in its incidence. We must go back to the problem of individual suffering in its most acute form: why should this painful illness happen to *me*, or to a member of *my* family? There are two groups of people who may ask this question when afflicted by suffering: those who have never tried to think out their religious beliefs, and those with a definite – and up to the present a tolerably compatible – belief in both the love and the omnipotence of God. There are also two groups of people who will not ask this question: those atheists who see the natural world entirely in terms of chance and mechanical determinism; and those theists who see the world and all its life as dependent upon God, yet at the same time possessing a real element of freedom. There is no "problem of pain" for the atheist, however deeply he may grieve that his wife has developed a cancer.

The incidence of individual suffering does not lead the theistic "process" thinker to doubt the love of God, since he is absolutely clear in his mind that the majority of suffering results from neither divine nor human interference, but from the inalienable freedom which he believes God to have rightly and lovingly given, in varying degree, to all his creatures. But the incidence of individual suffering poses so acute a problem for many Christians that I think it right briefly to examine the cause of this problem, namely the religious emphasis upon the "omnipotence" of God, before seeking the guidance of explicitly "process" thinking.

It is far from clear what we mean when we say that God is almighty and omnipotent. If we interpret omnipotent as meaning "able to do anything" we are immediately compelled to qualify this, since God cannot perform such logical impossibilities as making a square circle. St. Thomas Aquinas pointed this out, adding "It is better to say that such things cannot be done, than that God cannot do them". The first half of this dictum does, however, imply the second. "According to St. Thomas, therefore, the doctrine of divine omnipotence means that God can do everything which is intrinsically possible."* This is not very helpful because, as O. C. Quick goes on to point out in his great book *Doctrines of the Creed,* "with our imperfect knowledge we are unable to say, except within very narrow limits, what is and what is not intrinsically possible". Quick's adverb "intrinsically" is itself in need of definition, for it may be that certain things would be possible in other – perfectly possible – universes, but are impossible in the universe that happens to exist.

Behind the words almighty and omnipotent lies the Greek word *pantocrator,* or ruler of all things. Neither English adjective is an altogether happy translation, but the general feel of the word "almighty" is perhaps slightly the nearer to the Greek. I suggest that most English people take the opening phrase of the Apostles' Creed to mean that God possesses a might of power both greater than any other and able to be set against any other power or force in the universe, so that the other force is diverted or overcome. I shall myself use the words almighty and omnipotent in this sense. On this view God can, if he so chooses, deflect any bacterium (or the bullet that killed President Kennedy), prevent any storm or earthquake, or strike down any tyrant and his armed forces. The creatures' freedom is not inviolable, since God may at any moment intervene; God must, therefore, be held responsible for a great deal of preventable

* O. C. Quick, *Doctrines of The Creed* (Nisbet, 1938), p. 60.

suffering. Dr. Quick seeks to resolve the difficulties in terms of "the omnipotence of love":

"The Christian revelation . . . declares that the strongest power in the world is that of agape (love) itself, which does not work by force to achieve its highest purpose or win its greatest victories. The Cross is the power and the wisdom of God. And if St. Paul speaks truth, our whole conception of God's omnipotence must be transformed. The supreme manifestation of divine power is . . . in the complete self-sacrifice of Christ which has overcome evil by suffering, made atonement for sin, and opened the kingdom of heaven."*

This is in line with his earlier statement that "the value of the doctrine of divine omnipotence lies, not in enabling us to maintain that in some sense God can do everything possible, but in assuring us that certain things are possible for God to do, that the eternal salvation of men and the final victory of good over evil are not idle dreams".† These two quotations are valuable: love is indeed the highest quality in the universe, but it can scarcely be said to be either stronger or weaker than the force of gravity. God does bring good out of evil, and great good out of the great evil of the Crucifixion, but I could only feel entirely happy about Quick's phrase "the omnipotence of love" if I believed that God *always* brings good out of evil. Some suffering is indeed redemptive; no one can meet suffering that is bravely and selflessly borne without being thereby humbled and immensely enriched. But such cases are a tiny fraction of the whole of suffering. No one, surely, would deny that "good, even animal good, is a more fertile breeder of good on the whole – yes, even of moral good – than distress of any kind can be".‡

The possibility of life after death is no help in preserving belief in God as both loving and omnipotent. Admittedly God could use this second life to redress the balance of weal and woe by a system of spiritual rewards, with or without punishments. This is indeed one of the main reasons why people believe in a life to come. (I deliberately use at this point the language of the man in the street – we shall come back to the teaching of the New Testament on eternal life.) Heaven can make the overall balance "fair", but it cannot reduce the quantity of suffering

* *Doctrines of the Creed*, p. 65.
† *Doctrines of the Creed*, p. 60.
‡ *Love Almighty and Ills Unlimited*, p. 167.

some people endure here on earth. If it be said that earthly suffering is unimportant by comparison with heavenly bliss, this simply calls into question God's creation of a physical universe. If agonies of pain are unreal or unimportant, what value attaches to our universe, and why create it? If they are not unimportant, but are preventable, why does not God prevent them? If we look life squarely in the face we are bound to conclude that God, if he exists, may be *either* loving *or* omnipotent, but cannot be both.

Let us pause for a moment to examine the origins of these two beliefs about God, since we are forced to choose between them. The belief in God's omnipotence traces its ancestry back to the tribal gods of the ancient world, who were regaled for purposes of worship with all the trappings of an oriental court. To each god was attributed a definite and considerable range of power — limited only by that of other gods. Monotheism developed gradually during the Old Testament period, and is found in unmistakable form in the prophecies of Amos. With it came a concentration of all the powers of the many gods into the hands of one omnipotent God. In later centuries, the concentration of political power under one emperor made it the more natural that the omnipotence of the one God should be assumed without question. I imagine it was so assumed by Jesus and his disciples. Whitehead puts this succinctly:

"When the Western world accepted Christianity, Caesar conquered; and the received text of Western theology was edited by his lawyers. The code of Justinian and the theology of Justinian are two volumes expressing one movement of the human spirit. The brief Galilean vision of humility flickered throughout the ages, uncertainly ... But the deeper idolatry, of the fashioning of God in the image of the Egyptian, Persian, and Roman imperial rulers, was retained. The Church gave unto God the attributes which belonged exclusively to Caesar."*

The belief in God's love also has roots in the Old Testament, where this was seen to be one of God's attributes; but the belief that love is the *primary* characteristic of God was first given to us by Jesus. It is surely a measure of our human self-centredness that one of his great parables is known and referred to by the character in whom our self-interest is vested, the prodigal son, rather than by its central character, the loving father. It was

* *Process and Reality*, V.2.1 (p. 484 f.).

because he saw God's overriding, forgiving love so clearly that Jesus taught us to call God our Father. In choosing between God's overflowing love and his unqualified omnipotence, we choose between Christ's great intuition and something which he himself accepted as part of the thought-form of his century — as Jesus also accepted, for example, the belief that David had written the psalms from which he quoted.

A. N. Whitehead's thinking runs parallel to that of his contemporary O. C. Quick in seeing God's activity pre-eminently in terms of love; but then the two diverge. Whereas Quick goes on to describe "the omnipotence of love", Whitehead draws a firm contrast between love and power. This contrast appears most graphically in *Adventures of Ideas,* where Whitehead describes Plato's "final conviction, towards the end of his life, that the divine element in the world is to be conceived as a persuasive agency and not as a coercive agency. This doctrine should be looked upon as one of the greatest intellectual discoveries in the history of religion. It is plainly enunciated by Plato, though he failed to co-ordinate it systematically with the rest of his metaphysical theory." In his next paragraph Whitehead relates Plato's conviction to Christianity:

"The essence of Christianity is the appeal to the life of Christ as a revelation of the nature of God and of his agency in the world. The record is fragmentary, inconsistent and uncertain . . . But there can be no doubt as to what elements in the record have evoked a response from all that is best in human nature. The Mother, the Child, and the bare manger: the lowly man, homeless and self-forgetful, with his message of peace, love and sympathy: the suffering, the agony, the tender words as life ebbed, the final despair: and the whole with the authority of complete victory. I need not elaborate. Can there be any doubt that the power of Christianity lies in its revelation in act of that which Plato divined in theory?"*

I would add two comments. There is wisdom in the old priest who is said to have insisted that God decided each day's rain and sunshine, adding that if you fail to see God's hand in one small thing you will end by failing to find it in anything: the thinking of many people has ended in precisely that failure. The alternative, however, is not to insist that God must decide on the rainfall, but to recognize that there is a real element of freedom in the world, with which the traditional concept of God's omnipotence is incompatible. Charles Hartshorne here

* *Adventures of Ideas,* pp. 213–14 (170–1).

clearly distinguishes between the limitation of this concept and its rejection:

"It has become customary to say that we must limit divine power to save human freedom and to avoid making deity responsible for evil. But to speak of limiting a concept seems to imply that the concept, without the limitation, makes sense. The notion of a cosmic power that determines all decisions fails to make sense. For its decisions could refer to nothing except themselves. They could result in no world; for a world must consist of local agents making their own decisions. Instead of saying that God's power is limited, suggesting that it is less than some conceivable power, we should rather say: his power is absolutely maximal, the greatest possible, but even the greatest possible power is still one power among others, is not the only power."*

Secondly, I would stress the *positive* nature of process thinking about God's activity in the world. We saw at the end of the last chapter how this thinking affirms God's love in a way that does not contradict our experience of human love: we have now seen that this thinking denies that God's power is absolute or "omnipotent". This affirmation and this denial are two sides of the same coin: you cannot have the one without the other. In the present chapter I have attempted to show that the existence of suffering is in itself a reason for doubting the compatibility of God's love with his absolute power, and have suggested that the Christian will attach greater value to the former. But process thinking is not confined to a mere denial of the concept of omnipotence. Local agents *must* make their own decisions, so that God's power "is not the only power"; but it *is* "the greatest possible power". All process thinking about God's activity and power is in line with the conviction, derived by Whitehead from Plato, "that the divine element in the world is to be conceived as a persuasive agency and not as a coercive agency". We have seen that Whitehead described "prehensions" as vectors because they possess direction: it matters which way round "prehensions" work. The subject entity "prehends" all other entities (including God) as objects. "Prehension" is a form of awareness. Thus entities are aware (consciously or unconsciously) of other entities as objects, and "it is logically impossible that an object should dictate to awareness precisely how it is to respond to the object"†. This logic applies to God: he influences us, but

* *The Divine Relativity*, p. 138.
† *The Divine Relativity*, p. 139.

we have to accept and respond to that influence, which is persuasive and not coercive. Both God and the world influence, and affect, each other. We influence God by our actions:

"But do not thereby deprive him of freedom in his response to us. This divine response, becoming our object, by the same principle in turn influences us, but here, too, without removing all freedom. The radical difference between God and us implies that our influence upon him is slight, while his influence upon us is predominant . . . Hence God can set *narrow* limits to our freedom; for the more important the object to the subject, the more important is its effect upon the range of possible responses. Thus God can rule the world and order it . . . "*

In discussing biological evolution we saw God as supplying the "chance-limiting factor". We now see him as setting narrow limits to human freedom. The two are closely parallel.

"This divine method of world control is called 'persuasion' by Whitehead . . . [It] challenges comparison with the traditional view, which merely says that God creates out of nothing, and that his rule of the world is essentially the same as this creation. Scarcely the faintest glimmer of insight from experience seems to shine through such language. Our knowledge that objects influence but do not coerce subjects is left entirely unexploited. Is this the way to attain even the slight comprehension we are capable of—to pay no attention to the one mode of influence we in some degree understand?"†

We have pursued our discussion to a conclusion, but it is doubtful whether this has been of much use to those who are the most troubled by the problem of pain. Intellectual logic usually cuts very little ice where our emotions are involved. We may have shown the idea of God's unqualified omnipotence to be a fallacy, but it will linger on because it is emotionally helpful in our worship; unless one has an analytical mind it is probably easier to worship an Omnipotent Absolute than a God whose power is, in Hartshorne's words, "one power among others". We may have shown that a random distribution of pain and disease is an inevitable factor in our universe, so that individual instances are not attributable to God's specific choice, but it still seems cruelly and devastatingly "unfair" when someone we love dies slowly of cancer. This "unfairness" is strengthened in our minds because these focus more easily on the concept of divine justice, which we inherit from the Old Testament and from

* *The Divine Relativity*, p. 141 f.
† *The Divine Relativity*, p. 142.

passages in the Epistles, than on the infinitely forgiving love of God which Jesus proclaimed. As a result we have strong emotional reasons for wanting individual life to continue beyond the grave, so that those who endure excessive suffering here can receive "fair" compensation in heaven, on the lines of Dives and Lazarus. (We usually omit to see this parable in its other modern form, in which perhaps Dives is every Englishman, his castle a "semi-", while Lazarus is a beggar from the back streets of Bombay, fed from the few crumbs we give to Oxfam.)

All the same, our emotions are seldom good guides to careful thought, and we must put them in their place. We derive great comfort in many ways from the thought of an "after-life", but this is no proof that there will be such a life. Still less is such proof aided by the "unfairness" of this life; we must remind ourselves that pain and suffering are an inevitable, and in many cases a fundamentally random, element of life in this physical universe. One must not use the adjective "unfair" of a random element. The most one can do is to suggest that it would have been better if there had never been a physical universe at all — and few people would agree with that: the overall balance of joy and sorrow does not support it; most creatures *want* to live, and not only for the negative reason of being afraid to die.

We end with two thoughts about suffering that can give comfort to our emotions as well as to our intellect. If a priest has regularly visited a family throughout the father's long and painful illness, and seen his suffering reflected in their faces, he can sometimes help them afterwards in their bereavement to think of husband or father not as they so vividly remember him, in pain, but as he was in earlier and younger years: this is easier if the priest knew the man before his illness began. What one is saying, in effect, is that they must try to see their father's life as a *whole*, in which his last illness, however long, is but a fraction, and to remember him "as he really was". I suggest that there is theological truth in this, as well as emotional comfort. Is this not how God sees a person's life — as one integrated whole?

The second word of comfort is to remind ourselves that God is always longing to bring good out of evil. The power of his love can vanquish pain in our hospitals, as it did on Calvary:

"Peasants and housekeepers find what philosophers seek in vain; the substance of truth is grasped not by argument, but by faith. The leading of God through evil out of evil and into a promised good is acknowledged by those who trust in his mercy. The balance of the world is good to them, though in the eyes of onlookers their misfortunes go beyond endurance. I remember the happiest man in a hospital, lying broken-backed forever in pain on a waterbed, overflowing with gratitude to those who tended and those who visited him, and blessing us all by his prayers."*

God does not cause pain, but he does all that we will let him do to alleviate it. It is our duty, and ought to be counted our privilege, to help him to alleviate it by all possible means. We must continue Christ's work of healing by seeing that more of the benefits of modern medicine are available in every continent. We must see that poverty is fought and reduced in every corner of the world. We must proclaim the good news of God's love so that others, and we ourselves, can be helped in our hour of suffering by our faith, by prayer and sacrament, and by that inner strength which God alone can give, and of which Jesus Christ is our supreme example. Such proclamation will be helped by Whitehead's insight that "God is the great companion – the fellow-sufferer who understands".

(b) WHAT HAPPENS WHEN WE DIE?

Anyone who tries to help a group of people to think out their religious beliefs is highly liable to come up against the great difficulty that as soon as some particular item of belief comes up for discussion the group sub-divides into two parts: one set feels impelled, either by strong conviction or by the basic insecurity of their faith, to insist that this item be retained in its traditional form, without any amendment or restatement; whilst the other set regards that traditional form as frankly incredible, may perhaps be inclined to reject the item of belief altogether, and almost certainly regards any discussion of it in traditional terms as a waste of time. This particularly applies to any discussion of "life after death" and "what happens when we die?" The hope of everlasting life is, for some, the most highly treasured item in the Christian creed: it also today incurs very widespread disbelief.

Nowhere is it more urgent to sort out the true from the false, the God-centred reality from the myth inspired by self-interest: for there is a strong element of self-interest in much of our thinking about what happens when we die. There is no need

* A. Farrer, *Love Almighty and Ills Unlimited*, p. 187.

to point out that the Church as an institution has a colossal vested interest in the whole idea of heaven, even if it seeks less help than it did from painting pictures of hell. But let us be clear that all of us who were brought up to believe in it have a strong vested interest in the idea of a life to come. The desire for security goes very deep in human nature. Death is the one enemy against which all forms of physical or financial security are useless; life insurance can make provision for one's dependants, but only faith in a future life offers any dividend for oneself. Christians know that they ought to be willing to travel light in this life, as many of their number have done in every century. But we have also been taught that this life is but a short journey, leading as its goal to an eternal life in which we shall experience infinite joy. I find it a highly disturbing thought that it may be precisely our vested interest in this idea of future individual experiences in another realm which God is calling our generation to forgo, or radically to modify.

We shall consider the question "what happens when we die?" in three stages. First, we shall look at some of the things that traditionally-minded Christians are saying about it at the present time. Second, we shall examine some of the principal difficulties which confront modern man as he contemplates eternity. In the light of such difficulties as we have found to be valid, we shall then have to decide which elements of currently held belief must be rejected. Only then, and at the third stage, will we be in a position to start building up a *positive*, meaningful interpretation and hope of eternal life. I very much dislike putting the largely negative aspects of all this before the attempt at a positive re-interpretation. But people hold such a variety of views on what happens when we die, most of which bear little relation to the New Testament, that it is essential to begin by specifying what one is *not* saying or assuming. The theologically-minded reader may become inpatient at being asked to spend time on interpretations of "life after death" which may bear little resemblance to the Johannine promise of eternal life or the Pauline hope of resurrection in Christ, but the fact is that the hope of eternal life for many people, including many church-goers, is only very loosely connected with the teaching of the New Testament.

In the third and final stage I shall put forward what I believe to be a truly *positive* answer to our question, and one which attempts to interpret the biblical hope of "being raised in Christ" in a way that is entirely meaningful for modern man. But I shall find myself forced to reject several widely held beliefs as to life after death – a rejection which can at first seem quite shattering to those people for whom the outline which follows is a fair approximation to the way in which they were brought up to believe in individual survival beyond the grave. I emphasize this, for I am myself one of those people.

Some much loved ideas

Of all the theologians no longer living whose books stand on my shelves, I can think of none whom I would more dearly like to have known in the flesh than the two brothers Baillie.* The deep love alike of God and of people shines out from their writings, and it must have been a rare privilege to come within their pastoral care. When I re-open their books, I am sad to find how often I am bound to disagree not so much with their close reasoning as with some of their initial assumptions. But I always treasure John Baillie's account of a story told to him when visiting "a fine Christian gentleman, who was about to die":

"The story was of just such another dying man as himself who, when informed by his devotedly Christian doctor that the end was very near, asked the doctor if he had any conviction as to what awaited him in the life beyond. The doctor fumbled for an answer. But ere he could speak, there was heard a scratching at the door; and his answer was given him. 'Do you hear that?' he asked his patient. 'That is my dog. I left him downstairs, but he grew impatient and has come up and hears my voice. He has no notion what is inside that door, but he knows I am here. Now is it not the same with you? You do not know what lies beyond the Door, but you know your Master is there.' "

I value that little story as some consolation for not having known the Baillies in the flesh, and for its reminder that a life of prayer and Christian love can so increase our sensitivity that we may sometimes see the parables that lie around us, and use them, as Jesus so often did, to help those among whom we live.

* Donald, whose *God was in Christ,* is referred to on page 91, and John whose best known doctrinal work is *And the Life Everlasting.* Each dedicated one of his books to the other, and John added a memoir of his brother to Donald's *The Theology of the Sacraments* (1957), published after his death. John was Professor of Divinity at Edinburgh; he died in 1962. The quotation is from p. 199 of *And the Life Everlasting.*

I am also humbled by the content of this particular parable: that heaven is *an unknown place with one known Inhabitant*. How ill content we all are to accept this without asking for more, and how much we and our forebears have elaborated upon Baillie's picture of heaven. In part, this is done flippantly and with no thought of any intellectual difficulty. There are those endless stories about meeting St. Peter at the golden gate, which encourage the idea that heaven is simply a continuation of earth. A more sophisticated variant was supplied many years ago by Sir (then Mr.) Winston Churchill. Thinking of the entertainment he would get from a dialogue between Plato and his friend Lord Balfour, Churchill banteringly remarked, "When I go to heaven I shall try to arrange a chat between these two on some topic not too recondite for me to follow".

But we also add to John Baillie's parable of heaven in deadly earnest by assuming, or hoping, that we and others may become inhabitants of heaven, as well as God. Indeed Baillie himself assumed this: his book *And the Life Everlasting* is very largely a reasoned defence of the belief in life everlasting as applied to the individual. His assumptions, he says, lie deep in the faith he learned as a child in his father's manse in the Scottish Highlands: that God is both loving and omnipotent, and that each of us is important in his sight. He suggests that the assurance of immortality is enclosed in the discovery of the love of God, coupled with the fact that "something of intrinsic value resides in human individuality". Here is the nub of his argument:

"If God is the God of individuals, if individuals can enter into fellowship with Him, if individuals are precious in His sight, then our hope in God necessarily becomes a hope for the individual. The argument is unanswerable; and is indeed the only unanswerable argument for immortality that has ever been given, or ever can be given. It cannot be evaded except by a denial of the premisses. If the individual can commune with God, then he must matter to God; and if he matters to God, he must share God's eternity. For if God really rules, He cannot be conceived as scrapping what is precious in His sight."*

As will emerge, I find this reasoning unsatisfactory in several respects; but John Baillie's book is a fine example of a way of thinking which many Christians regard as essential to their faith, as I once did myself. I want now to return to another aspect of our vested interest in the belief that heaven contains

* *And the Life Everlasting* (Oxford, 1934: now a paperback), p. 137.

individual souls in addition to the one known Inhabitant, namely our very natural desire for reunion with those we have known and loved here on earth. Churchill spoke banteringly of a friend who may have been still alive at the time. But I recall – perhaps more vividly than any other I have heard – an Easter sermon given from his cathedral pulpit by a widower bishop, who told us that he had meditated deeply upon the nature of eternal life during the period following his wife's death. Returning his thoughts to the present life, he discussed the importance of the family and how it was, by God's intention, the fundamental unit in human affairs; it would, the bishop believed, be preserved and continued in heaven. He had therefore come firmly to believe that in the hereafter we would in some sense meet and recognize those who had been dearest to us on earth. He had pondered deeply whether recognition of others would be possible in heaven, and his sermon examined this question carefully before coming to a positive conclusion. I was much moved by this sermon, which I heard while at theological college. But my fellow students, mostly younger than I, seemed very unimpressed. So I asked my Principal for his opinion of the sermon, I think adding that I would like to get it duplicated. His reply, brief and spoken with great emphasis, was that the sermon had "no scriptural justification whatever". I mention this sermon because the bishop's deep meditation had brought him to a conclusion that people so often simply take for granted, and because his reasoning seems largely parallel to Dr. John Baillie's, though with the value of the family substituted for that of the individual.

I shall not attempt to summarize the more recent theological writing on the nature of "life everlasting". It is sufficient to say that Paul Tillich's denial of "supranaturalism", and John Robinson's repeated insistence in *Honest to God* that we must not think of God as "out there", appear to put most traditional ideas of heaven in jeopardy without offering any clear answer to the question "what happens when we die?" Let us now look at some of the difficulties which confront any attempt to answer that question.

Some of the difficulties

1. The overriding difficulty is the whole problem of time in

relation to eternity; indeed this difficulty is so great as to cause many people to regard all discussion of eternity as futile. We certainly cannot envisage an existence which is not governed by the interrelated dimensions of space and time, and in particular most of us cannot begin to imagine *ourselves* without these dimensions. And even if I could at least partially perform the feat of imagining "myself" as existing in a non-spatial, spiritual state, I could not do so without relying on the successiveness of time, which indeed pervades all our thinking. I can, however, both contemplate death and ask myself in what sense it is, and in what sense it is not, the end of my existence. I shall not, therefore, allow the problem of time and eternity to cut short our discussion.

2. The second difficulty seems insuperable to many young people with a partly scientific education. It is greatly reduced if one thinks in terms of being raised in Christ rather than in terms of "life after death" and the immortality of the soul; but so many people think in these latter terms that we must begin by doing the same. In those terms, the difficulty can be put as a question: *what is it* of a human being that can conceivably survive physical death? What is the modern equivalent to the word "soul"?

Spirit is often used as a synonym for soul, but this is of little help, for the word has so many meanings. The word spirit, like its equivalents in Hebrew, Greek and Latin, is akin to breathing, and so can mean the "animating or vital principle in man (and animals)": in this sense, it clearly ceases at death. The words spirit or soul can also denote "the immaterial, intelligent or sentient part of a person", "the principle of thought and action in man".* Is the human spirit in this latter sense capable of continuing beyond physical death? The plain meaning of the words and phrases I have quoted would appear to imply that it is not so capable, for intelligence, feelings, thoughts and actions as we know them all depend upon the interaction between the brain and its environment: this applies to the realms of aesthetics and of moral decisions just as much as to our simpler thoughts and actions. To suppose that any of these can exist apart from the physical world and the cells of the brain is to suppose that there is in heaven some spiritual equivalent both to

* See the entries for "spirit" and "soul" in *The Shorter Oxford English Dictionary*.

our brains and to our environment; the more man learns about each of these, the more difficult it becomes to continue to suppose that either has its equivalent in "heaven".

It is often suggested that the ancient idea of the "soul" is best conveyed today by the word personality. But can one think of personality surviving death? I quote from two short papers on "Death"; the author of the first, D. M. MacKinnon, is now a Cambridge Professor of Divinity:

"One cannot, if one is honest, ignore the extent to which metaphysical arguments, like those concerning immortality, have gained plausibility from a refusal to attend to the logic of our language. How much indeed does our glib talk about survival owe to our refusal to reflect on the very significance of the pronoun 'I' itself. 'I survive'—but what is 'I'? Do I suppose that 'I' is the name of a kind of ultimate substrate of qualities, clad with its states much as a clothes-horse is draped with towels, shirts, etc? Do I think that I am related to my biography in that kind of way? Yet much of our superficial talk about survival suggests that we do. Whether we think of survival or of the survivor, we are at once plunged into bewilderment. What exactly are we talking about?"*

The non-Christian philosopher Antony Flew is equally critical of the concept of personal survival:

"The great obstacle in the way of attaching sense to the talk of a future life, the reason why people suggest that it is self-contradictory to suppose we shall live after phycial dissolution, consists in the often neglected fact that person words mean what they do mean. Words like 'you', 'I', 'person', 'somebody', 'Flew', 'woman' . . . are all used to refer in one way or another to objects . . . which you can point at, touch, hear, see and talk to. Person words refer to people. And how can such objects as people survive physical dissolution? This is a massive difficulty . . ."†

This "massive difficulty" also applies to A. B. Starratt's recent suggestion that we should think of life after death in terms of "selfhood". Having agreed with modern physiology that a mind cannot exist without a brain he argues that:

"The self is neither the body, nor the mind, although it is in and through both of them. That the self is not identical with the body can be shown in fact that the changes in the body that take place in the process of physical growth and ageing neither increase nor diminish the basic feeling of selfhood . . . Our feeling of selfhood . . . is not the

* *New Essays in Philosophical Theology*, ed. Flew and MacIntyre, (1955; paper, 1963), p. 262.
† *New Essays in Philosophical Theology*, p. 269.

same thing as our body although it pervades all parts of our body. That the self is not identical with the mind can be shown by similar evidence. The mind of a five-year-old child and the mind of the same person at the age of fifty are very different, but the feeling of selfhood is the same in the mature adult as it was in the child . . . So long as the self is there, the living process holds an identifiable individual form which we know as mind and body. When the self withdraws, the form collapses and the elements that were in it flow outward into the other forms of the environment. Body and mind both dissolve, but the self continues."*

MacKinnon's plea that we reflect on the meaning of the words we use is highly relevant here. "Self" may not be identical with either mind or body, or both, but can it be entirely separated from these? Has "self" any meaning apart from self-awareness, which is awareness of oneself as a mind and body separate from one's surroundings? I cannot better Paul Tillich's definition:

"Being a self means being separated in some way from everything else, having everything else opposite to one's self, being able to look at it and to act upon it. At the same time, however, this self is aware that it belongs to that at which it looks. The self is 'in' it. Every self has an environment in which it lives . . ."†

There is nothing peculiar to his own system of thought about Tillich's definition of being a self: this *must*, surely, involve both awareness and separation – and it is far from clear how either of these can continue after death.

Not many Christians would think specifically of using the word "self" in this connection, but I suspect that there are a great number whose hope for individual survival is not dissimilar from Dr. Starratt's: they believe that there is some link, some element of personal identity, which can survive without either brain or body – and they would much prefer not to be asked to explain this belief. I cannot myself see any way round the difficulties raised in this section, but there is another which is very closely allied to them:

3. Even if personality or self were separable from all the organs which disintegrate at death, these are *dynamic* concepts: they change and develop throughout the person's life. Whether one thinks in terms of survival of personality or attempts an individualistic interpretation of being raised in Christ, one is

* A. B. Starratt, *The Real God* (S.C.M., 1965), pp. 85 and 87.
† *Systematic Theology*, vol. I, p. 188.

bound to ask *what* survives or is raised up: the lazy amiability of old age; the conceit of success, which even his wife found insufferable; the driving ambition of his forties, which had in turn gradually supplanted the real goodness of his early years of married life; the utter selfishness of the young fornicator of early adulthood; or the real but transitory attempt at Christian discipleship in the months that followed Confirmation? Each in turn has been the dominant characteristic of Mr. X, who might have been run over by a bus at any stage. *What* survives? – and what if the bus had killed him in his pram?

4. The possibility of young Master X being killed in his pram raises the whole question of the *range of possible candidates* for everlasting life. Austin Farrer ended his *Love Almighty and Ills Unlimited* with an appendix entitled "Imperfect Lives", in which he suggests that those who die in infancy, or are imbecile from birth, have never been rational beings and are therefore not capable of eternal salvation: we do not know where God draws the line, "but we may be sure that he loves and saves whatever is there to be saved or loved"; God does not wish to discriminate, but would do so "rather than suspend the designs of his mercy towards the human race". The *Church Times* strongly criticized Dr. Farrer for publishing an appendix that could give great unhappiness to the parents of these children, but made no attempt to argue out the truth or falsity of what Farrer wrote. Are we to seek after the truth, or simply to insist upon whatever we, or others, wish to believe?

Many of the boys I teach would criticize Farrer's argument at least as strongly as the *Church Times,* but in a quite different direction. They would call in question his underlying assumption that immortality can be bestowed on some members of the human race but not on any other forms of life: they refuse to believe in a heaven which includes only *homo sapiens,* or in the soul as an exclusively human prerogative. They hasten to ask, with polite sarcasm, whether *"homo habilis"* had a soul; they are quick to draw unfavourable comparisons between the mental prowess of a child of three and a chimpanzee or a dolphin – dolphins are a favourite item in the argument because of their high brain to body weight-ratio, and of their alleged ability to communicate with each other. Indeed most of these arguments were brought up recently by a small group of seventeen-year-old classicists, all of whom were about to sit university scholarships.

In short, a number of intelligent boys regard the traditional Christian concept of heaven as *sheer absurdity*. The rest of us need not be swayed by this fact, but neither should we ignore it.

For myself, I would agree with Dr. Farrer that our inability to know where God draws the line in no way precludes his drawing one, and that if God has to discriminate as regards eternal life he is likely to do so along the line of rationality. My difficulty is concerned with comparative value. Eternal life, or a soul saved for eternity, presumably has a value in God's sight that is of an altogether higher order than can attach to any purely temporal entity. If eternal salvation is limited to some or all of the human race, or to the rational beings on this and other planets, it follows that these "higher" forms of life are of *incomparably* greater value in God's sight than all the other entities which comprise 99·99 per cent of his universe. I have suggested earlier that one of the basic functions of theology is to help us to see a meaning and a purpose in our life and in our universe, and conversely that one of the main reasons why I believe in God is that I feel convinced that it *has* both meaning and purpose. But these concepts must apply in some degree to the *whole* of God's universe, and not be limited to one element within it. There will no doubt be gradations of value between a man, a cat, a mosquito, and an incandescent star – but not, surely, an infinite jump in value between man and all the rest.

Herein lies one of my difficulties with the passage from John Baillie that I quoted earlier: "If the individual can commune with God, then he must matter to God; and if he matters to God, he must share God's eternity." I shall seek to show that there is a sense in which everything except evil shares in God's everlastingness. I accept that ability to commune with God raises one's relationship with God to a higher level. But I refute the apparent implication that those that cannot commune with God do not matter, or do not matter to any significant extent. If I may return for a moment to the older boys to whom it is my privilege to try to commend the Christian faith, I would point out that the same boys who were so facetious about a heaven limited to humans listened with rapt attention to a recent lecture by the astronomer Professor Bondi, who spent a lot of his lecture explaining that modern cosmology *starts* with the assumption that our planet is in no sense in a privileged position in the universe. Those who accept that assumption are likely to reject any theology committed to the view that rational beings (on this or other planets) are in the uniquely privileged position of being the only candidates for everlasting life.

5. Is there free will in heaven? The other difficulties I have listed all start with this world and then find it hard, if not impossible, to believe that some elements or aspects of this life are projected into eternity. We will now approach the problem from the other end and try to think about the *quality* of life in the purely spiritual realm which we call heaven. During an "any questions" session after I had preached at a girls' "public" school, the headmistress told the story of an elderly cook-housekeeper who had asked the headmistress, putting great emphasis on the final phrase: "Do you believe in heaven, *harps and all*?" She regarded the harps as an essential, but somewhat unlikely, ingredient. The modern church is anxious to emphasize the symbolic nature of harps, wings and fleecy clouds – but finds it a great deal more difficult to suggest what the spirits or souls of the departed *do* in heaven.

The Book of Revelation, like the prophet's vision in the sixth chapter of Isaiah, allots to them the single occupation of worshipping God. But our modern minds question whether God would find any pleasure or value in the everlasting worship of beings with no alternative occupation. Our complete inability to envisage an existence that is not governed by space and time makes the question "what do the spirits do?" impossible to answer. But we can at least ask ourselves whether, in doing whatever they do, or in existing however they exist, the spirits possess free will: do they or do they not make decisions, in the sense of choosing between two or more alternatives?

In asking ourselves this question we can take up a problem we left over from our discussion of the problem of pain. We saw that pain and suffering are inevitable in a physical universe, and that no one can blame God for the world's suffering except in so far as God could have avoided creating anything physical at all. We were content to leave it there, assuming the creation of our world to have been desirable. In *Love Almighty and Ills Unlimited* Austin Farrer goes on to consider whether God could have avoided this and created only angels and archangels – pure spirits, without physical bodies. At first sight this arrangement would avoid all physical suffering, yet allow for the creation of other beings to share in and enjoy God's love; heaven without earth, if I may so put it. With an argument as closely reasoned as it is beautifully written, Dr. Farrer points out that this would not do. The angels would have no mind and exert no action of their own; with no creaturely core of their being, they would simply be mirrors of God's mind and will.

"God's desire was to create beings able to know and to love him. Yet, in the nature of the case, there lay a dilemma. In proportion to their capacity for such love or knowledge, the created minds or wills would be dominated by the object of their knowledge or their love; they would lose the personal initiative which could alone give reality to their knowing or their loving. The divine glory would draw them into itself, as the candle draws the moth."*

I should like to call beings without personal initiative robots, and to suggest that we have here two metaphors which are not identical: the robot metaphor, and that of the candle and the moth. The first seems to me of fundamental importance, and I greatly fear that it applies lock, stock and barrel to the traditional picture of heaven. The candle and moth metaphor implies some equivalent in the spiritual realm to a law of attraction and absorption, which seems to me a doubtful assumption. But it is in fact this second metaphor which Dr. Farrer pursues. He points out that if nothing existed but God, as candle, and purely spiritual beings, as moths, then there could be no shade or screen between them: there being by definition no third party, the screen would have to be either in God or in the angels. God would not darken his own being to baffle the "moths"; nor would he deliberately create only feeble spirits, spiritual feebleness being the only conceivable screen in a being whose only nature is spiritual: therefore, no screen. Therefore, abandon this myth and try again.

This time we follow the sequence alike of Genesis 1 and of scientific ideas of evolution: first a lifeless world, and then ascending orders of life up to man. Man's animal nature supplies the screen, with no need artificially to enfeeble his spirit. God "simply began his creation at the greatest remove from his own perfection and built it up from there towards himself". Dr. Farrer emphasizes the mythical character of all this, and I would only add that the element of myth extends, perhaps, to the idea of a moment in time when God "began"

* *Love Almighty and Ills Unlimited*, p. 69 f.

the creation of a universe whose age may be infinite. Dr. Farrer highlights his argument with a creation parable based on Noah's dove, which twice returned to the Ark because there was no dry ground. In Farrer's parable God, in the meditations of his creative thought, sent forth an archangel; and the archangel returned into the mind of him that sent him. After him, an angel, who also returned because there was no ground in which to take root. So God sent out a succession of particles "which returned not, not knowing the way"; these clung together, the earth built up, and in due course God set foot upon it, and made Adam from the dust of the ground.* Dr. Farrer's next comment is more important in relation to the nature of heaven than the parable itself, and I quote it in full:

"Is there anything to be said on the other side? We, who believe in angels and archangels on the authority of our religion, may be unable to accept a story which is based on the supposition that such beings are impossible. But the objection is not invincible; for the Ark-story need not absolutely deny angelic being. What it denies is that creation could begin with pure spirits, or that their existence could draw on the being of God alone. If they have one foot, as it were, planted on the material creation, the story has nothing to say against angels, any more than against mankind. For we, too, take hold of matter on the one hand, and God on the other. The hold of angels upon matter, or of matter upon angels, cannot be supposed the same as in our case. But may not their initial concern have been with the administration of the physical world, or with the guidance of its reasonable inhabitants? Angels, like men, may be freed at last from physical bondage. But they may have been so grounded in it first, as to obtain an individual existence: an existence which God afterwards liberates and glorifies, without destroying it. Belief in angels may be an article of faith; but we are surely permitted a great latitude of speculation regarding the nature of these mysterious beings."†

I am not here in the least concerned as to angels; not very many Christians of my acquaintance would share Dr. Farrer's view that belief in them is an essential article of faith. But his comment applies also, as he says, to men. The process envisaged is in two stages: in stage one angels (and men) are so grounded in the physical world as to obtain an individual existence. In stage two angels (and souls) are freed from such physical bond-

* Page 72. The parable is charmingly told, as are the other parables in chapter 4, in which pages 60–76 deal with the problem of why God created a physical universe.
† Pages 73–74.

age, and God liberates and glorifies their individual existence without destroying it. The purpose of all this is to surmount the difficulty shown up by the metaphor of the candle and moth. Earthly tasks supply a screen or, to vary the metaphor, an anchor during stage one. But we are not given even the most tentative explanation as to why the fact of having been given earthly tasks in stage one should make any difference in stage two, when angels and souls are "freed at last from physical bondage". If a "screen" of physicality is necessary to prevent individuality from being submerged by God, then how can God subsequently free us from physicality without at the same time destroying our individuality? Of what use is an ex-screen? It will be said that I have missed the entire point, and that their earth-connection is necessary to get angels, and men, started: to develop individual existence, and with it character and personality. But *can* these continue after the earth-connection is lost? If there is some spiritual equivalent, as between God and spirits, to a physical law of attraction, then – if I may so put it without seeming flippant – what keeps the spirits in orbit during stage two? Personality is scarcely equivalent to orbital velocity. The "moths" will get drawn into the candle once the screen is removed.

Let us abandon the moth metaphor, and with it any suggestion of a law of attraction in the sense of moving-towards. Heaven is, of course, dimensionless, whereas movement implies both space and time. Unfortunately, the robot metaphor remains. To preserve angels from being robots catholic doctrine attributed to them free will, and indeed talked of fallen angels: an angel could choose whether to obey or disobey God's will. To explain why an angel should ever choose to disobey God, it was necessary to attribute to them such motives as pride, jealousy and the like. But these human motives only arise because our physical and mental desires are stronger, closer and more immediate than our dim awareness of God and of the ultimate purpose of existence: remove both the dimness and the physicality and one removes all motive for disobedience on the part of either angels *or souls*.

Most of my generation were brought up to take the traditional picture of heaven fairly literally, and it closely corresponds to what I have called stage two in Farrer's account. Having acquired personality, with its mixture of sin and virtue, souls are freed from this earth and thereafter live in heaven. This is, of course, a state and not a place, but as souls are spirits they live in that spiritual state of existence which we call heaven: an unknown state with innumerable spiritual inhabitants, all in the presence of God. This general picture of immortal souls in heaven is slightly confused by the widespread use of "Rest in Peace", which properly belongs to the New Testament doctrine of a general resurrection at the Last Day. It is a prayer that for the interim of earthly time until that Day the dead may rest, not in heaven, but in perfect sleep. Those who think out their idea of heaven recognize that neither perpetual peace nor ceaseless worship supply a satisfactory concept; they therefore assume that God will find other, unimaginable things for our souls to *do*. It is precisely here that our popular idea of heaven goes beyond all scriptural authority in assuming meetings with our family, dialogues with Plato, and spiritual tasks which will be allotted to us. The one task referred to in the Bible is worship and adoration, and the Bible is perhaps wiser than popular imagination. For if heaven is a purely spiritual state entirely separated from the physical universe, its inhabitants can only mirror and reflect the love and beauty and glory of God. They would have no motive for disobedience, or for any other occupation than worship; they would therefore lack free will. In that case I find it difficult to see how life in heaven can be thought of as "higher" than our part-sinful, part-heroic life here on earth.

This difficulty is closely allied with (2, p. 113) above, for it may be said that spirits in heaven do possess free will in that they can choose between self-worship and worship of God, between love of self and love of their fellow spirits. But can they? Does an inhabitant of heaven possess an individual self, separated from his world? Even if he does, surely he also sees with absolute clarity the centrality of the two commands to love God with all one's being and to love one's neighbour as oneself. How, then, can self-love creep in? There would seem to be no place for it, or for free will, in heaven.

Towards a positive interpretation of everlasting life

The difficulties listed above do not all carry equal weight, and inevitably overlap. When added together they would seem to rule out the idea of an individual survival after death which includes the enjoyment (or otherwise) of new experiences. I fear that a number of our ideas about "life after death" will have to be scrapped, but this scrapping applies mainly to ideas that are largely non-biblical, and far less securely anchored to the New Testament than is the concept that we shall be raised in Christ and live on *in him* — and hence *in God* — for ever. I shall therefore begin our search for a positive interpretation of everlasting life not by re-examining the difficulties I have listed but by re-directing our thoughts from ourselves to God, and from our own ideas to those of the New Testament.

A full analysis of the relationship between God and time in process philosophy would be beyond the scope of this book, especially as individual process philosophers express this relationship rather differently. They all, however, envisage God as being in a real sense *involved* in the temporal process — thus differing fundamentally from those schools of thought which think of God as absolute and unaffected by the temporal world. As we have seen, Whitehead describes the nature of God as "dipolar": the primordial side of his nature is both underived and eternal; the consequent side is described as "everlasting". it "originates with physical experience derived from the temporal world, and then acquires integration with the primordial side". God's "physical experience" comprises his "prehensions" of temporal events; each "prehension" has its beginning point in time, and continues everlastingly.

It is what Whitehead calls the consequent side of God's nature which we must consider: I shall suggest that "heaven" can be thought of as — indeed *is* — the consequent side of God's nature. But first I wish to establish a general point which is not dependent upon process philosophy.

1. Our *hope derives from the everlastingness of God*. Many of us believe that we both can and do enter into a relationship with God. Perhaps the main reason why we believe God to be personal is our feeling that our relationship with him can best be described as a "person to person relationship"; but it is the existence, and not the nature, of a relationship between us and God that is my present concern. God's end of that relationship is everlasting, since God is everlasting. (In Whitehead's terms, our relationship is with the consequent side of God's nature, which is everlasting.) If we *start* from the belief that one end of our relationship with God is everlasting it helps us to accept in

faith that the whole relationship – or elements in it – may be raised by God into his everlastingness, and thus that we may in some sense be raised into everlasting life. This hope is derived from our belief in God, and is not limited exclusively to *homo sapiens*: other creatures have a relationship with God, but one that probably lacks conscious awareness on their part. This lack may affect the significance of their prospect of everlasting life, but it does not rule out such a prospect.

When I defend traditional Christian belief about heaven along these lines I find that it can begin to make sense to boys who had regarded it as an absurdity: they sometimes come to see that the possibility of belief in heaven depends in the first instance on belief in God, and not on some particular inter-pretation of human psychology. Our hope of everlasting life *derives from* the everlastingness of God. Jesus argued similarly against the Sadducees, *deriving* the livingness of those who are raised from the dead from the livingness of God:

> "But as touching the dead, that they are raised; have ye not read in the book of Moses, in the place concerning the Bush, how God spake unto him saying. 'I am the God of Abraham, and the God of Isaac, and the God of Jacob?' He is not the God of the dead, but of the living: ye do greatly err."*

2. *Heaven* is *the "mind" of God.* What has just been said can be expressed more meaningfully in Whitehead's terms. Instead of thinking of God raising some elements of his relationship with us into everlastingness, we can think of God "prehending" us, these "prehensions" becoming part of his "consequent nature", which is everlasting. All the entities in the universe are pre-hended by God; all therefore in some measure affect God's consequent nature: if "heaven" *is* God's consequent nature, the difficulty of "heaven for humans only" is avoided. But if rational beings are alone capable of a conscious relationship with God, then our prehensions of him, and his of us, possess a special significance. We can also see this if we dare to try to look at the universe through God's eyes: if we are right in believing that God is especially concerned with moral choices and with oppor-tunities for the growth and the giving of love, then his prehen-sions of our moral actions and mutual relationships will have particular significance. If God is also a God of beauty then he will also prehend with special significance everything in the

* Mark 12: 26, 27.

universe that has aesthetic value: this is worth saying, because some interpretations of heaven have great difficulty in finding any place for aesthetic, as distinct from moral, values. Whitehead did not see one type of value as inevitably more important than another:

"Importance is a generic notion which has been obscured by the overwhelming prominence of a few of its innumerable species. The terms 'morality', 'logic', 'religion', 'art', have each of them been claimed as exhausting the whole meaning of importance. Each of them denotes a subordinate species . . . No one of these specializations exhausts the final unity of purpose in the world. The generic aim of process is the attainment of importance, in that species and to that extent which in that instance is possible."*

Whitehead elsewhere used the term "value" instead of "importance", as in the great lecture on "Immortality" which he delivered to the Harvard Divinity School on 22nd April, 1941, two months after his eightieth birthday. It begins: "In this lecture *the general concept of Immortality* will be stressed, and the reference to mankind will be a deduction from wider considerations" (my italics). The essence of this lecture is that the universe has two aspects, which are presupposed in all our experience: the World of Activity and the World of Value. These two are in themselves only abstractions, and cannot be separated: they are intertwined, and each interacts upon the other. The World of Activity consists of a vast multiplicity of finite, self-creating acts: it is the creative world, which "creates the present by transforming the past, and by anticipating the future". Its emphasis is upon the present, upon "Creation Now". By contrast, Value is in its nature timeless and immortal; its emphasis is on persistence. It is the World of Value which gives purpose and direction to the World of Activity — which means that Activity is affected and *modified* by Value. But Value is simply the general name for the infinity of potential and often conflicting values, whose importance lies in their capacity for being *used* in the world of action.

I here confine myself to four short quotations, all from the earlier sections of this lecture:†

---

* *Modes of Thought*, p. 16.

† Whitehead's thinking in this lecture is difficult for the non-philosopher to assimilate, but those desiring a fuller treatment should study the whole lecture, which is printed in *The Philosophy of Alfred North Whitehead*, ed. P. A. Schilpp (Library of Living Philosophers, New York, 1941, pp. 682–99).

"The value inherent in the Universe has an essential independence of any moment of time; and yet it loses its meaning apart from its necessary reference to the World of passing fact. Value refers to Fact, and Fact refers to Value."

"Origination is creation, whereas Value issues into modification of creative action. Creation aims at Value, whereas Value is saved from the futility of abstraction by its impact upon the process of Creation. But in this fusion, Value preserves its Immortality. In what sense does creative action derive immortality from Value? This is the topic of our lecture."

"The two worlds of Value and of Action are bound together in the life of the Universe, so that the immortal factor of Value enters into the active creation of temporal fact."

"When we enjoy 'realized value' we are experiencing the essential junction of the two worlds. But when we emphasize mere fact, or mere possibility, we are making an abstraction in thought. When we enjoy fact as the realization of specific value, or possibility as an impulse towards realization, we are then stressing the ultimate character of the Universe. This ultimate character has two sides — one side is the mortal world of transitory fact acquiring the immortality of realized value; and the other side is the timeless world of mere possibility acquiring temporal realization . . . Thus the topic of 'The Immortality of Man' is seen to be a side issue in the wider topic, which is 'The Immortality of Realized Value': namely, the temporality of mere fact acquiring the immortality of value."

As regards our own human lives, all this can be put less precisely, but with great simplicity. The argument rests on the assumption that God is *affected* by what happens in his universe. God is everlasting, and if we affect God that effect is everlasting. So far from utterly perishing when we die, we have during our lives achieved an everlasting effect which cannot perish. Our later actions may modify the total effect that we have upon God, but when those actions cease their total effect lives on, in God, everlastingly.

Let it be said at once that if there is a sense in which it is the individual moments of our lives – our decisions and relationships – whose effect lives on everlastingly in God, then this is a deeply sobering thought. As long as it is "I" who may be raised from death to everlasting life, there is always the hope that with God's help and grace and forgiveness I may improve a little before I have "to meet my maker face to face". But if everything I do is being prehended *now* into God's everlastingness, then the hope of future improvement must be seen in a new and more realistic light. God may indeed grant his forgiveness if I truly seek it, and my subsequent actions may modify and improve the total effect of my life upon God – but my earlier actions have already had their everlasting effect, which cannot be expunged. In the case of the hypothetical Mr. X. whose biography I outlined earlier, the youthful disciple of Christ, the selfish young fornicator, the conceited, ambitious executive and the lazy, amiable old man *all* contribute to the total effect that Mr. X has on the everlasting God. This is what one ought to expect. There is no convenient time delay in our relationships with one another. My wife happens to be very understanding but even so she is not shielded from the hurt caused by today's ill-temper simply because my mood may be different tomorrow: the series of actions which constitute my life affects her *as it proceeds,* and not only in its final total.

This enables us to put in proper perspective the problem of death-bed repentance, which is one that boys often raise. We tend to think of God's forgiveness as retrospective: perhaps we should rather see it as looking forwards, and bestowing upon us a newness of life which frees us (but not God) from the burden of our sins, and strengthens us in our determination to do better, with God's help, in the future. Thus the forgiveness which God gives after a genuine death-bed repentance will alter the quality of the last hours of earthly life, and may indeed bring real peace of mind at the last, but it can do little to alter the total impact of the person's life both on the world and on God: how could it, for there is surely truth in the old saying "what's done can't be undone"?

Rose Macaulay made a similar point in her letters to Fr. Hamilton Johnson. She had returned to the Church and its sacraments after an absence of nearly thirty years, due to a prolonged clandestine relationship with a married man who had since died.

"I told you once that I couldn't really *regret* the past. But now I do regret it, very much. It's as if absolution and communion and prayer let us through into a place where we get a horribly clear view —a new view—so that we see all the waste, and the cost of it, and how its roots struck deep down into the earth, poisoning the springs of our own lives and other people's. Such waste, such cost in human and spiritual values. The priest says 'Go in peace, the Lord has put away thy sin.' But of course one doesn't go in peace, and in one sense He can't put it away, it has done its work. You can't undo what's done."*

In a later letter she described her regret at not having returned to God earlier, and how instead of giving God his rightful place in all her life she could now only make him the poor offering of the last years of an old lady's life: she was then about seventy.

Let us return to the suggestion that heaven *is* the mind of God, or in Whitehead's terms that heaven *is* God's consequent nature, and that our everlasting life consists in God's everlasting prehensions of each moment of our lives. The great difference between this and more traditional expressions of the Christian hope is that we are the object and God the subject of his prehensions of us, and therefore we live on objectively, and not subjectively, in the consequent nature of God. As I said at the beginning of this discussion, this seems a shattering difference to our self-centred minds: our vested interest in the concept of heaven is precisely the desire that *we*, as subjects, shall enjoy future rewards and future bliss.

We shall consider this vital difference in greater detail, and seek if there be any way round it. But let us first remind ourselves that the New Testament writings place a good deal less emphasis on the individual aspect of the resurrection life, and a good deal more emphasis on its corporate aspect, than we tend to do today. There is a fluctuation of view within the New Testament as to whether the resurrection life is to be thought of as beginning at death or at the Last Day: both views can be found in the letters of St. Paul; many Christians today unquestionably adopt the former, individual viewpoint. Perhaps we should give more heed to the great passage in Hebrews where the author describes some of the heroes and martyrs of the faith, and adds: "These also, one and all, are commemorated for their faith; and yet they did not enter upon the promised inheritance, because, with us in mind, God had made a better plan, that only in company with us should they reach their perfection."† This New Testament emphasis on the *corporate* nature of the resurrection life is epitomized in the phrase

* *Letters to a Friend from Rose Macaulay, 1950–1952,* ed. C. Babington Smith, p. 61 f. Her letters, but not the priest's replies, were published in 1961, three years after her death.
† Hebrews 11: 39, 40. *(N.E.B.)*

"raised in Christ". There is a parallel emphasis on the corporate nature of our *present* life as Christians, living "in Christ" and as "members of the body of Christ": this is a recurrent theme in the Epistles.

In recent years a number of theologians have attacked our Western tendency to individualize the gospel. I suggest that there is deep truth in this, particularly with regard to the resurrection life. If we could recapture a real sense of our present corporate unity "in Christ", we would surely expect an even stronger corporate element in the resurrection life – and be less tempted by the desire for a future individualization into separate "selves" or "souls". If we go back to the Old Testament, with its strong sense of the corporate unity of Israel as the people of God, we shall in the main – and certainly in the older writings – find no belief in an individual resurrection (other than the shadowy underworld existence that was often expected in the ancient world); in New Testament times this belief continued to be denied by the Sadducees, and was clearly a frequent source of dispute. Having been forced drastically to question my own earlier acceptance of this belief, I find great comfort in the fact that psalmists who appear to deny that there is an individual life beyond the grave also – in the same psalm – vividly display their unshakeable faith in the loving-kindness of God.

We consider the person and Resurrection of Christ later, but it is here appropriate to look very briefly at the doctrine of his Ascension. This implies that after his Crucifixion Jesus was raised not only "from the dead" but "to the right hand of God", so that his humanity has been taken into the Godhead. Admittedly the Ascended Christ is thought of as living on in some sense separately from God the Father, but the Resurrection and Ascension are held to be the proof and crowning of Christ's divinity: he lives on *within* the Godhead, not outside it. If we think of Jesus primarily as a supernatural being, then his Ascension remains an utterly unique event to which nothing in ourselves or our own future can have any parallel. But a number of contemporary theologians are urging us to start our thinking about Jesus from the fact that he was a man "like unto us". If we think along these lines (as we shall, in far greater detail, in chapter six), then we can at least ask ourselves whether God may not also raise *us* not into an unknown "heaven" but *into himself* – or, in the terms we have been using, whether God will not "prehend" us into his consequent nature.*

3. *Our everlastingness influences the world.* Whether or not they hope for an individual future life in heaven, most men and women seek some form, if not of immortality, at least of prolongation of influence here on earth. They seek this through the procreation and nurturing of children, and through making their mark upon at least their little corner of society, so as to ensure the continuing influence of their own ideas or ideals. If "immortality" be used to denote such continuation, even though this neither endures through infinite time nor transcends time, then we can agree with the psychologist Raymond B. Cattell:

> "From a broad scientific standpoint our immortality is plainly of two kinds. We have a biological, physical immortality in our children, who perpetuate the dispositions, temperaments, and intelligences of their parents. Through this similarity they are living forces tending to foster the same kinds of values as those which we have ourselves most naturally loved. It could reasonably be maintained that this biological immortality alone is more satisfying than any of the internally contradictory phantasies of traditional religion."†

The second kind of immortality described by Cattell is that of "Acts and ideas and feelings [which] reverberate down the ages, and coalesce and favour the development of their own forms". The most obvious instances are the example of the saint, the discoveries of the scientist, and the work of the artist, writer or musician. But this kind of immortality is not confined to those who make a great mark upon history:

> "The humblest men and women may achieve great immortality . . . The devoted mother, the common soldier giving his life for the group ideals upon the battlefield, are equally essential to the group development and share in great measures the foundational elements in its immortality. If we accept the intuitions of Christ in this as in other fields as being contingently the nearest approximation to truth that human wisdom may attain, it is evident that love and humility, sincerity and faith in fellow-men, have as great an immortality value as power, mental capacity, or creativeness."

* More precisely, it will be suggested that God "prehends" into his consequent nature not "us" but the totality of our thoughts and actions, except for those that are utterly incompatible with his nature.

† This and the following quotations are from *Psychology and the Religious Quest*, by R. B. Cattell (Nelson, 1938), pp. 72–76. These passages are cited in *Philosophers Speak of God* by Hartshorne and Reese, pp. 388–91.

Cattell points out that these two kinds of immortality are inter-connected. "A system of ideas sits most comfortably on minds similar in structure to those which created the ideas, so that the aristocrat and the Chinaman are correct in emphasizing the importance of familial persistence". One cannot say which is more important; "but it is evident that men of great vision, religious leaders, scientists, and artists have regarded their spiritual immortality as of more value to society than their biological survival, and a whole Church, by insisting on celibacy in its priesthood, has embraced the same view".

Neither the Christian nor the atheist should belittle either of these forms of "immortality" – or, more accurately, of prolongation. But they ignore the working of God's spirit, the interaction between God and the world. The supreme instance of this is to be found in the second half of the New Testament, in which it is clear that the disciples – Peter and John and the others as well as the latecomer Paul – were bolder, *more* decisive, *more* powerful figures after the Ascension and Pentecost than they had been before. This is discussed in greater detail later, but it is also relevant here. There would seem to be three reasons for it. Firstly, Jesus' death and the last week of his life formed the seal and climax of his total self-offering to God, and it was only after this that his followers were in a position to see the full significance of what their Master had both said and done – the more so as it was only his death which stripped some of them of their tenacious illusions of political success. Secondly, they were "filled with the Holy Spirit" at Pentecost. Thirdly, long after the series of Resurrection appearances had ended, the disciples continued to be very conscious of the powerful influence of the Risen and Ascended Christ, and especially so when they met together for prayer and for the breaking of bread.

These three reasons overlap to some extent in the New Testament itself: in the fourth gospel the Risen Christ breathes Holy Spirit into his disciples on Easter night; awareness of the significance of Jesus's life in the light of his death overlaps with awareness of the presence of the Risen Christ in Luke's beautiful account of the walk to Emmaus; Paul's theology often does not distinguish the indwelling of the Holy Spirit from the influence of the Risen Christ.

The three are seen as completely overlapping in the radical theology of Rudolf Bultmann, which is discussed in chapter six.

It is perhaps rash to attempt a summary in a single sentence, but for Bultmann and his followers the Spirit's indwelling and the guidance of the Risen Christ are two different "mythological" descriptions of the force and power accompanying a full appreciation of the significance of the life and death of Jesus. Again to anticipate and to summarize, I shall myself suggest that the greater spiritual power of the disciples after Easter arose from the fact that as they walked with God, and especially as they turned to him in prayer and sacrament, they "prehended" — and so were influenced by — the *total* event of their master's life and teaching and death, all of which God had raised and taken into the Godhead — had "prehended" into his own consequent nature. This influence of the total event of Jesus guided them *more powerfully* than Jesus had been able to do as they travelled round Palestine together.

If it is possible to draw any parallel between Christ's Ascension and our own, and to suggest that some of the totality of events which constitutes our life will be raised into God's consequent nature, then perhaps this parallel extends also to the sequel. Unlike Jesus, much of our life is *not* totally filled with the influence and spirit of God: but perhaps the part of one's life that one has allowed to be "of God" *will* be prehended into the Godhead, and thus exert a more powerful influence for good than it was able to do during one's lifetime. That our lives, or elements of them, will be prehended into the Godhead may sound a purely theoretical statement of no relevance to us and our world — especially so, from our selfish viewpoint, if "we" are not going to share in this experience. But once these elements are prehended into God's "consequent nature" they will, in God, reach back to influence the world — as happened in the case of Jesus and his disciples. Whitehead describes this reaching back in the short closing section of *Process and Reality*:*

"Each actuality in the temporal world has its reception into God's nature. The corresponding element in God's nature is not temporal actuality, but is the transmutation of that temporal actuality into a living, ever-present fact . . . This element in God's nature inherits from the temporal counterpart according to the same principle as in the temporal world the future inherits from the past. Thus in the

* The first of the quotations that follow does not escape the extreme difficulty inherent in all attempts to relate the temporal and the non-temporal. But Whitehead has something immensely important to contribute here, despite his admittedly difficult language.

sense in which the present occasion is the person *now,* and yet with his own past, so the counterpart in God is that person in God."

This "ascension" of the actualities of the temporal world into the Godhead is described as "the phase of perfected actuality, in which the many are one everlastingly, without the qualifications of any loss either of individual identity or of completeness of unity. In everlastingness, immediacy is reconciled with objective immortality." In the next and final phase:

"The creative action completes itself. For the perfected actuality passes back into the temporal world, and qualifies this world so that each temporal actuality includes it as an immediate fact of relevant experience. For the kingdom of heaven is with us today. The action of the fourth phase is the love of God for the world . . . What is done in the world is transformed into a reality in heaven, and the reality in heaven passes back into the world. By reason of this reciprocal relation, the love in the world passes into the love in heaven, and floods back again into the world . . .

"In this way, the insistent craving is justified—the insistent craving that zest for existence be refreshed by the ever-present, unfading importance of our immediate actions, which perish and yet live for evermore."*

I find this passage immensely moving, and worthy of deep and prolonged meditation. Even if "we" do not survive to experience it, such immortality, reflected back into the world, is no mean or meagre prospect. It may seem a lot "less" than many of us had been brought up to hope for, but it is also a lot *more* than many today either believe in or expect. It may be all that a loving Creator can do to "immortalize" his essentially mortal creatures. For I believe it to be important to admit that we *are* mortal and to see death for what it is: the termination of the sequence of experiences which comprise one's life, but not the destruction of its influence, still less of its existence.

4. *Birth and death, heaven and hell.*

"Prior to my first experiences, 'I' was not 'I', the individual which I am . . . there was once no such individual as myself, even as something that was 'going to exist'. But centuries after my death, there will have been that very individual which I am. This is creation, with no corresponding de-creation. But . . . what then is death?

"Death is the last page of the last chapter of the book of one's life, as birth is the first page of the first chapter. Without a first page there is no book. But given the first page there is, in so far, a book. The

* *Process and Reality,* final section (pp. 496-7).

question of death then is, How rich and how complete is the book to be? It is not a question of reality . . . reality, whether or not it is created, is indestructible . . . [George] Washington having died is at least Washington. Not just a certain corpse, for by 'Washington' we mean a unique unity of experience and decision and thought, and that is no corpse. So those are right who say to themselves upon the death of the loved one: It cannot be that beloved human reality is now nothing or is now something not human at all.''

This passage occurs in Charles Hartshorne's very fine essay "Time, Death and Everlasting Life", which is included in *The Logic of Perfection.** I find it valuable that Hartshorne considers birth and death together. People sometimes argue that if there is a sense in which we exist beyond death there must also be a sense in which we existed before our present life began, and hence that a series of reincarnations – which some people, and certainly some schoolboys, always find attractive – is at least likely as the traditional Christian concept of heaven. But if some ideas of heaven derive from a refusal to face the fact of death, the idea of a series of reincarnations surely derives from a refusal to face the fact of *novelty*, a basic element in a world of creative evolution. I reject the idea of reincarnation anywhere within the life of this planet on the grounds that it infringes this basic element of novelty. Some of the arguments against reincarnation can be countered by drawing up parallel arguments against traditional Christian beliefs, but there remains one argument against the reincarnation of one human being in another: since this is said to occur within the life of mankind, one could expect to find some evidence for it; whereas one would not expect to find evidence of a scientific kind for a future life in a purely spiritual realm. I have yet to hear of any evidence for reincarnation that is in the least bit convincing. I therefore hold, with most people, that conception and birth are the creation of a new individual.

Hartshorne insists that there is no corresponding de-creation. Death is the last page, as birth is the first page, of the book of one's life; after it is closed, the book remains. There was a belief in the ancient world that a person's shade or spirit was in a sense brought back to life whenever someone still alive remem-

* I would hope that this essay might be published separately. It merits the attention of a far wider public than can be expected to study this collection of philosophical essays; most of the other essays demand technical knowledge in the field of logic, but this one does not. I quote from page 250 f.

bered him: some theologians have suggested that this may in part lie behind the words "Do this in remembrance of me" which we repeat as we make memorial of Jesus' death in the Holy Communion. Hartshorne's insistence that reality is indestructible goes beyond the continuing memory of mankind. There will be a time when no one remembers Peter Hamilton — but God will still remember him. Our feelings, decisions and actions live on everlastingly in the "mind" or "consequent nature" of God, into which he "prehends" them as they occur.*

It is, however, one thing to suppose that our feelings and actions thus live on in "heaven", and quite another to suppose that there will be new ones. The belief that we shall continue as experiencing subjects, whose new experiences will include new meetings and discussions with loved ones and old friends, is very dear to many people — as it was to the Scottish theologian and the English bishop with whom we began; the difficulties we went on to consider largely spring from this belief. I have said that I can see no answer to these difficulties (except perhaps the first); they do not arise if we live on as "prehended" objects, and not as experiencing subjects, in the "mind" or "consequent nature" of God, which *is* "heaven".

What, then, is "hell"? The Church today seldom mentions hell. Perhaps this is because we have at last learned the truth that God is love, and that the divine love predominates over the divine justice. I do not myself see how one can possibly combine God's love with the idea of everlasting punishment, even modified by a doctrine of purgatory: I find value in the suggestion that the imagery of the flames of hell properly depicts *not* punishment but fire's usual function of destruction. Thus the concept of hell beyond the grave, as an alternative to heaven, uses the language of mythology to convey the warning that if there is nothing of any value in a person's life for God to "prehend" into his heaven, then that life must face *ultimate* destruction. This is the converse to Hartshorne's suggestion that "perhaps such [traditional] views of heaven are only mythical ways of trying to grasp the truth that death is not ultimate destruction but simply termination, finitude".†

* The metaphor "mind of God" should not be confused with Whitehead's terminology: God's "consequent nature" corresponds to his "physical pole".
† *The Logic of Perfection*, p. 251.

Scientists tell us that life on this earth cannot continue indefinitely; even if the life of the universe extends for infinite time *homo sapiens* seems unlikely to perpetuate itself by colonizing the planets of other stars. Thus the good or evil in men's lives can *ultimately* only live on in God. Without attempting to summarize Whitehead's concept of "negative prehensions", I will here just say that this allows all entities, including God, to prehend other entities selectively: thus God does not prehend into his consequent nature that which is utterly alien to it. God's prehensions of all that is good, true or beautiful ascend into "heaven": that which is utterly evil is excluded by his "negative prehensions", symbolized by the "flames of hell". God is indeed "the fellow-sufferer who understands": he prehends suffering into his consequent nature, but not sheer evil. Thinking in terms of the "group mind" and group welfare rather than Christian mythology, the psychologist Raymond B. Cattell makes a not dissimilar point as to evil:

"Evil actions, by the very nature and definition of evil as that which is opposed to group welfare, must in time, if not immediately, mutually cancel and destroy each other. Actions are evil because they are non-contributory, untrue to life, mutually contradictory, selfish rather than outwardly directed, tending naturally to become null and void. I think Whitehead is asserting the same view when he says, 'There is self-preservation inherent in that which is good in itself.' "*

Process thinking suggests that our "objective immortality" consists of God's "prehensions" of all that we do and feel, or rather of so much of this as is in any way compatible with his nature – hell being the complete absence of any such compatibility. It may be said in protest that the immortality of being "prehended" into God's consequent nature is less potent than the two forms – survival in one's children and "immortality" of one's ideas and ideals – which Cattell deduced from "a broad scientific standpoint".† I have just pointed out that the species *homo sapiens* will not survive indefinitely, so neither of these forms of "immortality" is strictly everlasting: true everlastingness resides in God. Furthermore it is only God who can know, appreciate, "prehend" *all* that is of value in a person's

* *Psychology and the Religious Quest*, p. 76; cited in *Philosophers Speak of God*, by Hartshorne and Reese, p. 390.
† See section 3 above, p. 130.

life. Clearly, only a small part of one's personality can be handed on biologically to one's children: quite apart from anything else, children are normally conceived and born before the parents' personalities have reached their full stature. As to the passing on of the influence of our acts and ideas and feelings, even those nearest and dearest to us can only be aware of a small fraction of these – whereas God is aware of them all. God's prehensions of the sum total of everything that constitutes myself and my life are far fuller than, say, my wife's prehensions of me could ever be.

It is a person's actual experiences, his actions and feelings and aspirations, which the omnipresent God "prehends"; and these are, surely, more personal, more truly "him", than anything that can be handed down through procreation or influence. I would indeed agree that:

> "It remains true that the Whiteheadian immortality is 'personal' in a literal sense. For all that is known to be actual of any human personality is the life of that person while on earth. And all this actuality, as actuality of experience – and what is value beyond all experience? – is just what, according to Whitehead, is immortalized in the all-receptive unity of God. Nothing is more personal about a man than his concrete experiences – which 'perish, and yet live for evermore' – in the divine, supremely personal life!"*

There remains the objection that this still denies an individual personal resurrection in the sense of a prolongation of our present personality, or personal identity, so that after death "we" begin a new series of experiences. The answer, as I have attempted to show, is that our *present* personality or identity cannot be prolonged. It is in itself merely an abstraction, the continuity-factor in the entire sequence of interacting events which comprises one's life; it is *utterly dependent* upon the interactions of the cells of our body and brain upon our environment. Our *present* personality or identity cannot be prolonged beyond death: "the within", cannot continue to exist in the entire absence of "the without".

No one can disprove the possibility that some different identity might be attached to us at death. "For personal survival after death with memory of personal life before death is hardly an absolute absurdity. Perhaps personal existence without a body is indeed impossible, yet the analogy to a

* *Philosophers Speak of God,* by Hartshorne and Reese, p. 285.

butterfly with its succession of bodies, while remote and implausible, is not necessarily strictly inapplicable."*

5. *God is more important than we are.* We can now return to part of the passage from John Baillie quoted earlier in our discussion:

"If the individual can commune with God, then he must matter to God; and if he matters to God, he must share God's eternity. For if God really rules, He cannot be conceived as scrapping what is precious in His sight."†

The main answer to this is that death is not "scrapping", but the setting of a limit. Our experiences can live on, in God, for ever. What about the experiences we have not had, or have not made time for, when death intervenes? The answer must be that we cannot now have them: the book of our life is not destroyed, but it is closed. "Death only says to us: 'More than you have already been you will not be. For instance, the virtues you have failed to acquire, you will now never acquire. It is too late. You had your chance.' This may be thought to be expressed in the notion of the Last Judgement. Our lives will be definitively estimated, the account will be closed, nothing can be added or taken away."‡

If new experiences cannot be added, neither can future rewards or punishments. In the entire field of religious thought there is probably no concept that does more harm than the idea that God – and in particular the Christian God of love – will compensate for moral good or evil, and for fortune or misfortune, by rewards and punishments *in a future life.* This idea may have seemed reasonable in earlier centuries, when it was assumed that God had created the different species in their present forms, with an absolute gulf between man and the rest, and when the largely static nature of human society encouraged people to think of rich and poor as living "in that estate into which it hath pleased God to call them". On this philosophy non-humans need not be considered, and God rewards the human dead in direct proportion to their moral goodness and in inverse proportion to the amount of health and wealth they had

* *The Logic of Perfection,* p. 253.
† Quoted on page 111.
‡ *The Logic of Perfection,* p. 255.

enjoyed in this life. This whole system of thought is untenable in terms of the theory of evolution. Once the evolving life of this planet is seen as a single whole, its individual constituents would all need rewarding for the misfortune of not having come higher up the ladder: ape-men for not being men, apes for not being either, and so on. Organic compounds being derived from inorganic, God might logically reward the latter for not having enjoyed the privilege of life. To speak like this is simply to repeat in another way my earlier insistence that we must not envisage any form of "heaven for humans only", since this inevitably denies ultimate value to the greater part of God's universe. This was one of my objections to that passage from Dr. Baillie.

The traditional concept of rewards in heaven, or punishments in hell, needs to be analysed in terms of continuity and of the relationship between present and future. The non-Christian philosopher Antony Flew says this on the question of continuity: "Unless I am my soul the immortality of my soul will not be my immortality; and the news of the immortality of my soul would be of no more concern to me than the news that my appendix would be preserved eternally in a bottle." He then says "it has been thought that the distinctively Christian doctrine of the 'resurrection of the body' (better perhaps reformulated as the 'reconstitution of the person') avoids this difficulty. But might not a sceptic argue that reconstituted Flew was only an imitation of the Flew that had been destroyed; and hence that I would not be justified in looking forward to the things that would happen to him as things that would happen to me?"*

I find Charles Hartshorne's analysis more penetrating. He queries not only whether we are justified in *expecting* such continuity but also whether we are justified in *wanting* it. He suggests that there is often a genuine confusion of thought between "good" and "my good", and cites the example of the middle-aged man who feels impelled to enjoy a young woman's beauty by leaving his middle-aged wife and marrying her himself – whereas he could have enjoyed the fact that her beauty was being enjoyed and appreciated by a husband of her own age. I fear the philosopher is being unduly sanguine if he regards such confusion of thought as altogether genuine – but it is an

* *New Essays in Philosophical Theology*, ed. Flew and MacIntyre, p. 270.

arresting example all the same. I find further food for thought in this passage:

"The common notion of immortality, that after death we begin a new series of adventures bound together by a prolongation of our present personality, is apparently ignored by Whitehead. But are we in a position to say that there ought to be such prolongation? The argument that only thus, through transcendental rewards and punishments, can the injustices of the present life be overcome, and only by the expectation of such future consequences to 'ourselves' can our acts be adequately motivated, leaves a Whiteheadian unconvinced, to say the least. For consider: the present occasion enjoys itself; this occasion has already all the reward *it* can ever have. The same human personality may be re-embodied in future occasions falling into the same personal sequence; but our interest in *these* future occasions is only one of our interests, with no absolute metaphysical priority. Whether future joys belong to the series constituting my personal life, or even to any human series now existing, is a secondary, not a primary, question, from the ethical, and from any imaginative or generous, point of view . . . there must be a thread of personal identity connecting our present act and any future good with which it can be concerned. Indeed, there must be, for truth itself depends on this thread, and so do the coherence and order of the world. But not *our* personality is this necessary, this primary, personal unity, but only God's. It is a hard lesson to learn—that God is more important than we are."*

When I first read those two final sentences I felt completely shattered, and remained so for several days, and in a sense for a much longer time. Together with the entire section on Whitehead in *Philosophers Speak of God*, those two sentences revealed to me all too clearly not only the probable falsity but also the basic *self-centredness* of the belief I then held as to what happens when we die. I should perhaps add that my own former belief—like that of so many Christians—owed a good deal less to the specific New Testament doctrine of resurrection in Christ than to the general concept of the immortality of the (Christian) soul.

God is more important than we are: that is why we ought not to expect, let alone to insist, that "we" will enjoy future rewards or suffer future punishments. Both the rewards and the punishments occur now: the reward of knowing—whether we think in specifically theistic terms or not—that our actions are helping God's loving purpose for his world; or the punishment of knowing, in the depths of our being, that our actions are incompatible

* *Philosophers Speak of God*, ed. Hartshorne and Reese, p. 285; italics in the original.

with this loving purpose. There is the third alternative of mere negativeness, of being too insensitive to know or to care either way. Human nature at its best and highest includes some understanding if not of God at least of the deepest values inherent in the life of man. It is our loss if we fall so far below that best as to lack all such understanding. And all of this, the joy and the shame, the gain and the loss, is shared with us by God, "the great companion – the fellow-sufferer who understands".

The main objection that may well be raised to all that has been said is that Whitehead's concept of immortality does not envisage our continuing as persons. Yet everything of any value in our life will be prehended into God and immortalized in his supremely personal life. "Nothing is more personal about a man than his concrete experiences." In God's prehensions of our experiences we *do* live on everlastingly as persons – but finite persons seen from the outside, not eternal persons as seen from the inside. Our "within" terminates at death; our "without" or "outside" – in so far as it is compatible with God – is privileged to share, in God, in his everlastingness. What ultimately matters is "not *our* personality . . . but only God's".

I now briefly sum up. We have found that the traditional ideas with which we began present serious difficulties to which there appears to be no solution that is compatible with our modern knowledge of the nature of the universe – a knowledge which also shows the dualism necessary for any form of personal survival to be remote and implausible, though not strictly impossible. By contrast, Whiteheadian "objective immortality" *is* compatible with our knowledge in other fields. It can be meaningful alike to the theologically uncommitted and to the Christian believer, once the latter has recovered from the shock of having previously expected "more". But I can myself testify that the initial shock is outweighed by the relief of finding an interpretation of this and other aspects of one's faith that *is* compatible with the rest of one's knowledge. This "more" is perhaps an instance of what Whitehead called "the fallacy of misplaced concreteness".* In any case, what moral right have we to expect "more"? God *is* more important than we are.

* See p. 233 below.

CHAPTER FIVE

The Living God

"God is *in* the world, or nowhere, creating continually in us, and around us. This creative principle is everywhere, in animate and so-called inanimate matter, in the ether, water, earth, human hearts. But this creation is a continuing process, and 'the process is itself the actuality', since no sooner do you arrive than you start on a fresh journey. In so far as man partakes of this creative process does he partake of the divine, of God, and that participation is his immortality, reducing the question of whether his individuality survives death of the body to the estate of an irrelevancy. His true destiny as co-creator in the universe is his dignity and his grandeur".*

This is the final paragraph of the *Dialogues of Alfred North Whitehead*: it supplies both a heading for this chapter and an epilogue to the preceding chapter on heaven. Its penultimate sentence is a remarkably courageous statement for an old man of eighty-six who, we are told, had looked frail and tired earlier in the evening, but was now speaking with vigour. The evening was that of Armistice Day, 1947; Whitehead died seven weeks later. Earlier in the *Dialogues* Whitehead is recorded as saying "Plato's God is a God of this world. Augustine combined Plato's God with St. Paul's and made a fearful job of it. Since then our concept of this world has enlarged to that of the Universe. I have envisioned a union of Plato's God with a God of the Universe."† The phrase "God is *in* the world, or nowhere" is typical of Whitehead's thought; it indicates the direction in which Whitehead's philosophy may help both our thinking about the nature of God and our attempts to express our image of God in terms that are meaningful for today.

One of the central problems of theology is that of the transcendence and immanence of God. To transcend is to climb, or go, beyond: to say that God is transcendent is to say, above all, that God is *distinct* from the universe; that God's being is not exhausted by that of the universe. Immanent means indwelling,

---

* *Dialogues of Alfred North Whitehead* as recorded by Lucien Price, (Mentor Books, New York, 1956), p. 297. (1954 edition, p. 366.)
† *Dialogues*, p. 177 f. (p. 214.)

or abiding in: this would appear to be the opposite of transcendent. Christian theology has never found it easy to bring these spatial opposites into a metaphysical harmony, but it has insisted that both are vital.

The New Testament emphasizes above all else the love of God, and thus by implication brings his immanence into clearer focus; for love is naturally associated with reciprocity and nearness, not with otherness or beyondness. Even so, several of Jesus' parables paint a clear picture of a transcendent God, with no reference whatever to his immanence. The parable, or rather allegory, of the wicked husbandmen is an important example, for St. Mark (12:1–12) gives it considerable prominence as Jesus' final challenge to the Jewish authorities. This portrayal of God as an absentee landlord who "went into another country" came naturally both to Jesus and to his hearers; the idea of God's transcendence comes easily to those who feel at home, as they did, in the dualism of heaven and earth. Neither I myself, nor many of the theologians I read, nor many of the boys I teach, are at all at home in this dualism. The "new" theology finds God's immanence much easier to express in meaningful terms than his transcendence, which some of the "death of God" writers explicitly deny:

"If there is one clear portal to the twentieth century, it is a passage through the death of God, the collapse of any meaning or reality lying beyond the newly discovered radical immanence of modern man, an immanence dissolving even the memory or the shadow of transcendence."*

No such explicit denial of God's transcendence will be found in *Honest to God*; indeed Dr. Robinson emphasized that "our concern will not be simply to substitute an immanent for a transcendent Deity . . . on the contrary, the task is to validate the idea of transcendence for modern man".† None the less it seems to me that in putting the whole emphasis on immanence, to the point of "dissolving" transcendence, Thomas Altizer's *The Gospel of Christian Atheism* is making explicit a tendency that is implicit both in *Honest to God* and in one of its major sources, the first two volumes of Paul Tillich's *Systematic Theology*. I shall not attempt to comment in any detail on the "death of God"

* Thomas J. J. Altizer, *The Gospel of Christian Atheism,* p. 22 (Philadelphia: The Westminster Press, 1966; London: Collins).
† Page 44.

literature, but a critical analysis of Robinson and Tillich will perhaps supply indirect comment on the whole contemporary denial of transcendence.

Dr. Robinson tackles his task of "validating the idea of transcendence" in his third chapter, "The Ground of our Being", the title and much of the contents of which derive from Paul Tillich, as the opening quotation and much of this chapter derive from A. N. Whitehead. Of these two great thinkers – each of whom has held the distinguished post of "University Professor" at Harvard – I suggest that the earlier, Whitehead, makes the more positive contribution to this particular task. I shall, however, start with Dr. Robinson's treatment of transcendence in *Honest to God*, since it is this precise point which formed the centre of both the popular and the theological controversy over the book – a controversy which, in the new form of the "death of God", is a continuing feature of our theological scene.

The cover of the follow-up paperback *The Honest to God Debate* reminds us of the initial newspaper headlines: *The Observer's* unfortunate "Our Image of God Must Go", *The Daily Herald's* "God is not a Daddy in the Sky" and *The Sunday Telegraph's* "Bishops Without God". The main talking point was not "the new morality" but whether Dr. Robinson had validated or lost the idea of God's transcendence, and whether the word "God" can retain any meaning and value if it be denied that God may be thought of as *a* Being. It is perhaps significant that so much of this important and widespread dialogue should have centred upon the transcendence of God – whether or not that actual phrase was used. I myself increasingly see this as the primary religious issue confronting thoughtful people today. Having heard the "secularists" and the "new" theologians,* having studied and in varying degree "demythologized" the gospels, each must decide for himself whether or not he will acknowledge a transcendent Creator, to whom he will turn in

* Notably Paul M. van Buren, *The Secular Meaning of the Gospel* (New York: Macmillan, 1963; London: S.C.M. Press); William Hamilton, *The New Essence of Christianity* (New York: Association Press, 1961; London: Darton, Longman and Todd); Thomas J. J. Altizer, *The Gospel of Christian Atheism,* already referred to; and Altizer and Hamilton, *Radical Theology and the Death of God* (Indianapolis: Bobbs-Merrill Press, 1966). Extracts and comments on these are to be found in Thomas W. Ogletree, *The 'Death of God' Controversy* (Westminster Press and S.C.M. Press, 1966).

prayer and worship and self-commitment, and from whom he will seek inspiration and guidance.

But those of us who seek to affirm the transcendence of God in terms that differ, perhaps fundamentally, from those used by Dr. Robinson must always remember that the controversey set alight by *Honest to God* has had the great merit of involving many thousands of people in serious discussion, some of whom had previously abandoned the entire concept of God. The many books and articles that have been published since *Honest to God* help to broaden the outlook of those of us who take part in this continuing discussion, and remind us that there are deeply committed and thoughtful people on either side in what I have called the primary issue of the transcendence of God—just as there were deeply committed people on either side in all the major controversies of the patristic period.

It was clear from the start that Robinson had undermined the idea of spatial transcendence; this was enough to lead some to denounce his book unread. It is, however, the second stage in the bishop's argument with which we are here concerned. He moves quickly from spatial to metaphysical transcendence: "For in place of a God who is literally or physically 'up there' we have accepted, as part of our mental furniture, a God who is spiritually or metaphysically 'out there'." He adds that the last thing he would want to do:

". . . is to appear to criticize from a superior position. I should like to think that it were possible to use this mythological language of the God 'out there' and make the same utterly natural and unself-conscious transposition as I have suggested we already do with the language of the God 'up there' . . . But the signs are that we are reaching the point at which the whole conception of a God 'out there', which has served us so well since the collapse of the three-decker universe, is itself becoming more of a hindrance than a help."

Robinson emphasizes that this second stage is a much bigger step than was the first:

"The abandonment of a God 'out there' represents a much more radical break than the transition to this concept from that of a God 'up there'. For this earlier transposition was largely a matter of verbal notation, of a change in spatial metaphor, important as this undoubtedly was in liberating Christianity from a flat-earth cosmology. But to be asked to give up any idea of a Being 'out there' at all will appear to be an outright denial of God."*

* *Honest to God*, pp. 13, 15 and 17.

It is all too easy to think that one has made both stages in this transposition when in fact one has only made the first, "so that we continue to picture God as a Person, who looks down at this world which he has made and loves from 'out there'. We know, of course, that he does not exist in space. But we think of him nevertheless as defined and marked off from other beings *as if* he did. And this is what is decisive. He is thought of as *a* Being ... What is important is whether such a Being represents even a distorted image of the Christian God. Can he be rehabilitated, or is the whole conception of that sort of a God, 'up there', 'out there', or however one likes to put it, a projection, an idol, that can and should be torn down?"*

We have quoted enough to clarify the negative aspect of Robinson's position. He will not accept as sound theology any thought of God as *a* Being, though he does not exactly "tear down" such language: there is nothing "intrinsically wrong with it" as symbolism. But "if Christianity is to survive, let alone recapture 'secular' man, there is no time to lose in detaching it from this scheme of thought ... and thinking hard what we should put in its place".†

In its place Dr. Robinson puts the theology of Paul Tillich, making use of this at the precise point at which this very great Christian thinker has been the most widely criticized, namely his doctrine of God. As the philosopher Karl Popper has said, one of the rules of rational method is to choose for criticism the strongest, not the weakest, form of the theories one rejects. My purpose is not to reject but to learn from Robinson's theology, and to suggest that its weaknesses are at bottom philosophical: it stands in need, as do we all, of a philosophy of process and of creative freedom. But Popper's rule can still be applied to our present task: if we would learn from a single book we often need to go back to its sources of inspiration, and for its doctrine of God we must go back from *Honest to God* to Tillich;‡ further-more, any assessment of Tillich's contribution to contemporary

* *Honest to God*, p. 30 f. and p. 41.
† *Honest to God*, p. 43.
‡ Thus the most thoughtful criticism, and on the whole rejection, of *Honest to God* that I have seen is Alasdaire MacIntyre's in *Encounter*, September 1963, which includes admittedly brief synopses of Robinson's three principal sources, Tillich, Bonhoeffer and Bultmann. This article is reprinted with abbreviations in *The Honest to God Debate*, in which—significantly— it is the only criticism to have subjoined to it a "Comment" by Dr. Robinson. Both the criticism and the comment merit attention.

theology must consider not only his doctrine of God but also other, perhaps stronger, aspects of his writing and preaching. So much has been written about the theology of Tillich that it would be quite out of place to attempt a detailed assessment.* But Tillich's influence on contemporary Christianity is so considerable that a brief consideration of Tillich and his doctrine of God is perhaps the best starting-point for an examination of the less familiar thinking of Whitehead and his followers.

GOD AS THE GROUND OF BEING: THE THEOLOGY OF PAUL TILLICH

Paul Tillich is rare among recent theologians of the top rank in having taken the trouble to acquire a detailed knowledge of one aspect of modern science; the branch he selected, psychoanalysis, is concerned with man and man's mind, but not with the rest of the cosmos. Indeed his largely existentialist philosophy and his interests in politics, sociology, psycho-analysis, and art, are all concerned with man and his situation, including his need of God, but are not primarily concerned with the transcendence of God. Compared with most modern theologians Tillich's interests are broad indeed, but perhaps less so than those of Whitehead, whose horizons are the physics of relativity and the quantum, and that extension given to the theory of evolution by the realization that organic matter was itself derived from inorganic. Beyond all differences of background, what basically divides these two thinkers is that Tillich used a philosophy of *being*, Whitehead one of *becoming*. If there be a God all roads can lead to him, but Whitehead's doctrine of God is more positive than Tillich's, whose greatest contribution to theology may perhaps be his doctrine of man, and of man's predicament and culture.

The Courage to Be,† is an example of this. The book is primarily an analysis of courage in relation to the phenomenon of anxiety. In it Tillich suggests that "we distinguish three types of anxiety according to the three directions in which non-being threatens being ... the anxiety of fate and death ... the

---

* Recent writings include J. Heywood Thomas, *Paul Tillich: An Appraisal* and Kenneth Hamilton, *The System and the Gospel.*

† Nisbet, 1952; Fontana paperback (to which page references refer), 1962. Here in England it is probably Tillich's best-known work, except for his sermons.

anxiety of guilt and condemnation . . . the anxiety of emptiness and meaninglessness".* All three types are found throughout history, but the first was predominant at the end of the ancient world, the second at the end of the Middle Ages, and the third today. Anxiety cannot be removed – and here Tillich is closely in line with the emphasis in the writings of Whitehead and Hartshorne on the essential and unavoidable element of tragedy in all life. Anxiety can be faced only by "the courage to be", which is in part the courage to participate, and in part the courage to be oneself (self-affirmation) : again there are parallels in Whitehead and Hartshorne. Tillich expresses all this with great power; it is relevant to our situation, and important. But the book ends with two sections dealing directly with the doctrine of God; these strike me as the least successful part of the book, quite apart from the fact that in them, as we shall see, he at least appears to reject the idea of God's transcendence.

Tillich's main work is his three volume *Systematic Theology*. The first volume was begun in 1925, when Tillich was Professor of Theology at Marburg. At that time Tillich himself was greatly influenced by existentialism; but he found that the students were mainly influenced by the neo-orthodox theology of Karl Barth, in which all the emphasis is placed on the uniqueness of the biblical revelation, and no dialogue with contemporary culture is permitted. *Systematic Theology* was begun as Tillich's answer to this. He left Marburg in 1928, and became Professor of Philosophy at Frankfurt the following year. He felt impelled to make his philosophy relevant to the problems of the day, and thus in part social-political: this brought him into such conflict with the growing Nazi movement that he was dismissed from his post when Hitler became Chancellor of Germany. Tillich moved to the Union Theological Seminary, New York, in 1933. After some years he resumed work on his *Systematic Theology*, and the first volume was published in America in 1951: the other two volumes followed in 1957 and 1963. The writing of these volumes thus covers a span of almost forty years, and it is scarcely surprising that there was a certain development in his thought. The third volume in fact shows a certain affinity with some aspects of process thinking, but we here mainly confine ourselves to the first volume, and in particular to certain themes in it which sufficiently indicate the

* Page 49.

general lines of Tillich's doctrine of God: these were not significantly amended in the later volumes.

Tillich's own starting-point is emphasized in its opening pages, where he gives two formal criteria for theology: "the object of theology is what concerns us ultimately"; "our ultimate concern is that which determines our being or non-being. Only those statements are theological which deal with their object in so far as it can become a matter of being or non-being for us." The comment that follows merits quotation in full:

"Nothing can be of ultimate concern for us which does not have the power of threatening and saving our being. The term 'being' . . . means the whole of human reality, the structure, the meaning, and the aim of existence. All this is threatened; it can be lost or saved. Man is ultimately concerned about his being and meaning. 'To be or not to be' in *this* sense is a matter of ultimate, unconditional, total and infinite concern."*

A basic feature of Tillich's work is what he calls the "method of correlation", which could be crudely described as the juxtaposition or bringing together of the two ends of a tension:

"In using the method of correlation, systematic theology proceeds in the following way: it makes an analysis of the human situation out of which the existential questions arise, and it demonstrates that the symbols used in the Christian message are the answers to these questions."†

The work-sequence here outlined is important, and illustrates Tillich's words in the preface to Volume I that the purpose of his theological system is to provide "a help in answering questions". His work is "answering theology". Thus Tillich's section on God *begins* with man's self-questioning as he contemplates his own being and his own finiteness. It is from these questions that the idea of God arises, for "God" is the name of the ultimate concern which determines our being or non-being.

"Many confusions in the doctrine of God and many apologetic weaknesses could be avoided if God were understood first of all as being-itself or as the ground of being . . . he is the power of being in everything and above everything, the infinite power of being. A theology which does not dare to identify God and the power of being as the first step toward a doctrine of God relapses into monarchic

---

* Vol. I, p. 17. Subsequent quotations are all from this first volume, unless some other reference is given.

† Page 70. See also *The Protestant Era* (1948), p. xxii of the abridged paperback edition (Phoenix Books, Chicago, 1957).

monotheism, for if God is not being-itself he is subordinate to it, just as Zeus is subordinate to fate in Greek religion . . . But God is his own fate . . . This can be said of him only if he is the power of being, if he is being-itself . . . Being-itself infinitely transcends every finite being. There is no proportion or gradation between the finite and the infinite. There is an absolute break, an infinite 'jump' . . . all beings are infinitely transcended by their creative ground."*

This is followed by two important paragraphs in which Tillich examines the two types of relation – causality and substance – which man uses to express the relation between God and finite things. Either relation on its own is inadequate. The substance relation leads to Spinoza's pantheism, which says, not that God is everything, but that he is the substance of everything: this rules out "substantial independence and freedom in anything finite. Therefore, Christianity, which asserts finite freedom in man and spontaneity in the non-human realm, has rejected the category of substance in favour of the category of causality . . ."† This seems to make God the first cause in a chain of cause and effect and, at the same time, to separate God from the world which he causes. The trouble is that "cause and effect are not separate; they include each other and form a series which is endless in both directions. What is cause at one point in this series is effect at another point and conversely." To postulate a first cause, says Tillich, is to deny causality, or rather to use it "as a symbol. And if this is done and is understood the difference between substance and causality disappears, for if God is the cause of the entire series of causes and effects, he is the substance underlying the whole process of becoming." But the phrase "underlying substance" is also a symbol, for divinity "underlies" in such a way as to preserve the freedom of things. Thus God is symbolically both "cause" and "substance", yet transcends them both. Hence Tillich's preference for "ground of being", which covers both without being identified with either and overcomes "both naturalistic pantheism, based on the category of substance, and rationalistic theism, based on the category of causality".

"Since God is the ground of being, he is the ground of the structure of being. He is not subject to this structure; the structure is grounded in him. He *is* this structure, and it is impossible to speak

* Pages 261–3.
† Page 263 f; note the close parallel here between Tillich and Whitehead.

about him except in terms of this structure. God must be approached cognitively through the structural elements of being-itself. These elements make him a living God, a God who can be man's concrete concern."*

In this first volume Tillich describes the statement that God is the structure or ground of being as the only statement about God which "means what it says directly and properly": all other statements about God as God point beyond themselves, and are symbolic. In his second volume Tillich qualifies this and says that the *only* non-symbolic statement that can be made about God is "the statement that everything we say about God is symbolic".† It remains clear that the description of God as the structure or ground of being is of very great importance in Tillich's theology, whether that description be classified as statement, or symbol, or in some other way. Some years later, Tillich expressed a preference for the phrase "being itself" *(esse ipsum)*; when asked "Why is it necessary to talk about a ground of being?" Tillich replied:

"It is not necessary. I would prefer to say 'being itself'. But I know that this term is even more disliked. And so I speak of the ground of being. I actually mean, with the classical theologians, being itself."‡

Tillich also emphasized God as *living*. This next quotation also includes a definition of the word "symbol" in Tillich's usage:

"Few things about God are more emphasised in the Bible, especially in the Old Testament, than the truth that God is a living God . . . Life is the actuality of being, or, more exactly, it is the process in which potential being becomes actual being. But in God as God there is no distinction between potentiality and actuality. Therefore, we cannot speak of God as living in the proper or non-symbolic sense of the word 'life'. We must speak of God as living in symbolic terms. Yet every true symbol participates in the reality which it symbolises. God lives in so far as he is the ground of life. ('He that formeth the eye, shall he not see?' Psalm 94. 9)."§

The symbol "personal God" is of great importance to Tillich, since man cannot feel "ultimate concern" about anything

* This and the preceding quotation are from p. 264. † Vol. II, p. 10.
‡ *Ultimate Concern: Tillich in Dialogue,* ed. D. Mackenzie Brown. Copyright © 1965 by D. MacKenzie Brown. Reprinted with the permission of Harper & Row, Publishers, Inc., New York.
  § Page 268.

that is less than personal. But personality includes individuality. God is a person "not in finite separation, but in absolute and unconditional participation in everything".* This God can only be called the "absolute individual" if he is also called the "absolute participant". The one term cannot be applied without the other. "God is equally 'near' to each of them while transcending them both."

"The solution of the difficulties in the phrase 'personal God' follows from this. 'Personal God' does not mean that God is *a* person. It means that God is the ground of everything personal and that he carries within himself the ontological power of personality. He is not a person, but he is not less than personal . . . Ordinary theism has made God a heavenly, completely perfect person who resides above the world and mankind. The protest of atheism against such a highest person is correct. There is no evidence for his existence, nor is he a matter of ultimate concern. God is not God without universal participation. 'Personal God' is a confusing symbol."†

I find value in Tillich's insistence that God "is called a person . . . not in finite separation but in . . . unconditional participation in everything", and that God is the "absolute participant". But does Tillich succeed in preserving the other half of this polarity, that God is also the "absolute individual"? The closing sections of *The Courage to Be* suggest that he does not. As we have seen, this book is primarily an analysis of different types of anxiety, and of the courage required to overcome it. In its closing pages Tillich states that "the ultimate source of the courage to be is the 'God above God' . . . [it] is rooted in the experience of the God above the God of theism". This is preceded by an attack on "the God of theological theism", who is:

" . . . a being beside others and as such a part of the whole of reality . . . He is a being, not being-itself. As such he is bound to the subject-object structure of reality, he is an object for us as subjects. At the same time we are objects for him as a subject. And this is decisive for the necessity of transcending theological theism. For God as a subject makes me into an object which is nothing more than an object. He deprives me of my subjectivity because he is all-powerful and all-knowing. I revolt and try to make *him* into an object, but my revolt fails and becomes desperate. God appears as the invincible tyrant . . . This is the God Nietzsche said had to be killed because nobody can tolerate being made into a mere object

* Page 270.
† Page 271.

of absolute knowledge and absolute control. This is the deepest root of atheism. It is an atheism which is justified as the reaction against the theological theism and its disturbing implications. It is also the deepest root of the Existentialist despair and the widespread anxiety of meaninglessness in our period."

This "theological theism" is transcended in the experience which Tillich calls "absolute faith. It is the accepting of the acceptance without somebody or something that accepts. It is the power of being-itself that accepts and gives the courage to be."*

Readers of Tillich's sermons will know many powerful passages in which he bids us accept the fact that we are "accepted, though unacceptable". This message has great force for modern man, to whom it brings home the biblical truth that God's forgiveness is a free gift which cannot be earned: that, while we were yet sinners, Christ died for us. But it is one thing to accept the fact that God accepts us; it is another to accept "the acceptance without somebody or something that accepts". This not only seems to deny that God is the "absolute individual", it denies his transcendence, if not his existence. I would agree that it is "the power of being" that accepts us. But that power is only one aspect of God, who *is*, also, "somebody or something that accepts".

In saying that God appears as the "invincible tyrant", making us mere objects of his absolute knowledge and control, Tillich is pursuing a line of thought not dissimilar from that of Whitehead and Hartshorne, and of much of this book: I suggested in the first part of chapter four that the existence of suffering makes it impossible to believe both in God's love and in his absolute omnipotence. Whitehead follows Plato in seeing God's activity as persuasive rather than coercive, whereas Tillich asserts that God is in no sense a separate self. This is perhaps the critical dividing point between these two doctrines of God. I believe Whitehead's to be the sounder and more meaningful doctrine, and one that provides a basis for suggesting *how* God is active in the world. Tillich's doctrine of God does not seem to provide such a basis. Much of what Tillich says about the nature or being of God is both true and vitally important: but it is also inadequate.

I would add that the particular aspect of Tillich's theology

* *The Courage To Be*, p. 178 f.

with which we are here primarily concerned – his doctrine of God – played a central part in the immense debt that I personally owe to Tillich's writings, and in particular to the first volume of his *Systematic Theology*. Reading this gave me the shake-up, the encouragement, and the enlargement of vision which *Honest to God* was later to give to a wider public; above all, it opened up for me the fundamental *largeness* of him whom we so easily label "God". I can never again think of God as less than the ground of all being, the source of all life and all creation. I hope God was always this for me implicitly: Paul Tillich first made this explicit in a way that nothing can ever remove or gainsay.* And yet this largeness can easily lose itself: it seems to me that Tillich's thinking here needs to be supplemented by Whitehead's. Emphasis on God as the ground and structure of all being may broaden our vision of God, but if our faith is to withstand the tensions of doubt and of suffering – above all, if we are to grow in depth of prayer – we need some more specific indications of God's *function* in the world, and of how we can make contact with him.

I shall try to show that Whitehead does indicate at least some aspects of God's particular function in the world, and in the last chapter I shall briefly discuss the relevance of this to prayer. By contrast, Tillich's repeated denials that God is in any sense *a* Being seem almost to preclude God from any specific, active function: God may *be* the structure of being, but what does he *do*, and how can we establish communication with him? I shall return to this question in the final section of this chapter, where we consider the Archbishop of Canterbury's question of *Honest to God*: "I ask where 'revelation' and 'grace' come in?"

In the first chapter of *Honest to God* Dr. Robinson describes how very moved he was on first reading Paul Tillich's great sermon entitled "The Depth of Existence",† in which Tillich discusses the liberating effect on traditional religious symbolism of transforming the imagery from the heights to the depths. The sermon speaks powerfully of the ultimate depth of human history, of both the psychology and the sociology of depth, and so of "the Kingdom of God". But the aspect of this sermon on which Dr. Robinson leans most heavily is its relevance to our

* In particular, in chapters ten and eleven of volume 1.
† This sermon is printed in full in *The Shaking of the Foundations*, p. 59 ff of the Pelican edition.

thinking about the meaning and nature of "God". Here are the most important sentences in the passage from this sermon that is quoted in the first chapter of *Honest to God* (on page 22):

"The name of this infinite and inexhaustible depth and ground of all being is *God*. That depth is what the word *God* means . . . Perhaps . . . you must forget everything traditional that you have learned about God, perhaps even that word itself. For if you know that God means depth, you know much about him. You cannot then call youself an atheist or unbeliever. For you cannot think or say: Life has no depth! Life is shallow . . . He who knows about depth knows about God."

This vision of God in terms of the depth of life is not dissimilar from our earlier consideration of the purposive element in evolution. But process thinking makes it clear that this purposive element is the *result* of God's activity, the result of the fact that every entity "derives from God its basic conceptual aim",* whereas Tillich appears to *equate* the element of depth with the meaning of the word God. Now the element of depth is a *quality* of life, and of all existence. One can admire the quality of a painting or a piece of music: indeed people sometimes describe music as their religion, and they bear witness to a truth, for they are giving worth-ship or worship to something whose beauty God assuredly values. (Let it be said in parenthesis that Tillich's writings supply a most valuable theology of aesthetics and of culture.) But one cannot separate the quality of a picture from the picture itself—or the depth in a person's life from that life—and give it an independent existence in its own right: we saw this, in a different context, in the previous chapter. All such attempts stand condemned as instances of what Whitehead termed "the fallacy of misplaced concreteness". Thus if the meaning of the word "God" be equated with the depth of existence, there would seem to be no sense in which God can be separated, even for purposes of thought, from the universe of which he is the depth. One can get inspiration from the depth and value that one sees in certain people's lives: one can indeed model one's life on theirs: but one cannot pray to that quality of depth, or seek guidance from it—not, at any rate, in the sense that would appear to be demanded by the Archbishop's question about "revelation" and "grace".

A similar difficulty arises in connection with Tillich's concept

* *Process and Reality*, III.1.5 (p. 317).

of "self-transcendence", which is praised by Dr. Robinson as "Tillich's great contribution to theology – the reinterpretation of transcendence in a way which preserves its reality while detaching it from the projection of supranaturalism".* I would agree that this concept detaches transcendence from supranaturalism; I question whether it preserves its reality. The key passage comes in the introduction to the second volume of Tillich's *Systematic Theology*:

"The term 'self-transcendent' has two elements: 'transcending' and 'self'. God as the ground of being infinitely transcends that of which he is the ground . . . To call God transcendent in this sense does not mean that one must establish a 'superworld' of divine objects. It does mean that, within itself, the finite word points beyond itself. In other words, it is self-transcendent. Now the need for the syllable 'self' in 'self-transcendent' has also become understandable: the one reality which we encounter is experienced in different dimensions which point to one another. The finitude of the finite points to the infinity of the infinite. It goes beyond itself in order to return to itself in a new dimension. This is what 'self-transcendence' means."†

It is the finite world, not God, that is here described as pointing beyond itself, and so self-transcendent. Quite apart from the fact that the universe may not be finite as regards either space or time, it is far from clear that it does point beyond itself, even in terms of "mind" rather than physics. Indeed many of our leading scientists would hotly dispute this suggestion – psychologists as much as astronomers. For example, psychologists have found that the forgotten experiences of childhood and infancy, and sometimes of life in the womb and of the pain of being born – even the earlier inherited experiences of the human race – are powerful factors in the human mind, and could be said to transcend the conscious mind. But this in no way implies that the human mind as a whole is "self-transcendent".

The student of Whitehead will interpret the world's self-transcendence in terms of the coexistence of freedom and order, which necessitates, in his philosophy, an entity whose character is boundless creativity and whose primordial nature is eternal. But it is far from clear on what grounds Tillich can say that the finite world is self-transcendent. Many people think it is, but they also call God transcendent; and many others disagree with

* *Honest to God*, p. 56.
† Page 8.

both these assertions. It seems that Tillich is here doing no more than produce a variant on the traditional arguments for the existence of God – indeed his whole theology has been described as the ontological argument in a new form. I cannot see that the world's self-transcendence tells us anything about the transcendence of God, or indeed anything at all about God beyond the bare fact that, if the world is self-transcendent, then God must exist.

Modern man does indeed reach out beyond himself, but he does so with rockets, with a two-hundred-inch telescope, and with electron microscopes. He is often quite unconvinced that either the physical world or man "points beyond itself" in a metaphysical sense. In this situation, theology's primary task is to suggest a comprehensive and coherent way of looking at the universe and its life which will make modern man even begin to entertain the possibility that it *may* point beyond itself in a metaphysical sense. I believe that we can be greatly helped in this by Whitehead's doctrine of God.

GOD IN PROCESS PHILOSOPHY

Alfred North Whitehead

We have already noted three of Whitehead's important statements about God: that "God is an actual entity"; that God is not an exception but the chief exemplification of all metaphysical principles; and that every entity derives its "basic conceptual aim" from God. We shall examine this third statement in more detail in a moment. We first pause to consider how these three statements interlock and cohere: this will show us the manner in which Whitehead envisaged the physical world to be "pointing beyond itself", and will help us to decide whether Whitehead's thinking includes a *transcendent* God – or, to put the same point in a different manner, whether in his thinking the word "God" stands for a unique existent or for a quality or facet of the universe.

The chapter entitled "God" in *Science and the Modern World* begins thus: "Aristotle found it necessary to complete his metaphysics by the introduction of a Prime Mover – God". Whitehead describes this as of double importance. Firstly, if we are to describe anyone as the greatest metaphysician "we must choose Aristotle. Secondly, in his consideration of this metaphysical question he is entirely dispassionate; and he is the last European metaphysician of first-rate importance for whom this claim can be made. After Aristotle, ethical and religious interests began to influence metaphysical conclusions." Having said that the concept of God as Prime Mover discloses Aristotle's erroneous physics and cosmology, Whitehead substitutes for it "God as the Principle of Concretion". He later defined this as "the principle whereby there is initiated a definite outcome from a situation otherwise riddled with ambiguity".* This "situation" is simply that in Whitehead's system each entity *is* a growing-together of its "prehensions", a process of becoming: this process *needs* an initial aim and purpose, without which it would never acquire any concreteness or definiteness. Every entity derives its initial aim – and thus acquires "concretion" – from an unique entity, God.

The fact that every entity must derive its initial aim *from another actual entity* follows from what Whitehead terms the "ontological principle", which "means that actual entities are the only *reasons*; so that to search for a *reason* is to search for one or more actual entities".† We now see how the first and third of the statements about God at the beginning of this section fit together: if we think of God as the reason or cause from which every entity derives its initial aim, then that reason must itself be an actual entity—a unique entity whose initial aim must be underived or primordial, and whose influence must be equally available to all entities throughout all space and time.

The starting-point that God is the "principle of concretion" may sound abstract and impersonal: we have already briefly considered some ways in which Whitehead's doctrine of God is in fact personal.‡ In these days of widespread agnosticism it is, I suggest, of the first importance that Whitehead's doctrine of God *derives* from his vision of the universe, which *requires* a source for each entity's initial aim – just as Aristotle's doctrine of God derived from his need for a Prime Mover. Whitehead's penetrating criticisms of Christian theology, and his equally critical use of Buddhist philosophy, suggest that on the question

* *Process and Reality*, V.2.3 (p. 488).
† Process and Reality, I.2.2 (p. 33).
‡ See above, ch. 3, p. 88 f.

of God he is almost, if not quite, as "entirely dispassionate" as Aristotle — whilst the vision of the universe which led to Whitehead's doctrine of God was itself derived from modern scientific knowledge.

Having been thus led to postulate a unique actual entity, Whitehead proceeds to identify this with the God of monotheism: "It is here termed 'God'; because the contemplation of our natures, as enjoying real feelings derived from the timeless source of all order, acquires that 'subjective form' of refreshment and companionship at which religions aim."* In this difficult sentence I take Whitehead to be saying that if we contemplate the unique entity required and described in this philosophy we enjoy "real feelings" of the type normally called religious experience — and therefore this unique entity can be termed "God". Whitehead thus includes religious experience as part of the data for his philosophy, but is not imperilled by the imprecise nature of this experience since he *bases* his doctrine of God upon the requirements of his philosophical system. Whitehead would, I think, have agreed both with Hartshorne's statement "that God is experienced, not just proved indirectly" and with his warning

"Is there perhaps a perception of divinity? It must be admitted that, if such perception occurs, it has not the same sort of obviousness and intersubjective communicability as characterizes ordinary perceptions. Hence the mere *claim* to perceive or experience God is hardly a rational justification, in the normal sense."†

We must now examine further the statement that "Each temporal entity . . . derives from God its basic conceptual aim, relevant to its actual world, yet with indeterminations awaiting its own decisions".‡ This is a crucial point in Whitehead's thinking. God supplies its basic conceptual aim, yet the entity retains freedom of manœuvre in its response to that aim, and in responding shapes and affects the aim itself. It would be easy to suggest that God supplies the *initial* aim, which the entity shapes thereafter. There is truth in this in that the "concrescence", or becoming, *is* the entity, and until it starts there is no subject to take decisions. But it is a metaphysical, not a temporal, priority; indeed it closely corresponds to the Christian

* *Process and Reality*, I.3.1 (p. 43).
† Both occur in Hartshorne's essay in *Religion and Culture*, ed. Leibrecht, pp. 179 and 173.
‡ *Process and Reality*, III.1.5 (p. 317).

doctrine of the "prevenience" of God. In the primary phase of the concrescence the initial aim is not genetically prior to the other feelings; it arises with them.* As soon as the process starts the entity develops its own aim, prehending or grasping at the influences of everything in its environment, assessing these, and modifying its own subjective aim as it proceeds. But it is never literally aimless, and God supplies its non-aimlessness. In Whitehead's terms, God's aim is for maximum intensity of experience: the initial subjective aim of each entity is directed towards maximum intensity for itself-plus-its-environment, which includes God. Thus God and the world interact upon and affect each other: the initial aim which God offers to successive entities is continually adjusted to allow for environmental changes, so as to aim for maximum intensity of experience according to the circumstances of the moment. The subject-entity, as we have seen, introduces further change in modifying its own "aim".

We must always remember that Whitehead's entities are occasions, not persons. Nevertheless, as we found earlier, much that he says about entities can be applied, at least by analogy, to persons. As its "concrescence" proceeds, an entity's subjective aim is compounded of God's influence, the environment's influence, and the subject-entity's own self-determination: a person's aim in life is similarly compounded, and similarly varying. God's influence aims at a maximum total of satisfactory experience for all concerned. A person may decide that he "doesn't give a damn" about all concerned, or even perhaps about God; neither, as we have seen, does an entity always follow its initial subjective aim. There are also human analogies to the way in which an entity's subjective aim develops and crystallizes. W. A. Christian suggests one:

"The initial aim is vague in the sense that the relations of its datum to other possibilities and to the physical data are not completely determinate. It includes indeterminations which the concrescence must determine. The concrescence aims at 'that sort of thing'. As the process goes on the aim becomes more specific so that it is finally 'this thing and no other'. It is as though someone started out to be a doctor, then had to decide what sort of doctor he would be, and ended up being just this sort of doctor and no other."†

* See W. A. Christian, *An Interpretation of Whitehead's Metaphysics*, pp. 312–4.
† On page 315 of his *Interpretation*.

In this connection, I recall a preacher at my theological college saying that most of us probably had no idea what we were letting ourselves in for when we first responded to a "call" to ordination, that we probably still had no idea, and that the full extent of God's call would only gradually be revealed "as we were able to bear it". His congregation are, I hope, still learning for ourselves the truth of what he said to us that evening.

The second of Whitehead's important statements about God that we noted once again at the beginning of this section was that "God is not to be treated as an exception to all metaphysical principles . . . he is their chief exemplification". The importance of that statement — which I earlier paraphrased as "God keeps the rules" — is a recurring theme throughout this book. Thus it was suggested in chapter four that God sympathizes, in the sense of the Greek derivation of "sympathy" as suffering-with, and that God reacts to our finiteness not by prolonging our existence as experiencing subjects but by taking into himself, into his consequent nature, all that can be taken of our thoughts and actions. It may help if we emphasize at this point that this keeping of the rules includes the fact that God is an object for us as we are for him, in the sense that we prehend or grasp him, as he does us. The contrast between Whitehead and Tillich is here extreme, for Tillich emphasizes that "Theology always must remember that in speaking of God it makes an object of that which precedes the subject – object structure and that, therefore, it must include in its speaking of God the acknowledgement that *it cannot make God an object*" (my italics).*

The third of the three statements at the beginning of this section, that every actual entity derives its "basic conceptual" aim from God, has already been examined, because of its close relationship to the first. I now return to it because of its bearing on the question as to whether Whitehead's vision or intuition of the nature of reality *requires* God, or whether his doctrine of God is a mere decorative addition to his system due rather – as has been suggested – to Whitehead's own upbringing and background than to any necessity within his system of thought. A full philosophical study of this question would require very extended treatment; a brief indication of the possible lines of such a fuller treatment must here suffice. The writings of those

* *Systematic Theology*, vol. 1, p. 191.

who knew Whitehead personally contain various conflicting comments on his attitude to the question of God. It is therefore unwise to attach importance to any individual comment. There are, however, several references to Whitehead having said that he had never fully worked out his doctrine of God. A study of Whitehead's writings confirms this – particularly the difficulty, discussed in the next section, inherent in his description of God as a single actual entity. Indeed such a study has led Dorothy Emmet to a position of considerable hesitancy as to whether this doctrine is really integral to his view of the world.* Most of those who have written extensively about Whitehead have, however, taken the opposite view.

Whitehead's system of categories at the beginning of *Process and Reality* does not itself include any reference to God, or indeed to any particular type or set of entities: mention of God, as of enduring objects and other "derivative notions", comes in the subsequent relating of his theoretical system of categories to actuality. Our world contains *temporal* actual entities, each of which has a beginning in time, and the concept of God is introduced to solve the problem of how the subjective aim of each such entity originates. This is a basic problem in the relating of Whitehead's abstract system of categories to our actual world: as we have seen, the concept of God plays a vital *role* in its solution.

Three conclusions follow, here put succinctly by Professor W. A. Christian: "The concept of God in Whitehead's philosophy is categoreally contingent, systematically necessary, and existentially contingent."† This triple assertion merits slight expansion:

(a) The concept of God is contingent, and *not* necessary, to Whitehead's system of categories.

(b) This concept *is* necessary to the applying of this system of categories to our actual world. It is perhaps significant that Whitehead began his chapter on God in *Science and the Modern World* by saying that Aristotle found it *necessary* to complete his metaphysics by introducing the concept of God as Prime Mover: when he later came to systematize his own metaphysics, Whitehead also introduced the con-

* See the Preface to the second edition of her *Whitehead's Philosophy of Organism* (Macmillan, 1966).
† In his important essay in *Process and Divinity*, p. 195.

cept of God in order to fulfil a necessary function in the application of his system to the actual world.

(c) The concept having been thus introduced, the existence of God must, in this philosophy, be contingent: the need for the concept depends upon the existence of temporal actual entities, which is itself contingent. (We are not concerned in this book with the philosophical problem whether God's existence is necessary or contingent. Students of Hartshorne's writings will know that he emphasizes the necessity of God in his primordial nature – his consequent nature being contingent. All that need be said here is that this facet of Hartshorne's thought is not derived from Whitehead.)

God is in the world. We can bring together three ways in which Whitehead emphasizes the immanence of God. (1) God supplies every entity or occasion with its basic conceptual aim. (2) God is also present with the entity throughout its concrescence, *in* its world, and as the entity prehends him, so God is one of the influences upon it. God's immanence in the world obviously presents no difficulty to Whitehead; if everything is inter-dependent, then in a sense everything is immanent in every-thing else – but immanent only objectively. It is often noticeable how the personalities and characters of a husband and wife converge and grow together, although they may have seemed utterly dissimilar on their wedding day. This is because each is willing to be influenced by the other. But they remain two distinct experiencing subjects; in this sense they cannot become "one flesh". Their personalities are objectively present in each other. God's immanence in actual occasions is also objective in this sense – which is another way of saying that, like other entities, God is also transcendent to his world. (3) We said above that an entity's environment includes its past, using the word environment in such a way as to include heredity. This leads to the third way in which, in Whitehead's system, God is immanent in the world: as the ground of the givenness of the past.*

... *or nowhere.* The next two words of the quotation with which this chapter opens follow at once from Whitehead's "ontological principle" "that actual entities are the only *reasons*; so that to search for a reason is to search for one or more actual entities".

* For a useful discussion of (3), see Christian's *Interpretation,* ch. 16.

163

This may seem a somewhat abrupt way of denying even the possibility of what Tillich calls "supranaturalism", a "superworld" of divine objects; but if Whitehead's imaginative vision of the nature of our total environment is in any way reliable then this environment does *not* include a superworld, but *does* include God. Whitehead's system here assumes what Tillich argues at some length. The justification for Whitehead's assumption is the self-consistent and all-embracing character of his system: there is neither room nor need for a superworld, or for a nonimmanent God. Without at this stage mentioning the word God, Whitehead makes his non-supranaturalistic position clear in the opening section of *Process and Reality*:

"This course of lectures is designed as an essay in Speculative Philosophy ... [which] is the endeavour to frame a coherent, logical, necessary system of general ideas in terms of which every element of our experience can be interpreted. By this notion of 'interpretation' I mean that everything of which we are conscious, as enjoyed, perceived, willed or thought, shall have the character of a particular instance of the general scheme. ... there is an essence to the universe which forbids relationships beyond itself, as a violation of its rationality. Speculative philosophy seeks that essence."

It remains to consider whether Whitehead's system can validate God's transcendence. The first point to note is that in Whitehead's writings, as in Tillich's, there are frequent references to transcendence as something by no means confined to God: "It is to be noted that every actual entity, including God, is something individual for its own sake; and thereby transcends the rest of actuality ... The transcendence of God is not peculiar to him. Every actual entity, in virtue of its novelty, transcends its universe, God included."*

On the other hand Whitehead's system does not admit of any absolute transcendence: no item can be considered as if it existed in isolation. According to his "principle of relativity" "every item in its universe is involved in each concrescence", so that "the notion of 'complete abstraction' is self-contradictory. For you cannot abstract the universe from any entity, actual or non-actual, so as to consider that entity in complete isolation. Whenever we think of some entity, we are asking, What is it fit for here? In a sense, every entity pervades the whole world."†

* *Process and Reality*, II.3.1,3 (pp. 122,130).
† *Process and Reality*, I.2.2,4 (pp. 30, 38).

We have noted Whitehead's insistence that the two "natures" of God are simply abstractions to aid our thought, neither having any separate existence without the other. It follows that not even God is absolutely transcendent, for although his primordial nature is independent and unrelated, his consequent nature is affected by the world.

Professor Hartshorne validates God's transcendence by maintaining *(a)* that everything exists in God, "pan-en-theism", "God literally contains the universe"; and *(b)* that "God is both this system [the cosmos] and something independent of it".*

The classic text of "panentheism" comes in St. Paul's Athens sermon: "for in him we live, and move, and have our being."† Whilst panentheism is much nearer than pantheism to Christian theism, it has difficulty in maintaining any real independence for the creatures if these are literally included in God. Professor W. A. Christian's pair of propositions avoids this difficulty: "*(a)* God is not the cosmos, nor does he include (in Hartshorne's sense) the cosmos; and *(b)* his activity is always conditioned though never determined by the cosmos."‡ Proposition *(a)* validates God's transcendence, and at the same time differs from both pantheism and "panentheism". I would agree with Christian that Whitehead is not strictly a "panentheist"; his complete insistence on freedom means that although we are influenced and indeed surrounded by God, each of us remains a separate subject. God includes us in his consequent nature by prehending us as objects: we are not included as subjects. "Panentheism" – in Hartshorne's sense that God "literally contains" us – would upset Whitehead's superb balance and interrelation between God and the world, and between the transcendence and immanence of each in relation to the other.

It is as an experiencing subject that every entity transcends its world: "every actual entity, including God, is something individual for its own sake; and thereby transcends the rest oí actuality". Here again God "keeps the rules" and is their chief exemplification. When discussing "subjective aim" we found a parallel to the doctrine of God's "prevenience" in his gift to every entity of its initial conceptual aim, which the entity proceeds to modify for itself. The "chief exemplification" of this

* *The Divine Relativity*, p. 90.
† Acts 17: 28.
‡ *An Interpretation of Whitehead's Metaphysics*, p. 407.

is God's own subjective aim, which is his "primordial nature". "In this aspect, He is not before all creation, but with all creation. The primordial nature of God is the acquirement by creativity of a primordial character";* from this, as we have seen, comes the possibility of *novelty* in the universe. God's unique function in the process of becoming of an entity is precisely that he elicits novelty and self-creativity, whereas the influence of actual occasions on each other is restrictive; they stipulate conditions to which subsequent occasions must in some measure conform.†

"Apart from the intervention of God, there could be nothing new in the world, and no order in the world. The course of creation would be a dead level of ineffectiveness, with all balance and intensity progressively excluded by the cross currents of incompatibility. The novel hybrid feelings derived from God . . . are the foundations of progress."‡

Whitehead here overstates his case. In his system novelty and order are functions attributed to God. But I certainly do not think it possible to assert that these *could not* exist without God, though I would assert that the God-hypothesis offers a better explanation of the elements of novelty, order and progress than does the atheistic assertion that these are simply inherent in the nature of things. The existence of a transcendent God is not intellectually essential: I doubt whether it ever was. But Whitehead's system is a valuable illustration of the claim that the existence of God is intellectually more satisfactory than the atheistic alternative.

We have drawn attention to some of the ways in which God "keeps the rules". We must also note some of the ways in which God, as an experiencing subject, differs from all other individuals. He differs first, and most obviously, in his "omnipresence": God is present throughout all space and all time. He is the God of Abraham, of Isaac, and of Jacob, of the most distant galaxy yet known to man, and of all that lies beyond. He is un-caused, primordial, without beginning or end. Entities become, and perish; God is equally present everywhere. Secondly, God's aim or purpose is unique in that he always aims at a maximum total of intensity of satisfaction for all concerned:

* *Process and Reality*, V.2.2 (p. 486–7).
† See Christian's *Interpretation*, p. 579 f.
‡ *Process and Reality*, III.3.2 (p. 349).

putting this in human terms, God never lazily aims only at second best, nor is he ever selfish or self-centred. Thirdly, God is unique in the intensity of his feelings. He perfectly and completely "prehends" everything in his universe; he is completely aware of what is going on in our innermost minds, and so is completely able to feel for us, and sympathize with us. He is "the fellow-sufferer who understands" – and he alone completely understands.

Whitehead's insight that God and the world each affect and are affected by the other has two consequences that are of momentous importance for theology. If what we do really affects God, then there will be a sense in which our actions and influence live on, in God, everlastingly; and if God affects the world then our actions, prehended into God's consequent nature, will also affect the world – as we saw in chapter four. Also, as was said in chapter three, a philosophy that envisages God as really affected by our weal and woe, and sees him as "the fellow-sufferer who understands", is able to offer a more meaningful interpretation of the love of God than does much traditional theology. I here let Hartshorne's words speak also for myself: "It is my conviction that in Whitehead Western metaphysics moved appreciably closer than ever before to a technical language capable of formulating without inconsistency the content of the ancient saying 'God is love' ".*

The writings of Alfred North Whitehead are, in my view, of the first importance for both the philosophy and the theology of our time. Whitehead was, however, a philosopher or metaphysician and not a theologian. He wrote about God and God's relationship with the universe and with man: he wrote very little about either Jesus Christ or the Bible. He also wrote about religion as an important part of the total culture of mankind: one of his books is called *Religion in the Making*; religious ideas also play a prominent part in his *Adventures of Ideas* (the title of whose tenth chapter – "The New Reformation" – anticipated by thirty years that of Dr. Robinson's recent book, except that in 1933 Whitehead saw no need to end this title with a question-mark). Whitehead thought of God as fulfilling a vital and necessary role in the universe, and attempted to describe those aspects of the divine activity which are most directly relevant to his philosophy: the poet in Whitehead also led him, as we have

* *Alfred North Whitehead: Essays on His Philosophy*, ed. Kline, p. 24.

seen, to paint many superb and moving verbal images of God, his "fellow-suffering" and his "tender care". But, as Charles Hartshorne has often said, Whitehead never worked out a fully developed doctrine of God.

Charles Hartshorne

Hartshorne is the most important of the several thinkers in America who are developing the theological aspects of process philosophy. Whilst Hartshorne is an important philosopher – theologian in his own right, and not only as an interpreter of Whitehead, the most prominent feature of his thinking and writing about God is the extent to which he emphasizes and develops more fully the *same* insights as did Whitehead: that God and the world affect each other; that our actions live on in God; that God supplies every entity with its initial aim; and that, in my phrase, God keeps the rules.

The significant difference to which I would here draw attention is that Hartshorne does not envisage God as *an* actual entity. A number of us here agree with Hartshorne: William Christian agrees with Whitehead, of whom he is a notable interpreter. Hartshorne has said of Christian "he can take Whitehead's 'God is an actual entity' literally, and I cannot".*
Whitehead himself was not always consistent on this point. In *Process and Reality*, as we have seen, he states quite specifically that God is an actual entity, but not an occasion. Occasions perish, and only live on objectively: God exists throughout time without loss of immediacy. (The entity who is God thus has at least the whole of time for his prehensions to grow together and "become"; whereas all other entities are also occasions, and have only an infinitesimal epoch of time in which to become.) Elsewhere, however, Whitehead seems to have accepted the idea that God is not an entity but rather a whole sequence of entities – a sequence of God-now-occasions comparable to the sequence of self-now-occasions which together comprise a living person:

"God is, as Whitehead agreed in a carefully noted conversation with A. H. Johnson, a linear sequence (which Whitehead terms 'a personally ordered society') of occasions—with the difference, as contrasted to ordinary personal sequences, that in God there is no

* *Alfred North Whitehead: Essays on His Philosophy*, ed. Kline, p. 23.

lapse of memory, or loss of immediacy, as to occasions already achieved."*

On this view, it remains true that *at any given moment* God is an actual entity; but when viewed over the entire span of time, God is seen to comprise a whole sequence of divine occasions of experience.

The difference between these two statements about God is significant, but not overwhelming: much that Whitehead says about individual entities can also be applied to persons. Furthermore, no statement about God can be precise in every aspect: "a being conceivable through and through without mystery, in the sense of aspects inaccessible to our knowledge, would not be God";† the relationship between God and time, with which we are here concerned, is one such aspect. Both Whitehead and Hartshorne recognize process in God—specifically, in God's consequent nature. The difference is that in *Process and Reality* Whitehead thinks of this process in God in terms of the process of becoming of an actual entity, whereas Hartshorne thinks of it as the process of an ordered sequence of entities.

This would seem to exemplify the fact that Whitehead never fully developed his doctrine of God, for it is basic to his philosophy that an entity cannot influence other entities until it has *completed* its infinitesimally brief process of becoming. (Entities become, achieve satisfaction, and perish; only then can they "live on" by being prehended and objectified by other entities.) But Whitehead is equally emphatic that the "process" or changing element in God, due to the world's influence upon him as he prehends it into his consequent nature, itself in turn influences the world *during its history*. We saw the importance of this when considering our own immortality.‡

There is here a contradiction that does not occur in Hartshorne's interpretation, in which each individual entity or occasion in the sequence that comprises God – each momentary God-now – affects, and is affected by, its world. In this respect it is Hartshorne's concept of God, and not Whitehead's, that is the "chief exemplification" of all metaphysical principles.

Hartshorne also avoids the need for Whitehead's exceptional statement that God is an actual entity, but *not* an occasion –

* *Philosophers Speak of God*, by Hartshorne and Reese, p. 274.
† C. Hartshorne, *The Divine Relativity*, p. 1.
‡ See chapter 4 (*b*) above.

whereas all other entities are also occasions. If God is an ordered sequence of entities which are also occasions, then at least in this respect he is not an exception to the normal categories of existence. Hartshorne's concept of God also the more naturally agrees with the vital religious intuition that God is *personal*; for in process philosophy a "living person" is an ordered sequence of entities, and not *an* actual entity. Thus Hartshorne's concept of God "keeps the rules" that process thinking applies to persons. What he says of Whitehead's philosophy applies, I believe, even more strongly to his own:

"It may indeed be said that this is one of the first philosophies which has any intellectual right to speak of divine personality. For personality, as any psychologist knows, is a sort of cluster of habits and purposes and ideas, and it therefore has a certain abstractedness, in that it expresses itself now in this particular experience and now in that, whether one looks out the window and sees rain or sunshine or opens a book and sees words. Thus personality is, in Whitehead's language, a 'defining characteristic' of a sequence of experiences, and the characteristic does not fully determine the sequence . . . All concepts of personality seem to imply this partial independence of particular experiences from the determining influence of the personality . . . we doubt if anyone can really, or other than verbally, mean by a 'person' more than what Whitehead means by a 'personally ordered' sequence of experiences with certain defining characteristics or personality traits. This is also how he conceives God, with the appropriate qualification that in God the imperfection involved in forgetting is denied."*

We have been emphasizing those respects in which God is not to be thought of as an exception. I am increasingly convinced that this emphasis is badly needed today. But God must differ from all the other entities or beings in our universe in that he is immediately present throughout all space-time. Tillich emphasized this truth by his insistence that "God is called a person, but he is a person not in finite separation but in an absolute and unconditional participation in everything".† Because God must be immediately (that is, unmediatedly) related to every entity, Hartshorne suggests that we think of the God–world relationship by analogy to the relationship of a human mind to its body. He thus comes near to the ancient Greek idea of God as the World-soul, and for this reason some Christians may feel inclined to reject his suggestion out of hand. Two things should,

* Hartshorne and Reese, *Philosophers Speak of God*, p. 274.
† *Systematic Theology*, vol. I, p. 270.

however, be borne in mind. First, Hartshorne emphasizes* that this is an analogy: to suggest that it is a useful analogy is *not* to say that God *is* the World–soul. Second, one must remember that for Hartshorne, as for Whitehead, there is an element of "mind" in everything: he rejects the conception of the body and its member cells as wholly passive in relation to its brain, and insists that the relations of individual cells with each other, and with the person in whose body they are, is in some sense a "social" relationship. The only relationship of which we have direct knowledge at both ends is that between two humans, and Hartshorne emphasizes that we can only think of the (social) mind–body relation by extrapolation from the human-to-human relation. Similarly, we can only think of "mind", freedom, spontaneity in an individual cell as some sort of rudimentary analogues of that which we know in ourselves.

Even so, the application of the mind–body analogy to the relationship between God and the world would seem to leave too little place for the freedom of the individual creatures in the world: our own freedom in relation to God is in some respects far greater than that of any individual cell or organism within the body in relation to its controlling mind. But no analogy should be pressed too far, and none is faultless. Indeed the familiar analogy by which we speak of God as Father fails to emphasize God's radical superiority over us. "The love of a parent for a child is the best we can know of a love having a human being for its object, the subject of which is or may be vastly superior in power and wisdom and goodness to the one loved. But the superiority is still not radical enough to serve as a very clear indication of the direction of divine superiority".† (Jesus used this analogy against a background of Jewish thought which assumed God's infinite superiority, but did not always find it easy to think of God in terms of personal love.)

The strength of the mind–body analogy as applied to God's relationship to the world lies both in the immediacy and the universality of that relationship: God is immediately related to, and indwells in, every entity. Analogously, some at least of the cells of the brain and central nervous system are immediately related to their controlling mind; the mind's communication

* Notably in chapter 5 of *Man's Vision of God,* in which this analogy is considered at some length.
† C. Hartshorne, *Man's Vision of God,* p. 202.

with other parts of the body is not strictly immediate, but there is an essential directness of control over all the cells in the body – the cessation of that unified control being one way of defining death. Thus Hartshorne describes the relation of a mind to its body as "something like an indwelling God".*

Both the father and the cosmic mind analogies fail to include any indication of God as creator. In his account of creation in the *Timaeus* Plato distinguished between the world–soul and the creator–god. Hartshorne has suggested that these two could be linked in terms of Whitehead's concept of the two natures or aspects of God, and that "it is not hopelessly far-fetched to see in the world–soul Plato's account of the consequent aspect, and in his ultimate Creator the primordial aspect".† Of the two analogies, that of God as the mind of the universe is perhaps the more inadequate in regard to the problem of evil. There is the further weakness that in this analogy the universe is likened to a single body or organism. The difficulty is partly that the universe as a whole does not possess an external environment, an essential requirement for any other body or organism, and partly that any other organism comes to life, renews parts of itself throughout life, and finally disintegrates – whereas the universe cannot shed unwanted members, and perhaps persists through infinite time. The analogy between the universe and a single body is, however, strengthened by the fact that the fundamental laws of nature – such as quantum mechanics and relativity – apply throughout the universe, just as certain biological properties apply throughout a body. But I suspect that Christian objections to the application of the mind–body analogy to the God–world relation stem mainly from the unfamiliarity of this analogy as compared with the great New Testament analogies, and from deep suspicion of any form of "pantheism". The merit of this analogy is its ability to indicate both the transcendence and the immanence of God by analogy to the corresponding properties of a mind in relation to its body. The fact that the controlling mind or personality transcends its body suggests that to use this analogy is not pantheism.

The analogy between God and the mind of the universe should not be rejected. But in this book more use is made of

* *Man's Vision of God*, p. 177.
† In *Philosophical Essays for Alfred North Whitehead*, "The Compound Individual," p. 211 (Longmans, New York and London, 1936).

Hartshorne's concept that God is a succession of entities with personal order – a "living person": this seems to express in the language of process philosophy the great biblical concept of the living God – and to express this better than does Whitehead's "God is an actual entity". It is along these lines – intermediate, in this respect, between Whitehead's *Process and Reality* and Hartshorne's "panentheism" – that I believe we shall best find a contemporary expression of the religious conviction that there is a personal Creator–God, immanent in the world and in ourselves, yet sufficiently transcendent for us to be able to pray to him and receive guidance from him. As regards the vital question whether God's nature is such that we *can* both pray to him and seek guidance from him, there is no great difference between Hartshorne's concept of God and Whitehead's, so that it is sufficient to consider Whitehead. But there is, as I now attempt to show, all the difference in the world between Whitehead and Tillich.

THE ARCHBISHOP'S QUESTION

I end this chapter by considering a penetrating question which the Archbishop of Canterbury asked of what he called "the new image" in *Honest to God*:

"I ask where 'revelation' and 'grace' come in? If there is ultimate reality which is love and personal, does not the initiative come not from us but from thence? That is what we have meant when we have spoken of 'revelation' and of 'grace': God finding us rather than we finding God."*

The Honest to God Debate contains no reply to this, and the Archbishop's question lies squarely in that doctrinal field in which the theology of Paul Tillich largely underlies that of *Honest to God*. I shall therefore apply this question first to Tillich and then to Whitehead. This will lead me to suggest that Whitehead's philosophy stands up to the Archbishop's question far more convincingly than Tillich's, although it is not the sort of question with which Whitehead himself was primarily concerned. Tillich always starts from man's end of the relationship between God and man; it is not surprising that he says far more about us finding God than about God finding us. "Revelation" and "grace" are closely connected in all theological thought,

* Michael Ramsey, *Image Old and New* (S.P.C.K. booklet, 1963), p. 8.

as they are in the Archbishop's question: rather than deal too briefly with each, I shall concentrate upon the first and begin by summarizing and criticizing Tillich's doctrine of revelation, to which he devotes the first of the five parts of his system. Much of this first part is immensely valuable, and provides material for deep meditation; we shall return to it in the next chapter in relation to the person of Christ.

Tillich defines revelation as "the manifestation of what concerns us ultimately. The mystery which is revealed is of ultimate concern to us because it is the ground of our being. In the history of religion revelatory events always have been described as shaking, transforming, demanding, significant in an ultimate way."* The term revelation should not be applied to any situation which is not a matter of ultimate concern and of essential mystery. "Revelation always is a subjective and an objective event in strict interdependence. Someone is grasped by the manifestation of the mystery; this is the subjective side of the event. Something occurs through which the mystery of revelation grasps someone; this is the objective side. These two sides cannot be separated." The objective occurrence has traditionally been called "miracle"; the subjective reception "has sometimes been called 'ecstasy'. Both terms must be given a radical reinterpretation." The word ecstasy is derived from two Greek words and means, in Tillich's phrase, "standing outside one's self". It "points to a state of mind which is extraordinary in the sense that the mind transcends its ordinary situation. Ecstasy is not a negation of reason; it is the state of mind in which reason is beyond itself, that is, beyond its subject–object structure. In being beyond itself reason does not deny itself. 'Ecstatic reason' remains reason; it does not receive anything irrational or anti-rational – which it could not do without self-destruction – but it transcends the basic condition of finite rationality, the subject–object structure."

I will defer comment on this until we have seen what Tillich goes on to say about both miracle and prayer. Since the word "miracle" is normally taken to mean a happening that contradicts the laws of nature, Tillich regards it as a misleading term; he prefers "sign-event". This cuts across the tendency to think that the more violently a miracle contradicts nature the greater

* The quotations in this paragraph are from *Systematic Theology*, vol. I, pp. 123–4.

is its religious value: Tillich says that this tendency is found in the later traditions within the New Testament, flourishes to absurdity in the apocryphal gospels, and "is still a burden for the life of the church and for theology". By contrast Tillich insists that

"The manifestation of the mystery of being does not destroy the structure of being in which it becomes manifest. The ecstasy in which the mystery is received does not destroy the rational structure of the mind by which it is received. The sign-event which gives the mystery of revelation does not destroy the rational structure of the reality in which it appears. If these criteria are applied, a meaningful doctrine of sign-events or miracles can be stated.

"A genuine miracle is first of all an event which is astonishing, unusual, shaking, without contradicting the rational structure of reality. In the second place, it is an event which points to the mystery of being, expressing its relation to us in a definite way. In the third place, it is an occurrence which is received as a sign-event in an ecstatic experience."*

Both nature and history are mediums of revelation. "There is no reality, thing, or event which cannot become a bearer of the mystery of being and enter into a revelatory correlation. . . Historical revelation is not a revelation in history but through history." Tillich distinguishes between original and dependent revelation. "Peter encountered the man Jesus whom he called the Christ in an original revelatory ecstasy", but as we meditate upon Peter's "Thou art the Christ" we receive a revelation dependent upon that confession of faith. "There is continuous revelation in the history of the Church, but it is dependent revelation." I consider this final quotation to be of the first importance; I shall similarly emphasize the elements of prayer and meditation in the life of Jesus, which we consider in the next chapter:

"A dependent revelatory situation exists in every moment in which the divine Spirit grasps, shakes, and moves the human spirit. Every prayer and meditation, if it fulfils its meaning, namely, to reunite the creature with its creative ground, is revelatory in this sense. The marks of revelation—mystery, miracle, and ecstasy—are present in every true prayer. Speaking to God and receiving an answer is an ecstatic and miraculous experience; it transcends all ordinary structures of subjective and objective reason. It is the presence of the mystery of being and an actualization of our ultimate concern."

* *Systematic Theology*, vol. I, pp. 128, 130; the quotations that follow are on pp. 131–41.

I support Tillich's insistence that the objective side of revelation be thought of as a sign-event. I do *not* wish to assert that any contravention of the laws of nature is in itself impossible: this is an *a priori* assumption, and cannot be proved. Our accurate knowledge and experience extends to only a tiny fraction of space and time: those who believe in God should not insist that there can have been no unique occasions on which he may have set aside some of the normal freedom of individual entities, and thus interrupted the "laws of nature". We can say that such events do not occur in our experience, and we can add that a God who uses ordinary events to convey revelation is surely "higher" – further removed from the old tribal gods – than one whose principal acts in this world's history have been contra-natural. It can scarcely be denied that there are places where the New Testament writers – not to mention the Old – seem deliberately to have heightened the miraculous element, with the result that our scriptures include a number of miracles which seem to many Christians both unnecessary and improbable – and improbable not mainly because they are "unscientific" but because they seem out of character with God's infinite wisdom and love. (I am not now concerned with those "miracles" and healings that are capable of a natural explanation.) The question of New Testament miracle is always a vexatious issue. In any group of Christians there are some who regard all miracle as impossible, and others who largely base their faith upon the miraculous element in the gospel story: and no one can say how many adherents to the former view have for that reason excluded themselves from the Christian religion. And yet I believe it is here almost possible to be "all things to all men". One should not deny all possibility of miracle, but one should insist that there is no point at which the Christian faith depends upon it. Those who have regarded miracle as a vital element will not like this at first, but they are not being asked to alter their own belief. On the other hand, they will find their faith enriched if they can come to see that it has other supports, and other interpretations, besides this element of "miracle".

I also find immense value and importance in Tillich's emphasis upon dependent revelation, and upon prayer as revelatory. Any thing or incident in life can be revelatory for those with eyes to see it, and hearts sensitive to God's will; but I am convinced that prayer in its widest sense – which includes both public worship and individual turning to, and waiting upon, God – is and always has been the activity in which the majority of us are most likely to receive a (dependent) revelation of God. I return to this in chapter eight.

I am much less happy about Tillich's other statement that ecstasy is "the state of mind in which reason is beyond itself, that is, beyond its subject–object structure". This comes dangerously near to the irrationalism which Tillich himself so roundly condemns. It is obvious enough that God is not just another person or thing that we perceive like all the rest. Revelatory experience differs in some measure from other forms of experience.* People can be urged to come to church, but the clergyman cannot "lay on" revelatory experience for them when they get there. There is a mystery about revelation, as there is about God, whom the Archbishop of Canterbury has described as "One who is not ourselves though it is never apart from ourselves that we know Him".† There is indeed truth in this, but I feel bound to ask whether there is not also a sense in which we *do* know God apart from ourselves, and whether this knowing does not lie within the orbit of reason without the latter, in Tillich's phrase, "being beyond itself". Is there not a sense in which both our finding God and God finding us come sufficiently within the normal run of things to be describable in terms not utterly dissimilar from those we apply to other forms of experience?

It is here that I find Whitehead's aim at complete generality more helpful than volumes of theological special pleading: he uses the same language, the same metaphysical terms, to describe both God's actions and everyday occurrences. The Archbishop speaks of revelation and grace in terms of "God finding us rather than we finding God". Whitehead's system of thought does not draw so sharp a distinction: we and God mutually "prehend" or grasp at each other, and in so doing each is influenced and affected by the other; in the moment of finding God we are aware that he has already found us. This agrees both with our religious experience – where we call it "the prevenience of God" – and with our everyday relationships with other people; someone may find me first, but I only become aware of the fact when his actions or proximity lead me

* See the quotation from Professor Hartshorne on p. 159.
† *The Sunday Times,* 20th December, 1964.

to focus upon him; I then find him, and in so doing I know that he found me first. It is here relevant briefly to repeat what Whitehead says about subjective aim: each entity's "concrescence" or process of becoming must have an initial aim, from which it is free to deviate according to its own decisions; it derives this from God, who is in this sense prevenient, although the entity's initial aim comes "not before but with" the process of concrescence.

A great deal of what Whitehead says about God is in strong reaction against the idea of God as absolute, omnipotent Monarch. Thus he strongly supports "Plato's final conviction, towards the end of his life, that the divine element in the world is to be conceived as a persuasive agency and not as a coercive agency". But there is much sheer compulsion in the universe, and Whitehead says very little about how God's persuasion is at all effective in a world so largely governed by brute force. Hence both the praise and the criticism in this comment by Professor D. D. Williams:

"When we turn to the question of how God acts upon the world we see that Whitehead has thrown important light upon some aspects of this perplexing problem ... But it still may be that Whitehead has underestimated the disclosure of the divine initiative in religious experience. I believe it can be shown that he has not carried through with his metaphysical method fully in his interpretation of the being of God. It is precisely in that aspect of God which makes him a fully actual, effective subject where Whitehead seems not to make clearly the affirmations which he needs to complete his doctrine. I suggest that it is because Whitehead has reacted so justifiably against the divine Monarch that he has given a partially inadequate account of the relation between God and the world."*

Of the two systems of thought we have examined, Tillich's seems inherently incapable of giving an adequate answer to the Archbishop's question, whereas Whitehead's points towards an adequate answer, although he himself never quite gave it. He did, however, supply the vital ingredients: a metaphysical analysis which includes God within its scope; the mutual prehending and mutual immanence of God and the creatures; an idea of God as something individual for his own sake, and as the fellow-sufferer who understands; and a real interaction between this fellow-sufferer and a changing world so that God's actions arise out of his primordial love yet are kept relevant to

* In *The Relevance of Whitehead*, ed. Leclerc, pp. 370–1.

our actual situation by the consequent effect that the world has upon him.

Using these ingredients, Hartshorne has come some way towards meeting Williams's criticisms. I believe that these criticisms can be met, and that Whitehead's doctrine of God *can* be completed without contradicting its own fundamentals. God's function as what Williams calls "a fully actual, effective subject" is most clearly seen in the Christian experience that God does help those who seek his guidance and make prayer a real element in their lives. It is here, above all, that we find God to be far *more* than an intangible force or power, and we can use this experience to complete Whitehead's doctrine of God. We "prehend" God as we pray to him for grace and guidance – and we receive his answer. This is something we can experience in our own lives: we also find it completely demonstrated in the life of Jesus Christ. As his life was deeply permeated with prayer, so it was also with God's grace and love: in the relationship between Jesus and the Father mutual "prehending" and mutual immanence reach fullest fruition, as we shall see in the next chapter.

CHAPTER SIX

"But Who Say Ye That I Am?"

"And Jesus went forth, and his disciples, into the villages of Caesarea Philippi: and in the way he asked his disciples, saying unto them, Who do men say that I am? And they told him, saying, John the Baptist: and others, Elijah; but others, One of the prophets. And he asked them, But who say ye that I am? Peter answereth and saith unto him, Thou art the Christ." (Mark 8: 27–29).

Our task in this and the following chapters is to seek an interpretation of the person and Resurrection of Jesus which on the one hand does justice to the beliefs of the first disciples and on the other hand does not violate our knowledge – nor our processes for seeking knowledge – in other fields of human thought and experience. In the course of these two chapters we shall apply process thinking first to the person of Jesus and then to his Resurrection: we shall see how this thinking enables us positively to affirm both that "God was in Christ" and that "Jesus is Lord", and to do so in ways that "keep the rules" of Whitehead's philosophy, yet are more positive than the corresponding affirmations of much contemporary theology.

Any inquiry as to beliefs about Jesus of Nazareth must begin with the records of his life and its immediate sequel. The New Testament writings contain most of the reliable surviving information about this.* In considering this information we shall need to examine the nature and purpose of these writings, and attempt to evaluate their reliability. In our brief consideration of the Bible in chapter one we saw the inadequacy of the concept of "inspiration", as applied either to its words or to its writers: we then considered Leonard Hodgson's penetrating question – applied in particular to the New Testament – "What must the truth have been if it appeared like this to men who thought like that?"

In seeking to estimate the impression Jesus made on his

---

* The apocryphal gospels and other early Christian documents yield comparatively little reliable information on this. Secular writers refer to the early Christians, but scarcely at all to Jesus.

followers *during his lifetime* we are, of course, up against this further difficulty: it is clear from the gospels—particularly St. John—that the disciples came to a deeper understanding of Jesus after his Resurrection than they had had before; but the only records of this process themselves date from some years—possibly a generation—after the Crucifixion. It is therefore quite impossible to tell how far later beliefs have coloured the records of earlier impressions and conversations.

It has long been generally accepted that the first three gospels are composite documents: that Matthew and Luke incorporated into their gospels whole sequences of material that had earlier been collected together by others; some of this material may have remained in oral form, but most of it was already written—and their largest single source was Mark's gospel, of which Luke used more than half, and Matthew almost the whole. (It is because these three use a common synopsis, Mark, that they are referred to as the synoptic gospels.)

It has also long been recognized that Mark itself is a composite document, incorporating a variety of material ranging, perhaps, from individual sayings or collections of such sayings to a connected passion-narrative. It is obviously harder to analyse the earliest gospel, and there is as yet no general agreement among scholars as to the nature or extent of Mark's dependence on written sources. The present decade has seen the introduction of modern statistical techniques—including the use of computers—into New Testament analysis. It is claimed by their exponents that these techniques both confirm that Mark contains whole *blocks* of earlier written material and show that the fourth gospel is also a composite document.

We shall return to this when we consider the records of the adult life of Jesus. It is here sufficient to say two things. First, it is probable that a significant amount of the material in Mark had achieved a written form earlier, perhaps considerably earlier, than the Neronic persecution during which (*c*. A.D. 65) Mark is most likely to have been written. I find this earlier dating of the sources helpful in combating those cynics who suggest that the gospels are wholly unreliable, but it in no way affects the very strong probability that *nothing* was written down during the lifetime of Jesus.

Secondly, if St. Mark is to be thought of as an editor assembling information about events and conversations at which he himself was not present (and doing so after the death of his principal informant, St. Peter), then it is at least possible that he assembled some of this information in the wrong order. In particular, the sequence that includes the question which forms the title of our chapter and Peter's reply "Thou art the Christ" may be part of the disciples' Easter experience – may indeed be the beginning of that experience – and not a conversation during the course of Jesus' ministry.

The position of this sequence is closely connected with the question whether Jesus saw himself as the Messiah, and whether his disciples so regarded him during his lifetime. In this matter much can be said on either side of the argument, and much depends on one's interpretation of the Resurrection narratives. Taken at their face value, the synoptic gospels imply that Jesus knew himself as Messiah at least from his baptism; and that his disciples came to share in that belief when near Caesarea Philippi, subsequently faltered in this faith, but found it again, more fully than before, when they met the risen Christ. There are, in brief, two principal difficulties here: the element of com-complete surprise in the Resurrection narratives, and the extreme difficulty – if not impossibility – of fitting together the Resurrection appearances in Jerusalem and in Galilee. The disciples' surprise suggests that they had no definite idea of Jesus' messiahship, still less of his divinity. The incompatibility of the details of time and place suggests that the Resurrection appearances were not external events, but rather the gradual dawning of the disciples' faith in Jesus as God's chosen one, crucified in the flesh yet in spirit still powerfully present with them.

But if the disciples' post-crucifixion faith arose in their minds, and not as a result of an external event, then it must have arisen out of their own earlier experiences and surmises, lodged in their memories and now seen in a new light: the gospel accounts of Jesus' ministry may be coloured, perhaps highly coloured, by this later faith, yet that ministry must have been such as to call forth that faith, even if it did not do so until the whole could be seen as "one single cross-completed act". Whilst keeping an open mind as to how far either Jesus or his disciples thought in terms of messiahship or divinity during his lifetime, I shall suggest that the gospel records are at least sufficiently authentic to lead us – even those of us with a critical attitude that sees

them as highly coloured and containing a good deal of myth —
to share in the two cries of the earliest Church, "God *was* in
Christ" and "Jesus *is* Lord".

Some New Testament scholars might wish to begin our
inquiry with the Resurrection of Jesus, on the grounds that the
Church began there, and the New Testament is the product of
the Church, entirely coloured by its Resurrection-faith. But the
Church also began as a group of disciples who shared certain
beliefs about someone they had known in the flesh. They may
soon have been joined by others who were primarily influenced
by the first disciples' fervent proclamation of Jesus' Resurrection and vivid awareness of his continuing presence, but the
faith of the original disciples had its first beginnings *during* the
lifetime of Jesus.

I suspect that in this respect many of us today resemble the
original disciples, rather than their converts. In past generations
people may have come to the Christian faith largely because of
the Resurrection, but today many people are highly doubtful
as to how to interpret this. They rather first put their trust in
the "tremendous person" of the gospel story, and then sense his
continuing presence with them in prayer and sacrament. We
shall therefore follow the same sequence, and consider the
impact of the adult life of Jesus in this chapter and his Resurrection in chapter seven. But it is impossible to approach this task
with no preconceived ideas. We therefore begin by comparing
some of the ideas about Jesus of our own day with the ways in
which the early Church sought to answer the question "But
who say ye that I am?"

(a) THE ANSWER OF THE EARLY CHURCH

As we turn from the nature of the gospel records to the doctrine
which they contain, and to the ways in which that doctrine was
developed in the four following centuries, we especially need to
try, as best we may, to clear our minds of preconceived ideas.
I know a number of people, some of them highly intelligent,
who believe that "Jesus is God", with no distinction between
the two words. I also know a number of practising Christians
to whom Jesus is simply a great and very good man. I agree
with Dr. Robinson that in popular Christianity the former view
is predominant, and often amounts to the idea that "Jesus was

not a man born and bred—he was God for a limited period taking part in a charade".* But I know a number of boys who take the second view. During my first term at Marlborough College I was a little startled when the eighteen-year-old prefect who had "served" for us in the College Chapel on the previous Sunday subsequently said in a seminar "I'm a *Godian* myself; I never have understood all this business about Jesus Christ".

Neither of these rather extreme views finds much support in the New Testament, though either can perhaps be supported from isolated texts.† The New Testament is, of course, not a book but a collection: there is no single New Testament doctrine either of the person or of the Resurrection of Jesus. But its various writers did have at least two things in common. They all wrote out of deeply held beliefs in which the person and Resurrection of Jesus played a central part. They also wrote as members of a growing and widening community whose members in some sense *experienced the continuing presence* of the risen Christ. The vividness of this experience is one of the most striking features of the parts of the New Testament we have as yet scarcely mentioned, namely the Epistles and the Acts of the Apostles.

Both the New Testament and the more formally doctrinal writings of the four following centuries are, in part, attempts to describe and explain that experience. In the main, these attempts share two common objectives: they wish to show the pagan world that their Christian faith is based not on a purely mythical character but on an historical *man*; they also wish to emphasize that that man is in some sense "divine".

Any adequate account of these attempts would need a chapter—preferably a book—to itself. What follows is merely the briefest sketch, with some suggestions for further reading in the footnotes. I shall confine myself to the two most important Councils of the early Church, Nicea (A.D. 325) and Chalcedon (A.D. 451), and to the two principal schools of thought as regards the doctrine of Christ (known technically as Christology), those of Alexandria and Antioch.‡

As with other aspects of Christian theology, the problem of

* *Honest to God*, p. 66.
† The fact that the New Testament "does not say that Jesus was God, simply like that" is discussed in *Honest to God*, pp. 70–75.
‡ The two schools are discussed—at no great length—in W. N. Pittenger, *The Word Incarnate*, and in detail in R. V. Sellers, *Two Ancient Christologies*, (1940).

how Jesus can be thought of as both human and divine was rendered far more difficult by the prevailing substance philosophy. It was assumed that God and man each possess different substances, and it was therefore extremely difficult – perhaps impossible – to explain how Jesus could possess both, and yet remain one person. The primary purpose of the Council of Nicea was to counter Arius by affirming unmistakably the full divinity of Jesus Christ. It did this by saying that Jesus is "of one substance with the Father": this phrase occurs both in the creed actually adopted by the Council and in the slightly later "Nicene" creed which is named after it. There was, however, no precisely similar affirmation that Jesus was also of one substance with mankind. This gave rise to the danger – always recurrent in Christian thinking – that the reality of Jesus' manhood would be lost sight of in the desire to emphasize his divinity.

"Popular and monastic piety was not satisfied with the message of the eternal unity of God and man . . . These pieties wanted 'more'. They wanted a God, walking on earth, participating in history, but not involved in the conflicts of existence and the ambiguities of life".* They wanted this because they found it impossible to believe that one who was "of one substance with the Father" *could* be involved in the conflicts and ambiguities of human life. This led Apollinarius to say that Jesus was entirely – perhaps one could say organically – human, except that his inner ego, his centre of consciousness, appertained to the divine "Word" or *Logos* and not, as we would put it, to a member of the species *homo sapiens*. Both this and the later monophysitism† were branded as heresies, but even the "orthodox" Alexandrians were at the least prone to the continuing danger of losing the reality of Jesus' humanity by denying its completeness in some vital respect.

The theologians of Antioch were more historical in their approach, and were therefore vitally concerned with the real, historical manhood of Jesus. They also laid an equal emphasis on his divinity: their recurrent difficulty was to explain how Jesus could be both divine and human *and still remain one person*;

* Tillich, *Systematic Theology*, vol. II, p. 166.
† This doctrine affirmed that in the Person of the Incarnate Christ there was but *one nature*, the Greek words here are *monos* and *phusis*, namely his divine nature.

the danger to which they were prone was that of losing the unity of the one Christ.

Here let it be said that the danger of this summary of the two schools – as of all summaries – is over-simplification. Both "schools" sought to maintain the divinity, the humanity and the oneness of Jesus Christ – and deep truth is enshrined in the writing of both schools. But the static ideas of "substance" and "nature" continually led to the danger of philosophical contradictions, and when this happened either the humanity or the oneness of Christ was liable to flounder. The one theologian of this period to whom I shall later refer – Theodore of Mopsuestia, a member of the Antiochene school – sought at one vital point in his writings to escape from ideas of substance and to interpret God's indwelling in Christ in terms of *activity*. This approach is particularly relevant to process thinking, and seems to me both to avoid the two dangers to which I have referred and to do so in a positive manner.

The Council of Chalcedon also sought to avoid these two dangers, but by a series of negations which has led it to be called "the signpost against all heresies". The Definition* produced by this Council avoided the danger implicit in Nicea by applying two substances to Jesus (as had the earlier "Athanasian" creed): "of one substance with the Father as regards his Godhead and at the same time of one substance with us as regards his manhood". The Definition then avoided the danger lurking behind the Antiochene position by its statement that Christ is to be thought of as one person with two natures: "one and the same Christ, Son, Lord, Only-begotten, made known in two natures (which exist) unconfusedly, unchangeably, indivisibly, inseparably ... " The Greek text here has four negative adverbs, and its strongly negative flavour at this vital point lends colour both to the phrase "the signpost against all heresies" and to the criticism that the Definition is most successful in telling us what we are *not* to believe. I would prefer to put it differently, and to say that Chalcedon succeeded in stating, though not in explaining, the great Christian belief that God was in Christ, that Jesus was truly human, and that Jesus Christ is one single person.

* Part of this is quoted in *Soundings*, p. 151, and in *Documents of the Christian Church*, ed. H. Bettenson, p. 73. For a full account see R. V. Sellers, *The Council of Chalcedon* (1953).

"In the two great decisions of the early church, both the Christ-character and the Jesus-character of the event of Jesus as the Christ were preserved. And this happened *in spite of the very inadequate conceptual tools.*"*

We shall attempt to use our own tools, first to examine and then to interpret the gospel picture of Jesus of Nazareth.

(b) TOWARDS AN ANSWER FOR TODAY

The birth of Jesus

Our reaction to the gospel story is inevitably partly intellectual and partly emotional. For most of us emotions run high as regards the Christmas stories. The "magic" of Christmas is among our most cherished childhood memories, and we want to preserve this for ourselves, our children and grandchildren; we do not *want* to analyse the story into its component parts of myth and history – and all the more so if we suspect that the former would predominate. Unfortunately, once we have begun to harbour that suspicion, our refusal to analyse bears a striking resemblance to the proverbial ostrich who buries his head in the sand when danger threatens. No real safety is to be found by such negative action. We do better to face the fact that parts of the story may be myth, and then seek the positive meaning and value of that myth. "The myth is there to indicate the significance of the events, the divine depth of the history. And we shall be grievously impoverished if our ears cannot tune to the angels' song or our eyes are blind to the wise men's star."†

If churchgoers had only themselves to consider, no great harm might result from this ostrich-like behaviour once a year, though a firm faith can scarcely be built on partly-suspect foundations which one refuses to investigate. But the main danger is to the uncommitted, who both disbelieve the story as it stands and see through the evasive attitude of their church-going friends. It is not only the question of whether or not it is still possible to believe in God "coming down", or in the Son of God "taking our nature upon him": Dr. Robinson's case

* Tillich, *Systematic Theology*, vol. II, p. 167 (my italics).
† *Honest to God*, p. 68.

against this is now well known. Nor is it simply a matter of the virgin birth. The nativity stories seek to combine two very different themes: that Jesus was born into an artisan family, the actual birth taking place in a cattle-shed; and that the birth-event was of such colossal and immediate importance that nearby shepherds received angelic visions, sages came from afar, and the court of the local puppet "king" was seriously perturbed. These two themes are not quite incompatible; they are in fact very beautifully combined. But one cannot help asking why, if God so planned it that Jesus came of humble stock, he did not leave him to be born in peaceful obscurity, and confine any necessary visions to Mary and Joseph. A critical reading of the opening chapters of Matthew and Luke must raise the question whether it was God or the evangelists who so arranged things that quite so many Old Testament prophecies should be fulfilled.

Some readers will be impatient at even this discussion of the nativity stories, having long ago accepted these as mythical. For them I would seek to "rescue" two elements as being historical. That Jesus was born of humble stock seems to be a definite fact, and is of some importance. Even the non-Christian must surely take account of Jesus' colossal impact upon his fellows and upon mankind, and must ask himself both how this came about and whether it affects his own scale of values in life; Jesus' sociological background will be a factor in any such assessment. Equally, the Christian will treasure his Master's humble birth as all of a kind with the humility he showed, and showed supremely, throughout his life.

The other element I would "rescue" concerns the whole childhood of Jesus and not only the infancy narratives. If we are to cease thinking of Jesus as a supernatural being whose virtues derive uniquely from God, then we must be prepared to give full credit – and more, perhaps, than we used to give – to those who supplied the influences that surrounded him: to the Jewish people and their religion for the overall background; and to his family, and above all his mother, for his immediate environment. The gospels tell us little about Jesus' mother, and I am myself highly suspicious of most of the non-biblical traditions about her, except for the tradition that she was widowed before, perhaps a long time before, Jesus' public ministry began: the complete silence as to Joseph supports this tradition. If so, it is significant that there is no suggestion that Mary objected to her first-born son ceasing to support his widowed mother in what, emphatically, was not a "welfare state". One of the few things we are told about Mary is that she followed Jesus to Calvary when most of the apostles had fled. It may have been less dangerous for a woman to do this, but it was a courageous, loving, humble and unselfish act, and typifies the humility and unselfishness that we see supremely in Jesus but also, in very high degree, in Mary. Whether they be myth or history, the nativity stories illustrate this most beautifully. If Protestants and Anglicans thus come to give greater respect to the mother of Jesus, and if Rome continues to discourage excessive "Mariology" and is joined in this by the Orthodox Churches, then perhaps one of the greatest stumbling-blocks at the parish level to Christian unity may, in God's good time, disappear.

I shall refer only briefly to the doctrine of the virginal conception and birth of Jesus, about which so much has been written. It is important to emphasize that, on almost any interpretation of what is meant by "the divinity of Jesus", his virgin birth is *not* essential for belief in that divinity. St. Mark, St. John, St. Paul, and the author of Hebrews all proclaim the divinity of Jesus Christ on almost every page, yet none of them relies upon the virgin birth or even mentions it (except for a possible allusion in John 1 : 13); this widespread silence* is fairly generally regarded as "making the historical evidence . . . inconclusive". These words are quoted from *Doctrine in the Church of England: the Report of the Commission on Christian Doctrine appointed by the Archbishops of Canterbury and York in 1922.* This report, published in 1938, is not an "official" statement of that Church's doctrine, but rather an examination of the views actually held within it between the two world wars. It sets out two views on the doctrine of the virgin birth of Jesus. First, the traditional view:

"It is a safeguard of the Christian conviction that in the birth of Jesus we have, not simply the birth of a new individual of the human

* A silence which also extends to the main body of Matthew and Luke. Indeed if one remembers that the Greek word translated "virgin" in A.V. and R.V. can equally mean "young woman", one finds that the virginal conception is only referred to in the Birth-sequence in Matthew 1 and the Annunciation-sequence in Luke 1: The Birth-sequence in Luke 2 shows no knowledge of it, and may well come from a separate source (as A. R. C. Leaney cogently argues in his commentary on St. Luke).

species, but the advent of One who 'for us men and for our salvation came down from heaven'."

Then comes this paragraph:

"There are, however, some among us who hold that a full belief in the historical Incarnation is more consistent with the supposition that our Lord's birth took place under the normal conditions of human generation. In their minds the notion of a Virgin Birth tends to mar the completeness of the belief that in the Incarnation God revealed himself at every point in and through human nature."

The Report then emphasizes that "both the views outlined above are held by members of the Church, as of the Commission, who fully accept the reality of our Lord's Incarnation".*

I have quoted from this report in the belief that it would be helpful if it were more widely known that these two views are far from new, and were held by a Commission of distinguished Anglicans who were still able to work and worship together, and presumably to say the Apostles' Creed: I find it is the need to refer to it when saying the Creeds which most bothers those who feel uncertain about the virgin birth.

For many Christians, the main value of the belief that Jesus was conceived and born of a virgin is probably the straightforward way in which it enables one to think of Jesus as uniquely related to God the Father, and thus as "the Son of God". And the main disadvantage of this doctrine – setting on one side the fact that many people today just cannot or will not believe it – is the uneasy feeling that if Jesus' conception was different from ours, then there is an initial and unbridgeable gap between him and us. I shall not consider the title "Son of God" at any length. As St. Paul emphasized, there is a sense in which we are all sons of God: the use of a capital letter, and sometimes the definite article, cannot prevent "the Son of God" from needing further definition as to just how it differentiates Jesus from us; the doctrine of the virgin birth of Jesus offers the most straightforward definition, which is why this doctrine and the title "Son of God" are closely connected in many people's minds. Whenever we refer to Jesus as "Son of God" we need to remember that he is also "Son of Man".†

* All the quotations are from page 82 f.

† Indeed a careful study of the gospels will reveal that this last phrase occurs repeatedly in passages which seem likely to stand extremely close to the actual words of Jesus, and that it is always used by Jesus himself and not

But the main point I would stress is that whilst the virgin birth supplies a convenient definition of the title "Son of God", the use of this title *in no way depends upon that doctrine*. The title was used by New Testament writers who show no knowledge of the virgin birth; indeed their information about Jesus may have been virtually confined to his adult life. Those who knew Jesus during his ministry felt the power of God in him so strongly that they came to believe in him as "Son of God". For our present purpose it does not matter whether they came to this belief before or after his Crucifixion: what matters is that their belief in no way depended upon the doctrine of the virgin birth. The title "Son of God" lacks precision, but it can be used meaningfully without necessarily implying any abnormality in Jesus' conception, birth or childhood.

There are at least three further ways in which the doctrine of the virgin birth is used to reinforce aspects of belief. Firstly, it emphasizes the divine priority or "prevenience" in the whole event of the life of Jesus. The visit of the archangel Gabriel to Mary illustrates this most beautifully, but God's prevenience does not depend upon the particular illustration offered by the Annunciation and its sequel. As has been said, God gives to every entity its initial conceptual aim. In this sense, God is prevenient to each moment of Jesus' life, and of every life. God's guidance – and it matters little in exactly what sense this is also his "prevenience" – is perhaps most clearly seen in prayer, and in particular in the prayer and meditation through which Jesus sought to put his whole life at God's disposal and to learn his will. I shall suggest that Jesus' deep prayer is a most significant aspect of his relationship to God the Father.

Secondly, the virginal conception and birth of Jesus is held to mark a new beginning for the human race, an act of divine begetting whose novelty and significance parallels God's initial act of creation. The classic texts here are the opening of the fourth gospel, whose "In the beginning was the Word" is a

---

by his questioners or disciples. There are two vitally important occasions where Jesus seems to have used "Son of Man" very deliberately, after the previous speaker had used a different title: after Peter's "Thou art the Christ" Jesus taught "that the Son of Man must suffer many things" (Mark 8: 31); and in reply to the High Priest's question "Art thou the Christ, the Son of the Blessed?" Jesus said "I am, and ye shall see the Son of Man sitting at the right hand of power and coming with the clouds of heaven." (Mark 14: 62; Jesus here seems to be quoting Daniel 7: 13).

deliberate parallel to the opening of Genesis, and the first chapter of Paul's letter to the Colossians (especially verses 15–20). But this concept of a new beginning for the human race cannot be pressed very far without impairing the real humanity of Jesus. In an evolutionary world there is always novelty and new beginnings, and furthermore each new beginning emerges not out of a vacuum but out of its own past. Thus Jesus emerges out of the Jewish nation with its prophetic tradition and its messianic hope; he also emerges with a deep novelty that far overshadows the detailed parallels between parts of his teaching and that of contemporary rabbis. But if his conception and birth mark a new beginning comparable to God's initial act of creation, then it is surely impossible also to affirm – as I insist we must – that Jesus is truly "one of us".

A third way in which the virgin birth has been used to rein-force belief is now, I hope, mainly a thing of the past. Because of the very close connection between sin and sexual intercourse in the thought of many centuries, it used to be convenient to be able to link belief in the sinlessness of Jesus with the belief that he was born of a virgin. Once again, the concept of Jesus' sin-lessness cannot be pressed too far without impairing his humanity: manifestly, it in no way depends upon the circum-stances of his conception.*

To sum up, the virgin birth is not doctrinally necessary: the historical evidence is inconclusive. What matters, surely, is to be able to understand, in terms that do not conflict with the rest of one's philosophy, the central belief which the doctrine of the virgin birth enshrines – that "God was in Christ". For this, we must consider Jesus' adult life.

The adult life of Jesus

We have no information as to the early years of Jesus' adult life. Tradition has it that he lived quietly in Nazareth and worked as a carpenter: perhaps, if Joseph was dead, Jesus ran the only carpenter's shop in what was no more than a large village. But the only firm evidence for this is the fact that in the gospel

---

* There is an interesting discussion of the sinlessness of Jesus—and of the impossibility of maintaining, for example, that the child Jesus never got annoyed with another child—in *Awkward Questions on Christian Love* by H. Montefiore (Fontana, 1964).

narratives Jesus is frequently linked with Nazareth; he is only once described as a carpenter.* It seems highly likely that Jesus lived at Nazareth: it does not follow that he spent all his time there up to the beginning of his ministry. It is not impossible, for example, that Jesus may have visited the Qumran community – although such a possibility seems more in character in the case of John the Baptist. It is more likely that Jesus spent a certain amount of time in or near Jerusalem: the fourth gospel depicts him as no stranger to that area, and recent research has confirmed the accuracy of its Judaean topography.

The fact is that we know virtually nothing about this period of Jesus' life, except its approximate duration. There is little reason to doubt St. Luke's statement that Jesus was "about thirty years of age" when he began to teach:† he had had many years in which to study and meditate upon the Jewish scriptures. This ties in with the fact that Jesus emerges at the start of his ministry not as someone remote from his fellows who propounds utterly new teaching and largely ignores what has gone before him, but on the contrary as one who stands in line with the great Jewish prophets, who enriches, deepens, and purges the teaching of the Jewish church, and in so doing builds upon it, not apart from it.

Jesus' deep knowledge of the Jewish scriptures and traditions is borne out by the fact that even prominent opponents appear to have called him "Rabbi": no self-taught provincial man of God would be given this honorary title unless his teaching was seen to be scriptural in its background, and to possess at least some affinity with rabbinical teaching. Some modern scholars have made considerable study of the writings of rabbis who were approximately contemporary with Jesus; they are able to point to several instances in which Jesus' words were highly

---

* "Is not this the carpenter, the son of Mary . . . ?" (Mark 6: 3). In the parallel passages Luke has "Is not this Joseph's son?" and Matthew "Is not this the carpenter's son?" Some Marcan MSS here follow Matthew (rightly, in V. Taylor's view – in which case it is only a later scribe of Mark whose alteration implies a knowledge of the virginal conception of Jesus).

† It seems quite unnecessary to reject Luke's "about thirty" (3: 23) as an artificial parallel to "David was thirty years old when he began to reign" (2 Samuel 5: 4). Admittedly Luke 3: 23 leads into a genealogy which traces Jesus' ancestry through David back to Adam, but the O.T. contains over 30,000 verses and such parallels are more likely to be coincidental than deliberate, unless there is clear evidence to the contrary. In any case it is Jesus' deep knowledge of the scriptures, not his precise age, that matters.

topical, and related to matters in dispute between the different rabbinic schools. Such scholars tell us that the element of absolute novelty in Jesus' teaching is smaller than is often supposed: there are rabbinical parallels to quite a number of Jesus' sayings. J. Klausner goes even further: "Throughout the gospels there is not one item of ethical teaching that cannot be paralleled either in the Old Testament and Apocrypha or in the Talmudic and Midrashic literature near to the time of Jesus."* The vital difference lies in Jesus' selection of certain themes and ideas, such as the loving fatherhood of God, to which he gives a completely new emphasis. Thus the new emerges not from a vacuum, not "straight from heaven", but from deep prayer, deep knowledge of the scriptures, and deep meditation upon them: "I am come not to destroy but to fulfil."

The probability that he had spent a number of years quietly observing human nature as he lived and worked at the centre of the small country community at Nazareth also ties in with St. John's statement that "Jesus knew what was in man" – a fact that emerges very clearly throughout the gospel story: Jesus' daily life is a recurrent illustration of this deep knowledge of human nature, combined with an equally deep love and compassion for those he met. His gentleness with the sick and the poor, and with the sinner who is in any way humble or penitent, is combined with a sternness against sin itself, against hypocrisy, and against any misuse of religion and religious authority. Above all, as we read the synoptic gospels we cannot fail to be struck by Jesus' utter selflessness: his passion was but the final, supreme example of his continual giving of himself for others. He refused no genuine request for help: he gave no thought whatever to his own comfort or convenience. He was indeed "The Man for Others"; and as we come to say with St. Paul that "God was in Christ" we are in no doubt that the God in him is a God of self-giving love.

There is an important sense in which Jesus' selfless humility extends to the subject-matter of his teaching. To see this one must concentrate one's attention on the accounts of his ministry in the three synoptic gospels, and exclude from one's mind the Resurrection narratives, the distinctive elements in the teaching of St. John and St. Paul, and any preconceived ideas of one's own. One then meets a Jesus who gave a great deal of teaching

* *Jesus of Nazareth*, p. 384.

about God and man, and relatively little about himself. I am not suggesting that the Jesus whom we meet in the synoptic gospels regarded his own person and function as of no importance, but simply that he did not put these in the forefront of his teaching, except where the situation demanded it. The sick in search of healing naturally focused their faith or their hopes on Jesus personally, and he allowed this. He had to refute the charge of healing by Beelzebub, and did so by saying that he acted not in his own power but by the finger (or power) of God. He also had to refute repeated opposition to his healings on the sabbath: whatever words Jesus used on these occasions, he must have in some way insisted that he had the right and authority to override Jewish law and custom in this respect.

The synoptic gospels describe Jesus' repeated calls for decision—including the calls to "follow me"—and his several parables of crisis and of the coming, or growth, of the kingdom of God. All of these can be taken as divine utterances, but none of them necessitates this. They all refer primarily to the critical nature of the times and to the vital message that is being proclaimed, rather than to the preacher himself. It is only in the fourth gospel that Jesus is portrayed as regularly putting his own person and function in the forefront of his teaching, for example in these "I am" sayings: "I am the good shepherd", "I am the door of the sheep", "I am the true vine", "I am the resurrection and the life", and "Before Abraham was, I am". Both the language and the emphasis differ so markedly from the synoptic gospels that these passages—or at least the three last—must, surely, be regarded as St. John's profound meditations, and not as words spoken by Jesus before his Crucifixion.

If careful study and comparison of the four gospels indicates that Jesus' own person and function were not prominent subjects in either his public or his private teaching, the question remains as to what Jesus believed about himself and his role, and how much—if at all—he discussed this with his closest disciples. In so far as we can even begin to do so, we can only infer Jesus' own thoughts from the records of his words and actions: so we must begin with the second part of the question. This brings us back to the problem of the sequence of question and answer "in the villages of Caesarea Philippi" and Jesus' subsequent teaching about his passion and resurrection, as recorded in Mark 8–10. We have referred to the possibility that this entire sequence has got misplaced and properly belongs to the Easter period: there is much to be said on either side, and this problem must now be considered in greater detail.

This sequence occupies a key position in the narrative of the synoptic gospels: before it, Jesus did not openly acknowledge his messiahship; once Peter had said explicitly "Thou art the Christ", Jesus – while still demanding secrecy in public – began to teach his disciples the *nature* of his messiahship;* much of his teaching in this section of the gospels is directed to this end, and the next section begins with his deliberate fulfilment of the prophecy concerning the king who "cometh unto thee, meek and riding upon an ass". It is fundamental to this narrative that Jesus knew himself to be Messiah and acknowledged this, at least in private, while interpreting his messiahship in an entirely non-political sense, and in a way that at least resembled the role of the servant in the prophecies of "Second Isaiah".

Criticism of this primarily Marcan narrative is not new. Wrede (1901) maintained that it is dominated by a group of fundamental conceptions which belong not to history but to the dogmatic beliefs of the circles to which St. Mark belonged: that Jesus always knew himself to be Messiah but kept his "messianic secret" until his Resurrection; that the "demons" also knew this, but were enjoined to secrecy; and that when Jesus' messiahship was revealed in private to his disciples† they were supernaturally prevented from understanding until the Resurrection. The details of Wrede's theory are no longer of importance: what matters is his suggestion – in 1901 – that Mark's narrative differs substantially, and for doctrinal reasons, from what had in fact occurred.

Rudolf Bultmann went further, and denied that Jesus knew himself as Messiah: "belief in the messiahship of Jesus arose with and out of belief in his resurrection": neither Jesus nor his disciples had held it earlier. "The scene of *Peter's Confession* is no counter-evidence – on the contrary! For it is an Easter

* *Christos* (Gk.) and *Mashiach* (Heb.) are equivalent titles meaning (God's) Anointed One.

† Peter's confession of faith is followed in the narrative by the Transfiguration, the two being linked by one of the few chronological references in Mark, "after six days".

story projected backward into Jesus' lifetime, just like the story of the Transfiguration."*

Many Christians are almost relieved at the thought that the mysterious Transfiguration scene may properly belong to Easter, but hesitate to make so major a disruption of the narrative as to say the same of Peter's "Thou art the Christ". But James McLeman sees this as "much more obviously a post-Crucifixion narrative than the Transfiguration, although there is no difficulty in accepting the transposition of the latter".† He denies that either Jesus or the disciples thought of him as Messiah before the Crucifixion: the narrative of Peter's confession of faith is a description of the first dawnings of faith in Jesus as the Christ, and thus of the birth of the Church—founded upon Peter's (Easter) faith.

One's attitude to all this must depend both on how one expects God to be active in the world and on how one interprets the psychology of the disciples and the nature of their initial Resurrection-faith. It is possible to take the view that the disciples never had any clear idea about—or definite faith in—Jesus during his lifetime, and only came to this when God raised him from the tomb and sent him back to them. This fits in with the disciples' poor showing after Jesus' arrest, with their complete surprise at his Resurrection, and indeed with most of the synoptic narrative, excluding Peter's confession of faith and Jesus' prediction of his Resurrection.‡ But in the realm of spiritual experience God normally seems to help those who in some measure help themselves: he does not, so to speak, work in a vacuum, nor does he suddenly give people a faith not only different but utterly discontinuous from all their earlier thoughts and ideas. Are we, then, to believe that the totally uncomprehending followers of a crucified carpenter-rabbi were suddenly turned into the fervent apostles of a risen and divine Messiah? Is it not likely, on *any* view as to the nature of the disciples' Easter experience, that God would have required—and helped them to achieve—at least *some* previous faith?

* *Theology of the New Testament* (Eng. trans., S.C.M. Press, 1952), vol. I, p. 26; pp. 26–32 contain a closely reasoned denial of "the messianic consciousness of Jesus".

† *Resurrection Then and Now* (Hodder and Stoughton, 1965), p. 187 f.

‡ It is easy to accept that Jesus foresaw and predicted his coming death: on no view is it easy to combine his predictions of his Resurrection with the disciples' complete surprise at Easter.

It is just possible to argue to the contrary, on the supposition that the disciples' entire outlook was revolutionized by the great miracle of the Resurrection of Jesus. It may be that in first-century Palestine messianic hopes were so closely linked with ideas of the "end-time", and of a general resurrection, that when their prophet-master rose from the tomb and appeared to them they realized both that the "end-time" had begun and that Jesus was – and had always been – God's Messiah. On this view of the Resurrection it *can* be argued that every suggestion in the narratives that both Jesus and his disciples were thinking in messianic terms is a reading-back into the earlier story of beliefs which did not exist before Easter. But there would today be little support for an attitude to the gospels that combines extreme scepticism as to the gradual growth of faith described in their main chapters with considerable literalness as to the Resurrection narratives. Furthermore, there are cogent reasons – discussed in the next chapter – for the view that the Resurrection narratives cannot be so literally interpreted, partly because they are not mutually consistent, but mainly because, on this view, the Resurrection of Jesus was not an external event of the type described in these narratives.

If it was not, if the Easter faith arose in the minds of the disciples and grew out of the shock of their Master's Crucifixion, then it follows from the normal psychology of the human mind that there must have been *some* continuity between the disciples' Easter faith and their earlier impressions and experience : this implies that during Jesus' lifetime his disciples must have begun to sense God's presence and power in and through Jesus *more powerfully* than they had ever sensed it in anyone else.

The existence of some such experience during Jesus' ministry is vital to all that followed : it matters comparatively little what precise form it took, or how explicitly it included the messiahship (or the unique Sonship) of Jesus. The gospel records may be highly coloured in this respect, but if Jesus was widely regarded as a prophet it seems more than likely that some people in Palestine will have begun to discuss Jesus in messianic terms during his ministry. Messianic expectations had been high for some time. There had been no major prophet for three centuries when suddenly first John and then Jesus appeared. People were almost bound to begin asking themselves messianic questions;

once this had spread to his disciples, Jesus would almost inevitably have been drawn into the discussion.

There is nothing improbable about a conversation on the general lines of that described in the villages of Caesarea Philippi. The difficulty lies in reconciling Peter's explicit affirmation of faith with the disciples' subsequent bewilderment and surprise. Perhaps these can be reconciled. Perhaps some such conversation took place, but the details of the synoptic narrative have been coloured at vital points by the faith of the post-resurrection Church. Or perhaps this particular sequence, with its full awareness of Jesus as God's Christ, does in fact belong to the Easter period: the prominence of Peter in the Resurrection narratives, and the fact that Matthew follows Peter's confession of faith with the only important use of the word "church" in the gospels, both give support to the suggestion that Peter's "Thou art the Christ" *is* the birth-moment both of the Easter faith and of the Christian Church.*

The problem of "the messianic consciousness of Jesus" includes the question whether or not he saw himself and his role in terms of the "suffering servant" of the prophecies of Isaiah 42–53. There has been a considerable swing of opinion in this matter. Many scholars still maintain what used to be at least the general English view: that Jesus specifically brought together the concepts of Messiah and Suffering Servant, and modelled his life thereon. But some scholars have claimed too much. Thus the heavenly voice at Jesus' baptism, "Thou art my

*This possibility does assume a major error of order in Mark (and hence in all three synoptic gospels). I am not here concerned with detailed New Testament analysis, but it should be said that there is nothing inherently improbable in this assumption. Mark is an editorial construction: statistical analysis of the text suggests that it is an amalgamation of large *blocks* of material; this entire sequence forms one such block, and the suggestion is that this block was inserted immediately before the passion narrative instead of immediately after it.

There is an early tradition of disorder in Mark, due to the famous fragment in which Papias (*c.* A.D. 60–130) claims earlier authority: "This also the Elder used to say: Mark, having been Peter's interpreter (or *aide-de-camp*), wrote down accurately—not, however, in order—all that he remembered . . . " This tradition could, as McLeman suggests, refer to the misplacement of Easter experiences: it could equally refer to the geographical sequence in Mark, in which Jesus only visits Jerusalem for the final Passover—whereas he pays several visits in John. (This sequence largely determines the order of events: the Elder may have known Mark to be incorrect.)

beloved Son, in thee I am well pleased", has been taken to imply a bringing together of the Son of Psalm 2 and the Servant of Isaiah 42: but in the second instance the linguistic parallel is highly tenuous, and should not be used to support weighty conclusions. Further analysis of this and other supposed parallels – notably Miss M. D. Hooker's *Jesus and the Servant* (1959) – has swung many people over to the view that there is no evidence that Jesus explicitly modelled himself on this Servant. Bultmann here expresses this viewpoint concisely:

"The tradition of Jesus' sayings reveals no trace of a consciousness on his part of being the Servant of God of Isaiah 53. The messianic interpretation of Isaiah 53 was discovered in the Christian Church, and even in it evidently not immediately ... The earliest passages in which the Suffering Servant of God of Isaiah 53 clearly and certainly appears are Acts 8: 32 f., 1 Peter 2: 22–25, Hebrews 9: 28 ... The synoptic predictions of the passion obviously do not have Isaiah 53 in mind; otherwise why is it nowhere referred to?"*

This last point is perhaps decisive. Jesus was a very great teacher. If he had accepted Peter's explicit affirmation of his messiahship and then reinterpreted this in terms of the Suffering Servant, Jesus would have made a sufficiently good job of it for at least some clear linkage with Isaiah 42–53 to have been recalled in the disciples' minds after Easter, and subsequently included in the synoptic narrative. One should therefore accept the view that Jesus' thinking did not include the explicit equating of himself with the Servant of Isaiah 42–53: neither the synoptic narratives nor the nature of the initial Easter faith – in so far as we can reconstruct it – supports such an explicit equation. But their Easter faith *does* imply that the disciples came to realize that Jesus had not been taken by surprise at his arrest and execution but had, in fact, believed it to be God's will that he should face probable death in Jerusalem. Because the disciples realized this, Jesus' death did not destroy but *reinforced* their earlier awareness of the presence and power of God in and through their Master.

It is not profitable to speculate in detail as to the self-awareness of Jesus. It may be that he did not explicitly think of himself as the expected Messiah: it certainly seems unlikely that he explicitly saw himself as the Suffering Servant. The gospel

* *Theology of the New Testament*, vol. I, p. 31.

picture both of his life and of his teaching – neither of which is in the least likely to have been distorted beyond recognition – makes it clear that Jesus *did* see himself, at the very least, as a prophet called by God both to reinterpret the deep truths implicit in the Jewish religion and its scriptures and also, in some sense, to suffer for the sins of the people. The concept of a prophet so suffering, or being ready to suffer, is implicit in a number of Old Testament passages – and not only in the Servant prophecies in Isaiah 42–53.* Thus we are again brought back – as were the original disciples – to the way in which both the life and the teaching of Jesus are in tune with the deep truths enshrined in the Jewish scriptures. Whatever may have been the precise form of Jesus' self-awareness, this seems to have emerged, like his teaching, not "straight from heaven" but from deep prayer and meditation upon his Jewish scriptures.

As I in turn try to meditate upon the life and ministry of Jesus as recorded in my scriptures, I see him as possessing an utterly unselfish character, a deep devotion to God, and a deep love of people. These characteristics are all interconnected, and cannot be put into a temporal sequence. The vital ingredient is prayer: the prayer of meditation upon the scriptures, to which I have just referred: the prayer of submission and self-dedication, which first seeks to learn what is God's will and then cries out "Thy will be done". Nor did Jesus confine that great phrase to his own life. He both practised what he preached and preached what he practised. He demanded of all men a radical obedience to God's will, as distinct from – and in protest against – the formal obedience with which the Jewish church of his day was all too often content.

One cannot obey God's will unless one has at least some idea of what his will is: but perhaps it is also true that one cannot learn God's will at a deep level except in proportion as one is willing in advance – as, I believe, Jesus was – to obey it.

"Radical obedience is only possible where a man understands the demand and affirms it from within himself . . . God requires radical obedience. He claims man whole—and wholly. Within this insight

* The equating of this servant-figure with an *individual* is primarily a *Christian* concept. In at least one prophecy the servant would seem to represent the whole people of Israel, the interpretation normally adopted in Judaism.

Jesus takes for granted that God requires of man the doing of the good and that ethical demands are the demands of God . . ."*

I sometimes think of Jesus as using an equivalent prayer to the ancient and beautiful Collect for the First Sunday after Epiphany (here transposed to the first person): "grant that we may both perceive and know what things we ought to do, and also may have grace and power faithfully to fulfil the same": or perhaps Henry VI's prayer, which has been a favourite of mine since my schooldays: "thou knowest what thou would'st do with me: do with me according to thy will, for thy tender mercy's sake". If one believes in a transcendent God and in prayer as a real relationship with him, if one has tried to pray Henry's prayer and had one's life altered as a result, can one doubt that when Jesus so prayed he would be led by God to formulate in his own mind the role which God wished him to fulfil?

The temptations of Jesus may perhaps illustrate a part of this process of learning God's will. Behind the pictorial language of miracle and of interrogation by the devil there may well lie a series of real decisions, perhaps arrived at gradually and after much thought and prayer – decisions to avoid using his undoubted popularity and powers of healing for the advancement of either himself or his teaching. St. Luke emphasizes particularly the element of prayer, often prolonged prayer, in Jesus' daily life: Jesus spends the whole night in prayer before choosing the Twelve. Luke also gives the clearest picture of how, in the closing months of the synoptic timetable, Jesus "stedfastly set his face to go to Jerusalem".† With or without the specific help of Isaiah 40–53, Jesus perceived all too clearly that God's will for him involved suffering and death; he did his best to forewarn his disciples; he steeled himself to accept this cup of suffering, and only wavered for a few moments in Gethsemane – to come back triumphantly with "nevertheless, not my will, but thine, be done".

I cannot regard all this as totally unhistorical, although many of the details may indeed be coloured by the disciples' later

* Bultmann, *Theology of the New Testament,* vol. I, pp. 12–13. It is Bultmann's extreme scepticism that is most often quoted, whether with approval or otherwise. This passage shows that there are also intensely positive aspects to his theology.
† Luke 9: 51–56.

faith. I admit that, as a Christian, I do not *want* so to regard it. But, as a critic, I think it highly unlikely that the early Church was as *inventive* as some highly sceptical New Testament theologians seem willing to assume. I also repeat what has just been said: that there would have been no Easter faith unless the disciples had, at the time, at least dimly sensed that Jesus' risking of arrest and death had been deliberately undertaken in the belief that this was God's will.

I think it more likely that Jesus sought to learn God's will through prayer and meditation and self-commitment than that he possessed some unique channel of communication – some unique relationship – with God. I also prefer to think the former, for the latter alternative places a great gulf between Jesus and ourselves. But most Christians, past and present, have put more emphasis on Jesus' unique relationship to God than on his exceptional use of the normal channels of communication between God and man. Both concepts must now be examined.

Jesus: true God and true man

"Unless it be agreed that he was 'truly man', it does not greatly matter what else can be said of him, because he will have been effectually separated from us and from our history ... Unless he had a human consciousness, he was not a man. If he did not think and feel, about himself and others, as a man does; if he did not take man's lot for granted as being intimately, entirely, and irrevocably his own; if he did not share, at the very deepest levels of his conscious and subconscious life, in our human anxieties, perplexities, and loneliness; if his joys were not characteristic human joys and his hopes, human hopes; if his knowledge of God was not in every part and under every aspect the kind of knowledge which is given to man, the creature, to have—then he was not a true human being ... If by being 'more than a man' we mean that he lacked the normal self-consciousness of a man, then we are saying that he was less than a man. We are rejecting his humanity at the really decisive point. It may be possible to think of him as being 'more than a man' in ways which permit us to think of him also as being a man, but we cannot think of him as *knowing* he was more than man without denying that he was man at all ... "

This striking passage from Dr. John Knox's *The Death of Christk* contains three elements that are highly relevant to our thinking at this juncture:

* Abingdon Press, Nashville, U.S.A., (1958), p. 70; this passage is cited in Pittenger, *The Word Incarnate,* p. 10.

1. Knox emphasizes that unless Jesus is seen to be "truly man" then he is both remote from our situation and, indeed, *less* than a man. The early Church came to a similar conclusion when it branded as heretical the teaching of Apollinarius.*

2. Knox lays special emphasis on the fact that if Jesus was truly man then his knowledge of God must have been the same kind of knowledge that we can have. This emphasis is important because it is with regard to his knowledge of God and of God's will for mankind that we most easily assume Jesus to have been "more than a man". It is widely accepted that in science, economics and other fields Jesus will have shared the prevailing beliefs of his day, but when they are dealing with some spiritual matter preachers and theologians often search the gospels for what they can regard as the authentic words of Jesus – his *ipsissima verba* – in order to claim for these an unquestionable authority. Behind this lies the unspoken assumption that in such a matter Jesus' knowledge will have been more than human. It is this assumption that Professor Knox first denies and then qualifies.

3. We now come to the tentative possibility to which Knox refers in the last sentence of the above passage: that it may be possible to think of Jesus as more than a man provided that he did not *know* himself to be so. If Jesus knew that God had made available to him some special means of communication, some special form of "grace", he would have been likely to tell his disciples of this, and if possible to show them how they might come to share in it. But in those passages where the gospels seem most likely to approximate to the actual words of Jesus we find that he teaches us that the way to a knowledge of God, and a relationship with God, lies through obedience to God's will as learned in prayer, through disregard of self, and through love and service of one's neighbour – none of which is wholly beyond our reach. It is not impossible that God had made some special provision for Jesus without his knowledge: there may indeed be ways of "prehending" God, channels for his grace, that are unknown to us. But to suppose that Jesus unknowingly possessed a unique means of grace is to deny the completeness of his humanity, whilst affirming that he himself believed it to be complete. It does not reduce the life and death of Jesus to the "charade" which Dr. Robinson condemns, but it does deny

* See above, p. 185.

that Jesus was "truly man". It should be rejected not because it is impossible but because it is unnecessary, and reduces the element of hope and joy in the Christian gospel.

I have repeatedly emphasized the importance of Whitehead's insistence that God is not an exception to all metaphysical principles but their chief exemplification; I paraphrased this by saying that God "keeps the rules". I find great value, and great joy, in being able to believe that God also "kept the rules" during the life of Jesus, so that the power and love of God and the understanding of God's will and purpose, with all of which Jesus was so richly endowed, came to him through prayer and self-commitment and not through some unique and unknown channel. In Whitehead's terms, prayer is a way of prehending God, a way that takes account of all other prehensions of everything in one's environment, including all earlier prehensions of God. In an interdependent universe all prehensions are interdependent: one's knowledge of anyone, for example one's wife, is affected by one's whole outlook and environment: so was Jesus's knowledge of God, which came to him as part of his total environment. It was a big part, for it seems clear from the gospels that Jesus gave top priority both to prehending God through all available means and to obeying these prehensions. Jesus thus kept his own "subjective aim" in alignment with God's aim and purpose: "thy will, not mine, be done".

This can equally be expressed the other way round. A prehending B means A as subject grasping at B as an object, and receiving influence from that object. Thus as A prehends B, so B becomes objectively, but not subjectively, present in A: everything is both open to its world and yet transcends its world. As a subject, A transcends and is distinct from B, however strongly he is prehending B; but in proportion as A both prehends B's influence and acts upon it, so we can say that B is influencing A, and is objectively present in A. It is a common fact of experience that a fellow-believer can sense the presence and power of God in a man or woman who is leading a really God-centred life. The "saint" or man of God is powerfully prehending God, and so God is powerfully, though objectively, present in him: the believer who prehends the saint will sense God's presence "in" him. If Jesus prehended God so unreservedly, then some of his contemporaries will have been likely to sense the presence of God in Jesus as something more powerful, more wonderful, than they had ever met before, or even dreamed of: the gospels suggest that this is precisely what happened.

One of the basic and recurrent Christian heresies, perhaps unfairly labelled Nestorianism,* consists in maintaining both the divinity and the humanity of Christ in such a manner that Jesus becomes, in effect, two persons rather than one. The "Athanasian" creed guards against this by insisting that "although he be God and man: yet he is not two, but is one Christ". In proportion as Jesus made his life available for God's use, so that his aim was aligned with God's aim and his actions resulted from that aim, so will God have been objectively present in Jesus. If we can say that Jesus made his life completely available for God, then we can also say that God's objective presence in Jesus was "complete", meaning by this "the greatest possible": God present objectively, while Jesus is the subject: not two, but one Christ. If objective presence sounds artificial, then substitute activity: God's activity powerfully – in a sense, perhaps, "completely" – present in Jesus.

Attempts to express the presence of God in Jesus in terms of activity have formed one of the strands of Christian thinking from the first. St. Paul's great phrase "God was in Christ, reconciling the world unto himself",† comes in this category. Such attempts are of importance because they get away from the static ideas of "nature" and "substance". I will quote one striking example from the early Fathers. Theodore of Mopsuestia was a doctrinal and biblical theologian during the period between the Councils of Nicea and Chalcedon. As Bishop of Mopsuestia in Cilicia from about 392 until his death in 426 he was widely respected for his learning and orthodoxy. A century and a quarter after his death his Christology led to his being declared "impious and heretical" by the Fifth Ecumenical Council at Constantinople, and he has been called "the Nestorius before Nestorius". There has been a great revival of interest in Theodore in modern times, and the justice of the Council's decision has been questioned by both Protestant and Roman Catholic theologians, who have come to regard Theodore as the best and most important representative of the

* The heresy is clear enough in Nestorius's followers, but it is not certain that he himself committed it.
† 2 Corinthians 5: 19.

Antiochene school of Christology. As we have seen, this school emphasized the humanity of Christ as well as his divinity, and was always in danger of ending up with so loose a union of these two natures as to amount to an unacceptable duality, sometimes almost to two persons, in place of the unity of the one Christ. Nestorius's followers certainly succumbed to this danger; whether Nestorius did so himself is doubtful; whether the charge of Nestorianism can fairly be lodged against Theodore is more doubtful still.

I am here concerned with just one aspect of his Christology, which happily occurs in the longest fragment of his *De Incarnatione* to have been preserved in the original Greek. Theodore is considering the relation of *indwelling*, which he uses to explain the union of God and man in Christ. He first considers the general mode of divine indwelling in men, and then applies this to Christ. Theodore is searching for the sense in which God's indwelling in men is not universal, being found in some men but not in all: for this purpose he rejects indwelling according to substance and indwelling according to activity (*energeia* = energy), both of which apply universally. He settles on indwelling by "good pleasure" (*eudokia*), and to show that this form of divine indwelling is selective (in our modern idiom) Theodore quotes Psalm 147: 11; "the Lord takes pleasure in those who fear him, in those who hope in his steadfast love" (R.S.V.). This indwelling by good pleasure manifests itself in the fact that "God is near to such men by the attitude of disposition of his will . . . He is willing to grant special assistance, special co-operation, to those in whom he is pleased".*

Theodore then turns to God's indwelling in Jesus, and makes a distinction. Here God is well pleased "as in a son". This "means that in coming to indwell he united the assumed† as a whole to himself". The question is whether this differentiation in the case of Jesus does or does not over-ride the general concept of indwelling by good pleasure. The Roman Catholic scholar F. A. Sullivan decides that it does not:

* In quoting from this fragment I have followed both the translation and the commentary in *The Christology of Theodore of Mopsuestia* by F. A. Sullivan, S. J. (Rome, 1956). See also *Manhood and Christ: a Study in the Christology of Theodore*, by R. A. Norris (Oxford, 1963).

† i.e. the assumed man, which is how Theodore considers and explains Christ.

"Now the first question which arises is this: does Theodore conceive of this 'dwelling by good pleasure as in a son' as a totally new genus of inhabitation by *good pleasure*? In this case, there would seem to have been little point to his previous discussion, wherein he established the general notion of this type of indwelling. It would seem rather that he understands the generic definition of inhabitation by *good pleasure* to hold even in this case."*

Eight pages later, Fr. Sullivan sums up his discussion:

"From the study which we have made, we believe this conclusion can be drawn: that as Theodore conceives this union of activity between Word and man, prior to the glorification of Christ, it seems to be a kind of divine co-operation, superior in duration and in degree, but not in essential character, to that co-operation which characterizes the inhabitation of God 'by good pleasure' in other saints."

Whatever may be said for or against Theodore's theology as a whole, this passage contains a valuable pointer towards a Christology which coheres with the general philosophy and theology which I am seeking to commend: God's indwelling by good pleasure in his saints corresponds to God's powerful objective presence, or activity, where there are strong mutual prehensions between God and man. That "the Lord takes pleasure" is God's gift: so is the future saint's "initial conceptual aim", which as we have seen derives from – or is a gift from – God. That the divine co-operation in the case of Christ is "superior in duration and in degree, but not in essential character" corresponds, as I see it, to a denial that God used some special and unique means of grace in order to indwell in Jesus.

This statement also raises the old question "does Christ differ from us in kind or in degree?" There is now wide agreement that this is an unsatisfactory question: as William Temple put it in a footnote in *Christus Veritas*, "this question has an appearance of precision which is utterly illusory".† He quotes the logical conundrum "Is the difference between differences of kind and differences of degree a difference of kind or a difference of degree?" Others have pointed out that enormous differences of degree (say of the order of 10^{10}) can amount to a difference of kind: this is highly relevant to our question about Christ. If it has to be answered in its own terms, then I must follow Dr.

* op. cit. p. 246.
† Page 147.

Pittenger "in maintaining . . . that the difference is of almost immeasurable degree and not of absolute kind".*

William Temple concludes his footnote by approaching the matter from the other end: "But if the question means, 'Is Perfect Man *eo ipso* God?' the answer is, 'No. Nothing that happens to a creature could possibly turn him into his own Creator. At that point the gulf between God and Man is plainly impassable' ". Whitehead would certainly have agreed with this. There is, as Whitehead emphasized, a sense in which the creature is self-creative: but he is only partially so. The creature, or individual entity, cannot create its own environment, although it can influence it. Neither can it create its own basic conceptual aim, which it derives from God. It can alter this aim by deviation, which in ourselves we call sin, but it cannot create it. No one else can have the subjective aim which God willed in the first instance for Jesus, and from which, as Christians believe, Jesus did not deviate. No one else, however hard he prays for God's guidance "that he may both perceive and know what things he ought to do", will ever receive the same answer, the same role, that Jesus received. We have strayed from Temple's point, but we have hit upon an important sense in which we can affirm the "uniqueness" of Christ. Each man's environment and role in life is unique to himself, and is in turn affected by himself. The significance of the "uniqueness" of Christ, or as I would prefer to say his "extreme specialness", lies partly in the extreme importance of his particular situation and role, partly in the way he accepted that role to the uttermost "becoming obedient even unto death, yea, the death of the cross",† and partly in what happened after that death.

Jesus' role is put superbly in the opening words of the Epistle to the Hebrews, which are read on Christmas Day: "God, who at sundry times and in divers manners spake in time past unto the fathers by the prophets, hath in these last days spoken unto us by his Son, whom he hath appointed heir of all things . . ." In an interdependent universe everything is in a sense "heir of all things": Jesus was in an extremely special sense heir to the long line of prophets, and to the whole religious hope and expectation of the Old Testament. There is nothing unique in

* *The Word Incarnate*, p. 243.
† Philippians 2: 8.

accepting a martyr's death: what made the impact of Jesus on some of his contemporaries "unique" was the combination of selfless obedience even unto death, selfless love of his fellows, and the extremely special role in which they came to see him, and in which he had in some way come to see himself. Even so, none of us would even have heard of Jesus of Nazareth, whom his Church rejected, had it not been for the "everlastingness" of his life, in Whitehead's terminology. We normally call this the Resurrection, the Risen Lord, the presence of Christ in his Church.

All that I have said about Jesus of Nazareth will, I fear, seem quite inadequate to some, who will feel that the concept of the mutual prehensions between God and Jesus does not maintain the full "divinity" of Jesus Christ. I would ask such readers to defer judgement until the next chapter, in which I attempt to use process philosophy to explain and give positive support to the Church's continuing cry "Jesus is Lord". I see this cry as the *present tense* of the Resurrection, the most outstandingly "unique" feature in the total event of Jesus Christ. In describing the life of Jesus up to his Crucifixion, the theologian must continually guard against saying things which would indeed emphasize the "uniqueness" and "divinity" of Jesus, but only at the cost of losing the reality of his manhood. This danger recedes, although it does not vanish, when we move on to his Resurrection. Thus the difficulty with certain of Jesus' miracles is not that God could not have performed them as unique events if he saw fit — I repeat that there is no justification for the *a priori* assumption that God has never performed a unique act — but that he could not have done so through the agency of Jesus without compromising the fullness of Jesus' humanity. This difficulty does not apply to his Resurrection, for the New Testament is emphatic that it was not Jesus, but God the Father, who raised the Crucified.

CHAPTER SEVEN

The Livingness of Jesus Christ

IN everyday life there is often a deep psychological difference between the novelty of a new experience and its frequent repetition. As the father of growing children I am well aware of how the intense excitement of doing something for the first time changes all too soon into the more sophisticated acceptance of a routine activity: this change is, of course, gradual. In not so many years' time my daughters will doubtless learn to drive, and at some stage each will, I imagine, pass her test: perhaps my most important function in all this will be to emphasize that the removal of "L-plates" does *not* mean that one has become an experienced driver overnight.

To take one more example, we give the special name of honeymoon to the holiday with which married life usually begins, but we expect an element of honeymoon to carry over into the months that follow. I remember my grandmother once saying that for the first twelve months a bride took precedence over a duchess at formal dinners: a charming custom, whose equivalent certainly survives informally. But distinctions get blurred now that so many people in so-called society marry more than once: would a former model in the third month of her second marriage be given precedence at a formal dinner over a countess, let alone a duchess? The point needs no further labouring: in everyday life the novelty of a new experience or situation distinguishes this from its subsequent repetition, but the distinction is not abrupt, and certainly not absolute.

Traditional Christianity *has* drawn an abrupt and absolute distinction between the initial Resurrection appearances and the subsequent presence of Christ with his followers and his Church: this distinction is represented or symbolized by the Ascension of Christ. The absolute nature of this distinction rests on the assumption that the initial Resurrection appearances were unique, and more objective, or visible, or tangible —

whichever adjective is preferred – than any subsequent individual or corporate experience of the "livingness" of Jesus. The abrupt nature of this distinction derives from the belief that the initial Resurrection appearances ended at Christ's Ascension.

Our Church calendar follows the timetable of Luke–Acts in allotting forty days to Easter, the last of which, Ascension Day, is followed by our commemoration on Whit Sunday of the pentecostal gift of the Spirit, and with it the beginning of the apostles' public preaching as recorded in Acts. We tend to forget that it is only St. Luke who describes the Ascension as a separate event. St. John telescopes the whole Easter to Whitsun timetable by his description of the risen Christ breathing on the disciples on Easter evening and saying "receive ye the Holy Spirit: whose soever sins ye forgive they are forgiven … "* The annual commemoration of Ascension Day has obvious difficulties for "modern man" – so obvious, indeed, that they are not too difficult to overcome. It also has its value: as Dr. A. M. Ramsey has pointed out, the Resurrection and Ascension are to be distinguished as theological truths, although "it is possible … that the apostolic writers often made little or no separation between the Resurrection and the exaltation to heaven, and that where a distinction is made it may be due in part to the existence of two kinds of imagery: (1) the raising of Jesus from death, (2) the entrance of Jesus into the heavenly Lordship foretold in Psalm 110."†

The danger inherent in the Lucan timetable is that it clearly implies two distinct types of awareness of the risen Christ, with the final removal of his visible presence at his Ascension as the dividing point. Dr. Ramsey's comment on his next page makes this quite clear: "the tradition in Luke concerning the Ascension as a distinct event cannot be dismissed. There is nothing incredible in an event whereby Jesus assured the disciples that the appearances were ended and that His sovereignty and His presence must henceforth be sought *in new ways*" (my italics).

"New ways" certainly implies an absolute distinction. The majority of Christians would, no doubt, agree. A typical viewpoint could perhaps be summarized in some such words as

* John 20: 23.
† *The Resurrection of Christ*, p. 122 of the Fontana edition.

these: "I'm a Christian because I believe that Jesus is the Son of God – God's unique revelation of himself. I believe this primarily because his own disciples saw him several times after he rose from the dead – a fact which the New Testament emphasizes over and over again; I also believe it because I myself sense the presence of Jesus from time to time, particularly at Holy Communion. But I don't see or sense Jesus in the way the apostles did at Easter, nor do I expect to do so: those appearances stopped at his Ascension; we live today in the age of the Holy Spirit." Such a belief has two major disadvantages: a faith in Christ that rests largely on miracle is – rightly or wrongly – unacceptable to a number of "modern men"; but a far deeper disadvantage is the absolute distinction that it inevitably draws between our present experience of Jesus Christ and the Easter experience of his original disciples.

A "philosophy of process" can help us to understand this *present* experience of Jesus Christ, and to see the "livingness" of Jesus as the chief exemplification of our own hope of "everlastingness". It is, surely, far more important to understand and to share in the continuing awareness of the presence of Christ which successive generations of his followers have experienced through prayer and scriptures and sacrament, and at decisive moments of their lives, than to inquire as to precisely what happened during the period immediately following the Crucifixion. As to the latter, the evidence is scanty and often – as we shall see – conflicting: I do not believe that such an inquiry can ever be brought to a positive conclusion. Indeed I would gladly say no more of this initial period than these two things: first, that it represents the vital turn-round of fugitive disciples whose Master had been executed; and second that the disciples emerged from this period with a far deeper and richer faith than they had ever possessed before – a faith in which it is our privilege to share. But this would omit all discussion of the empty tomb, which is so central an item of belief or disbelief that its omission might render all that I wish to say about our *continuing* awareness of the risen Lord unintelligible to the orthodox and perhaps irrelevant to the sceptic, who might think that I was evading the issue. Before coming on to the supremely important present tense of Christ's Resurrection – affirmed in the cry "Jesus is Lord" – we will therefore consider the initial Easter period and its cry of faith:

"Christ is risen"

"Christos aneste", "Christ is risen", is the cry with which Greek-speaking Christians greet each other on Easter morning, while the other replies "He is risen indeed" – a very ancient, and a very beautiful, greeting. No doubt the overwhelming majority of those who use this greeting link it so closely as virtually to equate it with the belief that Jesus' tomb was found to be empty on the first Easter morning, and that he then appeared to his disciples in visible, indeed tangible, form. Those who find this extremely difficult to believe will none the less, for the most part, regard it as an essential part of the Easter faith and the Easter greeting, to which they perhaps add in their minds that other New Testament cry "Lord, I believe: help thou mine unbelief".

There is, however, a small but growing minority of Christians who no longer make this equation, but affirm their faith in the continuing presence of the risen and living Christ in ways that do *not* depend historically upon the empty tomb. Some of them also feel obliged to deny all possibility of Jesus' body having been raised from its tomb. Others in turn react very strongly against this viewpoint and insist, with great emphasis, that Christendom must stand firm on its belief in the empty tomb and in the visible and tangible nature of Christ's Resurrection appearances during the six weeks following his Crucifixion: they find their path to the faith that Christ *is* risen, and to this present tense, *through* their belief that certain events occurred in a particular way during those six weeks.

For myself, I pray and I plead that each of these schools of thought may cease from trying to over-ride the other, and may instead concentrate on developing a viewpoint which they both share, namely that the *continuing* fact of Christ's presence with his followers matters far *more* than the precise nature of his initial Resurrection appearances. This much is common ground: let us build upon it, so that we may the more powerfully affirm, both to ourselves and to the world, our faith in the present "livingness" of Jesus Christ.

Those who regard the accounts of the empty tomb and its sequel as incredible, and as a great stumbling-block to the faith of "modern man", should pause to reflect that it is impossible to disprove these accounts, except in so far as they conflict with each other. One can affirm that unique events never occur, but this is as assumption: it cannot be proved without a knowledge of every single event that has ever occurred. Those who believe in God as living and, in some sense, transcendent would presumably attribute at least some uniqueness to God: it cannot be impossible that a unique God should sometimes act uniquely. One may think the unique event of a visible Resurrection unlikely: one may feel that a faith that depends upon such an event is weaker than one that does not; but one ought not to maintain that the traditional interpretation of Christ's Resurrection is impossible.

But I suggest that the traditionalist school of thought should equally refrain from insisting – as many do insist at the present time – that belief in the empty tomb and in the visible and tangible nature of the Resurrection appearances is the only way in which it is possible meaningfully to affirm the present livingness of Jesus, and the only legitimate way of interpreting the Resurrection narratives in the gospels. In the next section I shall lay great emphasis on this present livingness of Jesus, and affirm this in a way that is quite independent of the emptiness or otherwise of Jesus' tomb. In this present section I seek to show that belief in the empty tomb *is not the only way* of interpreting, without rejecting, the New Testament faith that "Christ is risen".

It is often said that the first disciples could never have continued to believe and to proclaim that their master had risen if, in fact, his dead body had continued to lie in its burial place: either the authorities or, perhaps, their own doubts would soon have led to the finding and the display of that body. But this very largely depends on when and where the Resurrection faith began. If the disciples came to this faith in Jerusalem within two days of Jesus' death, and began publicly to proclaim it in the Temple precincts within two months, then these traditional arguments do have considerable force. But if the Resurrection faith arose gradually, and if the principal disciples were in fact in Galilee during the period in which this faith began, then the whole question of the tomb and the Resurrection appearances takes on a different aspect. A quick reading of the four gospels appears entirely to confirm the traditional time and place of the first appearances; but a careful study of the New Testament as a whole shows this to contain significant pointers to the existence of a tradition within the church of the New Testament period which emphasized Galilee as the scene of the Resurrection appearances, and did not insist that these were confined to so limited a period.

Let us, then, look briefly at the New Testament. All four gospels agree that the empty tomb was first found by one or more of the women who followed Jesus, and all emphasize Mary Magdalene's part in this. In Mark* and Matthew the women met an angel, who told them to inform the disciples that Jesus had risen and was going before them into Galilee, where they would all see him. Matthew adds a brief meeting with Jesus himself, who gives similar instructions. Luke's description of the finding of the empty tomb is similar to Mark's, but he locates the entire sequence from Good Friday to Pentecost in or near Jerusalem: the lovely description of the appearance on the Emmaus road is followed by that to the eleven and others in Jerusalem on Easter evening, at which reference is made to an earlier appearance to Peter.

St. John's account of Easter Day is the best known: the detailed account of Jesus' appearance to Mary Magdalene, into which is inserted the visit to the tomb by Peter and John; then the appearance on Easter night to which I have already referred; then, a week later, the appearance to Thomas and the others. Some scholars think that the fourth gospel originally ended, in Jerusalem, with Thomas's great cry of faith "my Lord and my God" and Jesus' reply, in which Thomas is both contrasted and linked with those who have believed without having seen. John 21 may have been added later, either by the evangelist himself or by a disciple: even so, it represents a significant tradition of Resurrection appearances in Galilee, in which prominence is given to Peter.†

The second half of the New Testament is full of references to

* The original ending of Mark is uncertain: 16: 9–20 is almost certainly a later addition by a different author, summarizing and conflating the other gospels in order to round off Mark. It may be that the original ending got lost: verse 8 in the Greek ends at "they were afraid for"—and St. Mark is scarcely likely to have ended with a preposition, and on this note of fear. (See the footnotes in the larger edition of the *N.E.B.*, and also the commentaries—among which R. H. Lightfoot's *The Gospel Message of St. Mark* is unusual in arguing that Mark did deliberately end his gospel at this verse and on this note of fear, or dread.)

† John 21 is, on any reckoning, far more important than Mark 16: 9–20. The latter is clearly a secondary conflation from the other gospels; John 21 is a primary source, whoever wrote it.

the Resurrection faith that Jesus is risen, is alive, is Lord. Such references are sometimes assumed to imply the writer's knowledge of, and belief in, both the empty tomb and the appearances in Jerusalem on the day of its discovery: if so, the New Testament evidence for the empty tomb becomes overwhelming. But the tomb is not specifically mentioned except in the gospels, and I would challenge any general assumption that this lies behind all St. Paul's references to the Resurrection of Christ, the most detailed of which is the fifteenth chapter of 1 Corinthians. This is the earliest document to discuss the Resurrection at any length, and in it Paul claims to do no more than repeat "that which also I received". Those who wish to make up their own mind about the empty tomb should read this chapter as a whole, and ponder the meaning of its contrasts between the natural and the spiritual, and between the body that is sown and the body that is raised. Unfortunately, there seem to be almost as many explanations as commentaries: one must ask oneself how far any particular commentator is reading meaning out of the text of this vital but difficult chapter, and how far he is reading his own presuppositions into it. Here are three significant points to consider:

1. Paul ends his list of Christ's Resurrection appearances with one to himself, and makes no distinction, except as to date, between this and the others.* This clearly implies some modification of Luke's two-phase timetable, for Paul's conversion is usually dated from two to four years after the Crucifixion. Does it also imply either that the "appearance" to Paul was *more* "physical", or that those on Easter Day were *less* "physical", than the New Testament accounts would seem to describe?

2. Paul does not refer to the empty tomb in verses 3–10, nor does he give any description of the Resurrection of Jesus beyond the statement "and that he hath been raised on the third day according to the scriptures; and that he appeared to Peter . . ."; this is followed by a list which simply says each time "he appeared to". If Paul knew about the empty tomb, why did he never mention it? If he regarded the appearances – including that to himself – as "objective" or "public" facts, why does he

* "His claim is that the resurrection appearance of Christ granted to him, albeit 'out of due time', is strictly parallel with that given to the rest of the brethren. He also had seen the Lord in His risen body." (J. A. T. Robinson, *The Body*, p. 57 f.)

never describe any of them in greater detail? (He refers to the one to himself in Gal. 1: 15 ff, where he certainly does not imply anything more "objective" than an inward vision.)

3. In this chapter Paul is up against two problems: the delay of the expected Second Coming, which was a major stumbling-block to the faith of the early Church; and the fact that "some of you say there is no resurrection of the dead" (verse 12, *N.E.B.*). Our present concern is with this second problem, which perhaps shows that some at Corinth were influenced by Hellenistic ideas of immortality, and found the Jewish and Pharisaic doctrine of Resurrection crude and improbable. Paul tackles this by going a long way towards accommodating these Hellenistic ideas. He draws repeated and emphatic contrasts between the natural body and the spiritual body, between the mortal and the immortal.*

Now perhaps the principal reason why belief in the empty tomb is widely assumed to be implicit in this and other Pauline passages is the author's Jewish and indeed Pharisaic background. "Paul cannot relinquish the bodily resurrection idea in spite of the difficulties."† But this chapter indicates the extent to which Hellenistic ideas of immortality had influenced even the thinking of Paul. It therefore prompts this final double question: are we so sure that in this matter we *can* estimate the effective background of Paul's thought? Is it not possible that we approach this problem with minds unduly influenced by the Resurrection narratives in the gospels?

A few days after the opening verses of this chapter had been read during morning chapel an intelligent schoolboy, who at least partly regretted being unable to accept the Christian faith, told me that he had for the first time begun to regard the Resurrection as a possibility: "I had always heard it read from the gospels, which speak of Jesus' resuscitated corpse. I couldn't begin to believe this – but Paul says nothing about it, and he speaks with authority because he says he had one of these visions himself." The boy's description of the gospels' claim is not, of course, accurate – though I often meet it. The actual claim is for a double miracle: first, that the body of Jesus ceased

---

* In particular verse 50: "Now this I say, brethren, that flesh and blood cannot inherit the kingdom of God; neither doth corruption inherit incorruption."

† J. McLeman, *Resurrection Then and Now*, p. 112.

to exist as a physical object – the tomb was found empty, and the grave clothes unmoved;* second, that Jesus then showed himself, always only to disciples, using the same scarred body, yet now so different that he could make it appear and disappear at will, even behind closed doors. Each appearance is described as a separate miracle: there is, for example, no suggestion that Jesus hurried back from Emmaus to Jerusalem late on Easter afternoon.

Descriptions of the Resurrection of Christ along traditional lines normally assume the main details of time and place in Luke, Acts and John 20 to be historical. But these details are not above suspicion. Firstly, there is the sharp conflict between Jerusalem and Galilee for the privilege of providing the scene of the Resurrection appearances: we shall shortly return to this issue. Secondly, Acts is our only evidence that Peter began proclaiming the Resurrection in Jerusalem within seven weeks of the Crucifixion, and Luke's account leaves little room either for the gradual renewal of Peter's faith in Galilee, which is clearly implied by the fishing scenes in John 21, or for the appearance to "about five hundred brethren at once" (1 Corinthians 15: 6), which St. Paul emphasized by adding in parenthesis that most of them were still alive when he wrote. A Resurrection appearance to even three hundred people would be extremely difficult to fit into the timetable of Luke-Acts.†

* St. John's detailed description of the grave clothes – including the napkin, which was found "wrapped together in a place by itself" (20: 7) – is surely a deliberate contrast to the raising of Lazarus, who "came forth, bound hand and foot with grave-clothes: and his face was bound about with a napkin" (11: 44). The implication seems clear: that Lazarus emerged through the opening in his tomb, whereas God's raising of Jesus began with the removal of his body from within the grave clothes, which remained undisturbed as the body – as I put it above – ceased to exist as a physical object. (This last phrase may be cumbersome, but I prefer it to the verb "dematerialize" which is sometimes used in this connection.)

† According to Acts 1: 15 there were not as many as five hundred followers of Jesus in Jerusalem until after Pentecost, and even the Mount of Olives scarcely provides the Jerusalem area with a suitable setting for an appearance to so large a number, granted that all these appearances possessed a sufficient element of privacy to be *limited* to the followers of Jesus. This appearance has been equated with the gift of the Spirit at Pentecost: Dr. Dodd has described this as "pure speculation"; on practical grounds it seems more probable that it took place in Galilee. Furthermore, even in Galilee, a gathering of this number of believers must presuppose a period of time during which the Resurrection faith had been proclaimed.

Once the details of time and place in the Resurrection narratives cease to be sacrosanct, the authorities' failure to produce the body becomes just one factor in an unanswerable conundrum, for which we have far too little firm evidence. The Jews did not have a modern Criminal Investigation Department; Pilate was probably quite unwilling to help. I do not believe that one can profitably discuss "Who moved the stone?" along these lines. The real alternative to belief in the empty tomb is to regard the Resurrection narratives *not* as describing a series of partly-historical events *but* as conveying the great truth that, during their "turn-round period", the disciples were in some sense *reunited* with their Lord.

Paul Tillich describes the Resurrection as "the restitution of Jesus to the dignity of the Christ in the minds of the disciples". For the rest, he is highly sceptical of the Resurrection narratives. His most recently published collection of sermons* contains one of great power entitled "God's Pursuit of Man". Its theme is that God pursues us, although we continually flee from him. The text for this sermon is the sequel to Jesus' arrest: "then all the disciples forsook him and fled". Tillich comments: "We are used to imagining the Crucifixion in terms of those beautiful pictures, where, along with his mother and other women, at least one disciple is present. The reality was different. They all fled, and some women dared to watch from afar. Only an unimaginable loneliness remained." Tillich links this with the cry "My God, my God, why hast thou forsaken me?". He admires the disciples' honesty in recording their flight (and, I would add, Peter's denial) in the gospels. Then comes this passage:

"And yet, even in the same records, man's desire to cover up his own ugliness makes itself felt. Later traditions in the gospels try to smooth the hard and hurting edges of the original picture. Apparently, it was unbearable to established congregations that all the disciples fled, that none of them witnessed the crucifixion and the death of the master. They could not accept the fact that only far away in Galilee was their flight arrested by the appearance of him whom they deserted in his hour of agony and despair. So, it was stated that Jesus had told them to go to Galilee; their flight was not a real flight. And still later, it was said that they did not flee at all, but remained in Jerusalem. From earliest times, the Church could not stand this judgement against itself, its past and its present. It has

* *The Eternal Now* (S.C.M. Press, 1963). I quote from pages 85 and 86 f.

tried to conceal what the disciples openly admitted—that we all forsook him and fled. But this is the truth about all men, including the followers of Jesus today."*

Tillich is here concerned with the initial flight of the disciples—in particular the men—and not with whether they subsequently returned to Jerusalem. He perhaps overstates his case, for there is no evident necessity for the assumption that they all fled to Galilee: they could well have scattered; "the disciple whom Jesus loved" may have stayed behind with the women, while Peter and most of the others fled to Galilee. But those who affirm Christ's Resurrection in traditional terms seldom give due weight to the point here emphasized by Tillich: it is in the *later* strands of the New Testament that the Resurrection appearances of Christ are said to have centred in Jerusalem; the earliest documents emphasize Galilee. In Mark 16: 1–8 the disciples are ordered to go to Galilee as soon as the empty tomb has been discovered. In 1 Corinthians 15 Paul emphasizes that the Risen Christ appeared to Peter: he does not say where this occurred, but it is the Galilee and not the Jerusalem Resurrection narratives that give the greater prominence to Peter.†

As I endeavour to study the Resurrection narratives dispassionately—something that is never easy for a Christian—I am forced to admit that there is a far higher degree of discrepancy as to details of time, place, etc., as between these various narratives than there is between the different accounts of any period of Jesus' life before his Crucifixion. Comparison of these narratives presents both a minor and a major difficulty. The minor difficulty is that several of the Resurrection appearances listed in 1 Corinthians 15 do not appear anywhere in the gospels—notably the appearance to Peter that heads this list. Dr. Dodd has made an interesting comment here: he commends St. Paul for passing on the list as he himself "received" it, and for resisting any temptation to "write it up"; "otherwise, what a story we might have had of the appearance of Christ which was (to judge from various indications) crucial for the whole

* Tillich here implies that the synoptic gospels were written in the order Mark, Matthew, Luke: not all would agree that Matthew preceded Luke, but this is not greatly material to Tillich's argument, the force of which can be judged by comparing the gospels in that order, in particular Mark 16: 7./ Matthew 28: 7, 10/Luke 24: 6, 7.

† Notably John 21, Mark 16: 7, and—if it belongs to Easter—the conversation near Caesarea Philippi.

history of the Church, but which has inexplicably failed to enter into the Gospels!"* It may be, however, that Peter's great confession of faith "Thou art the Christ" in fact belongs to the Easter period, and specifically relates to this first and crucial Resurrection appearance.

The major difficulty is reflected in these words written by Dr. A. M. Ramsey: "The accounts of the appearances of Jesus are difficult to harmonize into a coherent story. The events of the first Easter are difficult to form into a consecutive plan."† It is often said that the narratives can be harmonized by assuming that the first Resurrection appearances took place in Jerusalem, after which all or most of the disciples went for a short time to Galilee, returning to Jerusalem before Pentecost.‡ But the Galilee narratives do seem to have the purpose of renewing the disciples' faith, in a way that would scarcely have been necessary if there had been a number of earlier appearances in Jerusalem. I cannot avoid the conclusion that if there were appearances in both places these *began* – at least as regards the (male) apostles – in Galilee. "The appearances of the risen Lord probably were not confined to Galilee but also occurred at Jerusalem after the disciples had returned there."§

James McLeman advances this viewpoint one stage further by suggesting that the Galilee tradition "arose through concentration on the primary fact that the first awareness of the total event must have been private", whilst the Jerusalem tradition arose "through concentration on the fact that the reference of the total event is public, indeed universal": in its desire to emphasize Jerusalem as the birthplace of the Church, Luke-Acts excludes all reference to Resurrection appearances in Galilee. He also suggests that the evident need to convince doubters will have led to increasing pressure on the original disciples to make their testimony as convincing as possible, and therefore to push back the first dawning of their Easter faith and bring this as near, in both time and place, to the death of Jesus as would carry conviction – and thus to the tomb, at dawn

* From C. H. Dodd, "The Appearances of the Risen Christ: an Essay in Form – Criticism of the Gospels," in *Studies in the Gospels,* ed. Nineham, p. 29.
† *The Resurrection of Christ,* Fontana edition, p. 48.
‡ Thus, for example, William Lilly's essay, "The Empty Tomb and the Resurrection," in *Historicity and Chronology in the New Testament* (S.P.C.K., 1965).
§ Bultmann, *Theology of the New Testament,* vol. I, p. 45.

on the third day. (There was a contemporary belief that the spirit of a dead person hovered about the body until the third day, so that if it had been said that Jesus rose earlier than this people could have said that he had never died.)

"But the public manifestation of the event must be subsequent to the private aspect—indeed, consequent on it. The beginning of the Church as the agent of the Gospel in the world is possible only because the necessary dynamic for its creation is already a reality in someone's consciousness. And it is this facet of the event which is creative to the Galilee tradition. Priority in time belongs to Galilee. Priority in importance as far as Luke-Acts is concerned belongs to Jerusalem. These two priorities are not mutually exclusive. The total event embraces them both ... The Jerusalem tradition can be understood if it follows the Galilee tradition, but not vice versa."*

None of these views of the Resurrection narratives can escape dispassionate as well as passionate criticism. Both Tillich and Bultmann appear at times to overstate their case. Tillich is not primarily a New Testament scholar. Bultmann's approach to the New Testament is regarded with suspicion by many scholars in this field. Dr. Robinson says of him "the fact that he regards *so much* of the Gospel history as expendable (e.g. the empty tomb *in toto*) is due to the fact that purely in his capacity as a New Testament critic he is extremely, and I believe unwarrantably, distrustful of the tradition".† Such criticism may be justified: Dr. Robinson is himself a notable New Testament scholar. But it could be that our great Anglican scholarship in the New Testament field has suffered in recent years from being too conservative.

Be that as it may, the Churches in Britain have certainly been too insular: many people are uncertain, to say the least, as to the empty tomb, yet until very recently only our scholars have had any inkling of the scope of contemporary criticism of it. Tillich and Bultmann are now discussed in our theological colleges, but their interpretation of the Resurrection of Jesus remains little known in our parishes and schools.‡ Their general point of view is too widely held to be regarded as belonging to one particular school of thought; its contemporary exponents are usually more positive in their approach than the old

* *Resurrection Then and Now*, p. 152.
† *Honest to God*, p. 35.
‡ *Honest to God* is of no help here: it contains no reference to the empty tomb, except in the brief criticism of Bultmann quoted above.

"modernists", and are far less concerned to remove "miracle" than to emphasize the disciples' vital element of *personal decision* during the period following their Master's Crucifixion.

"The decision which Jesus' disciples had once made to affirm and accept his sending by 'following' him, had to be made anew and radically in consequence of his crucifixion. *The cross*, so to say, raised the question of decision once more. Little as it could throw into question the content of his message, all the more it could and did render questionable his legitimation, his claim to be God's messenger bringing the last, decisive word. The Church had to surmount the scandal of the cross and did it in the Easter faith."*

This concept of the disciples reaching the Easter faith *through* the scandal of the cross has close analogies in psychiatry. A patient can often be led out of serious mental illness only by first going back into the depths of his anguish, seeing this for what it is or was, and then – and only then – beginning to emerge from its grip. Bultmann suggests that the Easter faith arose, not from unique visible and tangible Resurrection appearances, but from the disciples' re-thinking, *out of the depths of their despair,* of the meaning and value of Jesus' whole life of self-giving love and utter obedience to God.

Tillich tentatively advances what he called his "restitution theory", according to which the Resurrection is "the restitution of Jesus to the dignity of the Christ in the minds of the disciples", "a restitution which is rooted in the personal unity between Jesus and God and in the impact of this unity on the minds of the apostles".† Both Tillich and Bultmann insist on the importance of the fact that the disciples' experience of the power of God in Jesus' ministry *preceded* their Resurrection faith – however fragmentary, however little understood, that earlier experience may have been at the time. Tillich's word "restitution" implies a restoration: it should also be emphasized that this rekindled faith reached a far deeper level, and like their new-found courage proved far more persistent, than anything that had preceded it.

Any suggestion that the Resurrection appearances were "less" than visible – and perhaps tangible – visitations may attract the charge of making them "purely subjective", self-generated in the disciples' minds, whereas the four gospels and St. Paul's

* R. Bultmann, *Theology of the New Testament*, vol. I, p. 44 f.
† *Systematic Theology*, vol. II, p. 182.

letters all agree that the Resurrection experience came from outside: "he appeared *to* Peter". The old phrase "telegrams from heaven" was intended to safeguard this aspect; the writers we are now considering preserve this divine priority by insisting that the first Resurrection faith was a rekindling and deepening of what had gone before. As they relived old memories, the total life and action of Jesus suddenly had a far greater impact than it had ever had before that entire action came to be seen in perspective.

But if the impact of Jesus was now greater, so was the stumbling block. The first rekindling of their faith came at the moment when they began to *accept* the death of Jesus, rather than rebel against it. They very soon needed to explain it as well as accept it. "The rise of the Easter faith made necessary *a way of understanding the cross* that would surmount, yes, transform, the scandal of the curse which in Jewish opinion had befallen the crucified Jesus (cf. Galatians 3: 13)."* They did this by coming to see his death as an expiatory sacrifice. Convinced at last of Jesus' messiahship, they remembered how he had died as the passover lambs were being slain, and how the previous night he had enacted his death with bread and wine, and described it as being *for them,* and as a new covenant. They also remembered the "Servant" prophecies of Isaiah. Perhaps Paul did indeed repeat the faith of the very earliest Church when he claimed to have "delivered unto you first of all that which also I received, how that Christ died for our sins according to the scriptures".† Bultmann emphasizes this juxtaposition of "for our sins" and "according to the scriptures". He affirms that "faith in the Resurrection is nothing other than faith in the cross as the salvation-event, or, as may also be said, as the cross of Christ."‡

The last quotation shows very clearly two of the advantages which accompany this way of thinking. First, as I have said, it bridges the gulf between us and the disciples. All down the centuries Christians have felt God's forgiveness of their sins to be closely linked with the death of Jesus. If we humbly accept that death and all that it implies, then we, like Peter and Mary

* Bultmann, the same, p. 45 (his italics).
† 1 Corinthians 15: 3. Scholars have suggested that in these verses Paul is quoting a very early credal formula: thus E. G. Selwyn in *A New Commentary on Holy Scripture*, N.T., p. 302.
‡ Quoted from "Kerygma and Myth", I, p. 41 in S. C. Ogden, *Christ without Myth*, p. 99.

Magdalene, will feel the power of God's forgiving love, and join in their Resurrection faith. Secondly, if faith in the Resurrection, acceptance of the cross, and the belief that God forgives sins, are three aspects of the same thing, then the death of Jesus is automatically freed from any suggestion of a transaction, a making possible of something (namely God's forgiveness of our deepest penitence) which had not been possible before. God's forgiving love has always been available, and is not confined to Christendom. But we feel the power of that forgiving love most deeply as we come in contact with the total act of Jesus' life and death, which also brings us to deepest penitence by its sharp contrast with our own self-centred motives.

Some will find great advantage in the fact that these views on the Resurrection avoid the need to believe in a contraphysical miracle. I prefer to put it differently: these views avoid all suggestion of a divine intervention so catastrophic as temporarily to remove the disciples' free will. It is true that, in Jesus' parable, Abraham tells Lazarus that his brothers would not be persuaded even if one rose from the dead. But if the tomb was found to be empty, after which Jesus appeared repeatedly, ate food with his disciples, and continued his earlier teaching so as to underline its meaning, then this must have amounted to divine compulsion of the disciples. The viewpoint we are considering assumes no such compulsion at any time. (This may seem a great advantage to some, but it would be unsound philosophy to regard it as decisive. It is our present experience that neither human free will nor the normal processes of nature are subjected to, or interrupted by, divine compulsion; but we cannot state categorically that this is impossible even in a unique instance. The gospels, and the tradition of the Christian Church, are *prima facie* evidence that such a unique instance did occur.)

This brings me to the obvious disadvantages of the various "liberal" interpretations of the Resurrection of Jesus. First, they involve taking a very critical attitude as to the detailed reliability of the narratives in the gospels. I have quoted Dr. Robinson's criticism of Bultmann on these grounds, and commented upon it. The degree of reliability of these narratives is primarily a matter for those scholars who are specialists in the New Testament and its background. My personal view – I am not one of those scholars – is that the gospels do give a fairly reliable account of the ministry and teaching of Jesus, although this is coloured by the later beliefs of the New Testament Church: it is often, of course, extremely difficult to distinguish the former from the latter. In the case of the Resurrection narratives, the far greater discrepancies between them would seem to indicate that they are less historically reliable than the main body of the gospels. It would also seem only reasonable to *expect* a considerable heightening of the miraculous element within the New Testament, as there is in so many other writings of the ancient world. But it remains questionable whether the historical events of the first Easter are likely to have followed so *very* different a course from that described in Luke 24 and John 20.

Secondly, this approach to the Resurrection of Christ differs greatly from that of most of Christendom. Sadly, this is all too true. The traditional interpretation of the Resurrection is a major item in the religious belief of many churchgoers in most branches or denominations of Christ's Church. It is also a major stumbling-block to many outside—and to a largely silent minority inside — the body of regular worshippers. But here most of all — whatever the relative numbers adhering to either viewpoint — it is the *truth* for which we must all strive, as best we may.

Thirdly, this way of thinking removes the main plank from any attempt to quote miracle as *proof* of the divinity of Christ, an attempt which we find in the gospels themselves. I can only say that I just *cannot* regard this as a disadvantage: was not Jesus himself highly critical of those who were continually "seeking a sign"? And yet a "sign" of some sort was given to the followers of Jesus: "events do commonly have causes; there must, for example, have been something that somehow aroused the belief that one who had suffered what was in Jewish eyes the ultimate degradation of being hanged on a tree (Galatians 3: 13), was alive and present with his disciples".* In my view, the continuing existence and vitality of the apostolic Church is evidence both that "there must have been something" and that this "something" must have transcended the minds of the disciples: the "telegrams" must have come *from heaven*; there would seem to be no place for this in some "radical" interpretations of the Resurrection, *until* these are supplemented by process thinking.

* W. Lilly, "The Empty Tomb and the Resurrection," in *Historicity and Chronology in the New Testament,* p. 119 f.

Before turning to that task, let us summarize this section of our discussion. There are some people who reject the possibility that either the Bible or the Church *could* be even superficially misleading on a major item of faith, either because of their interpretation of "inspiration" or because they simply cannot believe that God would have allowed so widespread an error. Others will assume that God *never* interferes with free will, or maybe with science: for them this "liberal" viewpoint may be the only possible road to the Christian faith. My own plea is that *both* of these are *a priori* assumptions, and both are incapable of proof. Each extreme viewpoint on the Resurrection is coherent, and makes out a case for itself. *They should be allowed to stand side by side,* as they do in many churches. It is the various compromises between these views that prove to be invalid. If the newer viewpoint is correct, it will gradually substantiate itself: if it is not, it will fall away — as Gamaliel's advice to the Council implied:

"If this counsel or this work be of men, it will be overthrown: but if it is of God, ye will not be able to overthrow them; less haply ye be found even to be fighting against God."*

* Acts 5: 38 f. Thus the report *Doctrine in the Church of England* contains (pp. 83–88) two viewpoints as to exactly what lay behind "the unanimous faith or conviction of the earliest Christians that Jesus was risen and alive from the dead". These two viewpoints are founded upon a wide area of common ground as to the significance of Christ's Resurrection. The Commission are agreed in seeing this as the Father's vindication of Jesus, the victory of God over the powers of evil: they also see it as an indication of the Christian answer to suffering, and a confirmation of man's hope of immortality. But, as they put it, "When we attempt to go behind the *kerygma* [or apostolic proclamation], and ask 'What was it exactly that happened?' a variety of answers is possible." Two such answers are given in an Appended Note (pp. 86–88):
"To some of us it appears to be of vital importance that the supremacy of spirit should be vindicated *in* the material creation, and not merely outside or apart from it. In their view it is essential to the full Christian hope that the physical dissolution of life should be reversed by resurrection; and the basing of this hope on Jesus becomes intelligible and justifiable only if it is believed that His physical organism underwent some such transformation as the Gospel narratives suggest . . . Others of us who would not bind themselves so closely to traditional beliefs would urge, nevertheless, that both in the Apostles' Creed and the Pauline Epistles the resurrection of the dead and the Resurrection of Christ are made correlative the one to the other, and that the beliefs are connected not only by their historical origin, but also in their essential nature. They would maintain that the general freedom long claimed and used in the interpretation of the clause, 'the resurrection of the flesh', cannot leave the interpretation of the other clause, 'the third day he rose again from the dead', unaffected."

"Jesus is Lord"

"Both the individual Christian and the gathered Church experience in faith the fact that Jesus lives and continues his work. The Church as the Body of Christ is founded on faith in the exalted Christ who still intervenes in earthly events. The first Christians expressed this deep conviction in their confession of faith *Kyrios Jesus*, 'Jesus is Lord'."*

Thus, as Luke records it in Acts 2, St. Peter's great Pentecost speech reaches its climax with the cry "God has made him both Lord and Christ, this Jesus whom you crucified". The lordship of Jesus is here proclaimed with – even given verbal precedence over – his messiahship, and both are set firmly in the context of his Resurrection. This close linking together of Jesus' lordship and Resurrection – again in that order – is also found in Paul's letter to the church in Rome: "If on your lips is the confession, 'Jesus is Lord', in your heart the faith that God raised him from the dead, then you will find salvation".† The great New Testament scholar Oscar Cullmann cites this verse, Philippians 2: 11, and 1 Corinthians 12: 3 as the clearest evidence that the cry *"Kyrios Jesus"*, "Jesus is Lord", was in regular use as a confession of faith in Paul's day.

On the verse from Romans just quoted, Cullmann comments: "It is significant that to 'confess with the lips' quite self-evidently refers to this one confession, 'Jesus is *Kyrios*'. This is without doubt *the* confession, the 'original confession' which includes all others. When the topic is simply 'confession', this is the formula which forces itself upon Paul's mind. It is thus unquestionable that already before him this formula was in general liturgical use."‡ The cry "Jesus is Lord" reverberates in various forms through the Acts and the Epistles, and we use its equivalent each time we end a prayer with the words "through Jesus Christ our Lord".

The two affirmations "Christ is risen" and "Jesus is Lord"

* O. Cullmann, *The Christology of The New Testament* (1957), p. 195. (Quotations are from the English edition, S.C.M. Press, 1959.) A full treatment of the affirmation *Kyrios Jesus* would involve a detailed consideration of the word *Kyrios* and its probable meaning in this phrase. Cullmann does this with great care (pp. 195–237). Suffice it to say here that in this cry of faith *Kyrios* almost certainly carries the meaning "divine ruler", as did the Aramaic *Mar* in the liturgical cry of the first Aramaic-speaking Church *Maranatha*, "Lord, come!"
† Romans 10: 9 (N.E.B.).
‡ Page 217.

are both *in the present tense*, and both express truths that apply in the present as much as in the first generation of the Christian Church. But "Jesus is Lord" directly expresses the present lordship of Jesus, whereas "Christ is risen" has a primary reference to the events following Christ's Crucifixion, although it also expresses the Easter faith in the all-important present tense.

My difficulty with what can for simplicity be described as the Bultmann approach to the Resurrection of Jesus is that — unless and until it is reinforced by the insights made available by process philosophy — it fails to attach any real meaning to this present tense of Jesus' Resurrection, however admirably (or otherwise) it may express the minds of the original disciples during the Easter period.

Tillich's doctrine of God seems to fail to account for our experience of receiving "revelation" and "grace" *from* God. In a not dissimilar way, Bultmann's doctrine of the Resurrection of Jesus seems to fail to account for *our* experience of the risen Christ. Theological doctrines do not become true simply because we want them to be, nor are they necessarily inadequate simply because they fail to account for aspects of our inevitably subjective experience. But throughout the Christian era the followers of Jesus have believed that they experience the living presence and power of Jesus as they meet together for prayer and, in particular, for the Holy Communion. This experience of the living Jesus may be a personalized form of the more general experience of the grace of God, but it is a highly significant form.

We have seen how process philosophy *requires* the existence of the living God, who supplies to every entity its "initial conceptual aim". A philosophy cannot require the existence of Jesus, let alone his present "livingness". But in what follows I attempt to show that this concept of the livingness of Jesus is entirely compatible with a philosophy of process, and that this way of thinking helps us to interpret his livingness in a way that *also applies to ourselves.*

I must first draw attention to the confusion that may well arise from the two different ways in which belief in the Resurrection of Jesus is used in Christian circles. The traditional picture of the Resurrection of Jesus is partly used as evidence for his divinity, for which it is well suited. But it is also used as evidence for *our* future resurrection, or at least as the main grounds for our hope of resurrection: the traditional picture is far less suited to this second task. As William Lilly admits:

"There is one thing to be said against a corporeal resurrection. St. Paul taught in I Corinthians 15 not only that the Resurrection of Jesus is the ground of the Christian hope of life after death, but also that there is an analogy between the Resurrection of Jesus and that of Christian believers (vv. 20–23). This analogy breaks down in the fact that in the case of no Christian believer has the physical body left the grave and been recognized by those who knew previously the person whose body it was."*

My rather mathematical mind finds it in no way surprising that the more one emphasizes the uniqueness both of the person and of the Resurrection of Jesus, the harder it becomes to see his Resurrection as in any way analogous to ourselves. This could lead some Christians to want further grounds for their own hope of resurrection. Protestant Christendom was hurt and upset when Pope John's predecessor, Pius XII, pronounced the Assumption of the Blessed Virgin Mary to be a dogma of the Roman Church.† But many Roman Catholics were deeply pleased; indeed there had been repeated petitions for such a dogma from 1870 onwards. It would be easy to assume that this was entirely motivated by a desire for the greater veneration of Mary. But the writer Graham Greene made the interesting suggestion that behind it may also lie the feeling that the bodily assumption into heaven of the highest of mortals conveys a greater assurance than does the Resurrection of a divine being.‡ Greene is in fact suggesting that what happened to Mary is considered to be more relevant *to us* than what happened to Jesus.

The newer viewpoint I have outlined sees the initial Resurrection faith not as a separate piece of evidence for the divinity of Christ but rather as the first deep and permanent awareness of that divine indwelling in Jesus which makes him both Lord and Christ. Its adherents do not need to turn to Mary for an

* "The Empty Tomb and the Resurrection," in *Historicity and Chronology in the New Testament*, p. 131.

† According to this dogma, St Mary's body was assumed (or taken) into heaven at, or shortly after, her death.

‡ Greene's article is quoted by H. Chadwick in the *Journal of Theological Studies*, October 1951, p. 164; the original article is in *Life*, international edition, 20th November, 1950.

assurance of what Whitehead calls "everlastingness". The "everlastingness" of Jesus is to be found in the fact that the Church continues to cry "Jesus is Lord", and continues to believe in the presence of Christ where Christans meet together for prayer or sacrament. And if there is no abrupt and complete distinction between Jesus and his saints, then the "everlastingness" or "livingness" of Jesus *does indeed offer both hope and relevance to us, his followers.*

I have suggested that throughout his ministry – and indeed before it – Jesus "prehended" God to the uttermost: he turned to God in self-giving prayer and in deep meditation upon the scriptures. It was in this prayer and meditation that he both asked God to show him how to use his life and learned God's reply; this was itself intertwined with Jesus' total environment, including the scriptures. Jesus never deviated from the implications of that reply, as he interpreted them. Thus the total action of Jesus was devoid of self-interest and filled instead with God's grace and power, which showed itself in Jesus' deep love for all men; "God was in Christ, reconciling the world unto himself". Whether or not the disciples glimpsed this at all fully before the Crucifixion, whether or not they were given a unique corroboration of it at Easter, those who had known and followed Jesus in the flesh continued for the rest of their lives to be powerfully aware both of the past presence of God in the total action of Jesus as they remembered it, and in the *continuing* presence with them of that total action or, as they thought of it, of Jesus himself.

Now one does not normally distinguish between one's memory or recollection of another person and one's memory of that person's actions. It is the remembered actions, small and great, which convey the person to us. Is this not precisely what happens in the Church today? Groups of Christians are particularly conscious of the presence of Christ when they meet together for the Holy Communion, or for an evangelistic service based on the reading and proclaiming of the gospels. In each case, they deliberately bring themselves into contact with a part of the total action of Jesus: in the Holy Communion they make memorial of his death and re-create the Last Supper; in other services, and in our individual meditation on the gospels, we deliberately bring ourselves alongside Jesus. The sense of Jesus' presence may seem less vivid in this modern age, but it often runs deeper than people realize. It may suddenly be felt in moments of prayer to God the Father when there is no explicit thought of Jesus Christ, and in vital moments of decision when there is no conscious thought of God at all. Those who have sensed God most powerfully in and through part of the total action of Jesus will equate Jesus with his total action, and equate both with God. They will be in good company: the earliest Church did the same. And the great truth which they sense matters far more than any imprecision in their reception of it.

It is important to remember this when pondering Tillich's words about the difficulty of overcoming "the identification of the medium with the content of revelation."* Whitehead expressed the same thought in a wider frame of reference with his phrase "the fallacy of misplaced concreteness".† We succumb to this fallacy if we try to insist that Jesus' presence in prayer and sacrament is that of a second experiencing subject alongside ourselves, or that God was present as a second experiencing subject "within" Jesus of Nazareth. The danger in this is that those who feel such insistence to be fallacious may not go on to search for the greater truth, the content of the revelation, which lies beyond: the truth that Jesus so "prehended" God, so opened his whole being to God, that God was indeed powerfully present in him and in his total action, which fact we in our turn prehend today.

Jesus, or to be more precise the total action of Jesus, lives on in his Church, and thus possesses a livingness and everlastingness which is, however, dependent on the continuity of the Church, or at any rate of the race of *homo sapiens*. But his total action is literally everlasting in that it is included, and completely included, within the consequent nature of God. I have not embarked on a detailed study of what Whitehead calls " 'negative prehensions', which are said to 'eliminate from feeling' ": thus a concrescing subject can in some measure reject elements in its environment by prehending them negatively. There are no "negative prehensions" in the primordial nature of God, but it is not said that there are none in his consequent nature. I have assumed that God can and does prehend negatively in this respect, and there is therefore a sense in which

* See above, chapter five.
† See particularly *Science and the Modern World*, pp. 64–72.

our good actions achieve an everlastingness in God's consequent nature which our evil actions, mercifully, do not.*

If, as Christians believe and the New Testament affirms, Jesus completely opened himself to God, "prehended" God to the uttermost, then his total action will have been in conformity with God's aim for him: there was nothing of Jesus that God needed to reject, so God made only positive prehensions of Jesus' life and actions, the whole of which thus came to be included within God's consequent nature, and is therefore everlasting. In this sense Jesus – or if we must be precise the total action of Jesus – "ascended into heaven", and *is* "seated at the right hand of God". In prehending God we prehend not his primordial but his consequent nature, and as we do so we find that the total action of Jesus forms an element in God's consequent nature which is particularly accessible to us: this is equivalent to saying, in traditional terms, that the incarnate Jesus and the risen Lord together represent the most complete and the most comprehensible revelation of God that we in this life are capable of receiving,

God's power and grace and Jesus' own human decisions are so parallel, so inextricably intertwined, as to defy all human unravelling. In any Christology, the element of mystery remains. All one can hope to do is to express this in terms which may be the more meaningful because they do not conflict with one's other thinking; and then to show that these terms preserve the fundamental truth which underlies the more traditional expressions of Christological belief. The danger of "misplaced concreteness" is that in a largely scientific age the man in the pew, and perhaps the preacher in the pulpit, is likely to take it literally, and to say things which others regard as meaningless. But any element of "misplaced concreteness" which Whiteheadian thinking discloses is of small importance compared with the great truths which it enables us both to affirm and to bring into line with our other thinking: God was in Christ; Christ has been raised to the "right hand" of God; and his Resurrection, his *livingness, is* real evidence for our own.

* See above, chapter four, p. 136, especially the quotation from R. B. Cattell in which he supports the view taken here.

CHAPTER EIGHT

Conclusion

THE significance for Christian thought and theology of the "philosophy of process" can be summed up in four phrases of Whitehead's that have recurred throughout this book:

1. "God is not to be treated as an exception to all metaphysical principles, invoked to save their collapse. He is their chief exemplification." (I paraphrased this by saying that "God keeps the rules".)

2. "The divine element in the world is to be conceived as a persuasive agency and not as a coercive agency."*

3. "The fallacy of misplaced concreteness."

4. More symbolic than the other three: "God is the great companion – the fellow-sufferer who understands."

The first two have both positive and negative aspects: their positive significance for theology is underlined by Whitehead's further statement that "God is an actual entity" – or, in Hartshorne's thinking, a sequence of actual entities – and that God and all other entities mutually "prehend" each other, as the fourth phrase implies.

Whitehead's third phrase, "the fallacy of misplaced concreteness", is also important, but is entirely negative. Throughout this book I have concentrated as far as possible upon the *positive* aspects and consequences of process thinking: indeed the primary *raison d'être* for this book is its author's conviction that process thinking offers contemporary radical theology a fundamentally positive means of expression for the central truths of the Christian faith. We return to these positive aspects in the final section of this book.

"The fallacy of misplaced concreteness"

The urgent need for a more positive radical theology must not obscure the complementary need to prune away unsound

---

* As we saw in chapter three, Whitehead derived this from Plato.

doctrinal forms and over-statements – mostly due to "the fallacy of misplaced concreteness" – if the Christian faith is to continue to attract thoughtful people, and is to overcome the charge of falsity with which our first chapter began.

We have considered this need in relation to the concept of the unqualified omnipotence of God, and in relation to the tendency to over-emphasize the uniqueness and the divinity of Jesus in ways that seem to preclude his full humanity. We have applied Whitehead's "fallacy of misplaced concreteness" to the concepts of individual resurrection and of individual immortality, and seen how Whitehead and Hartshorne have reinterpreted these concepts. This reinterpretation may at first have seemed almost a denial of resurrection – and this precisely because our role is seen as less individual and thus, to our self-centred minds, less "concrete": but our subsequent thinking about the Resurrection of Jesus interpreted his present *livingness* as the "chief exemplification" of a livingness or resurrection that can also apply to us.

We have not yet considered the doctrine of the Trinity. The doctrines of Christ and of the Trinity are closely connected in Christian theology: indeed this is inevitable, since the person of Christ forms the second person of the Trinity. The "fallacy of misplaced concreteness" therefore sounds a warning to Trinitarian as to Christological thought. But whereas process philosophy has also an important positive contribution to make to the doctrine of Christ, it can only contribute positively to one facet of the doctrine of the Trinity. It is mainly for this reason that the doctrine of the Trinity does not feature in the main chapters of this book and will here be only briefly discussed.*

As we shall see, the one facet of this doctrine that is reinforced by process thinking is also the one that receives support in two penetrating but highly critical essays on the doctrine of the Trinity written, quite independently, in 1956–7. One author,

* A further reason is that this doctrine is not in the forefront of contemporary thought. Those who are concerned to think out their beliefs may wish to consider the person of Jesus Christ, and to ensure that their thinking about God includes not only the transcendence or otherness of the Father but also –and more emphasized today–the nearness of his invisible presence or Spirit: they are less interested in combining all this in a single doctrine. But the regular churchgoer–asked to make frequent use of Trinitarian formulae and occasionally to sing hyms about "Three in One and One in Three"– does come up against the doctrine of the Trinity, and is often puzzled by it.

Cyril C. Richardson* of Union Theological Seminary, New York, will have been aware of the general lines of process thinking, and his underlying philosophy shows a certain affinity to that of Charles Hartshorne. But the other author, Maurice Wiles,† Dean of Clare College, Cambridge, had not, I think, been influenced in any way by process thinking. This makes it the more interesting that his conclusions as to the doctrine of the Trinity are similar to those that can be associated with process philosophy.

The doctrine of the Trinity is not specifically to be found in the New Testament. It emerged later, fulfilling the need felt by the early Church to affirm beyond all doubt the divinity both of Jesus Christ and of the Holy Spirit. We cannot concern ourselves with how this doctrine emerged: the history of this is more complex than in the case of the doctrine of Christ, on which indeed Trinitarian thinking has always been partly dependent. The doctrine of the Trinity has fulfilled two historic functions that continue to be of vital importance today. It has emphasized that God is not limited to one mode of self-revelation: we can both "prehend" and learn of him as Father, as Son, and as Holy Spirit. It has also insisted that the God whom we address as Father, the God whom we meet in Christ, and the divine Spirit who inspires us are *all one with* the Creator-God from whom we originate, and in whom we live and move: there are not three Gods but one God; there are no demi-gods, nor grades within the Godhead – "but the Godhead of the Father, of the Son, and of the Holy Ghost, is all one: the glory equal, the majesty co-eternal".‡

The doctrine of the Trinity thus posits *unity-in-multiplicity* both in God's self-revelation and in his own inner nature. This same unity-in-multiplicity is also to be found, though in different terms, in the various aspects of process thought that have been examined in this book. We find it in the phrase "The many become one, and are increased by one", which Whitehead uses in describing his "category of the ultimate". We find it in the concept of God supplying its "initial conceptual aim" – the

* *The Doctrine of the Trinity* (Abingdon Press, New York, 1958).
† "Some Reflections on the Origins of the Doctrine of the Trinity", in *The Journal of Theological Studies*, April 1957, p. 92 ff.
‡ "Athanasian" creed, verse 6: the creed goes on to apply equally to all three Persons the adjectives "uncreate", "incomprehensible", "eternal" and "almighty".

starting-point for its own "subjective aim" – to every entity, and thus to the sticks, the stones, the living things: we see this in another way when we recall the thought that God's persuasive love is the "lure" for the processes of biological evolution. We again find unity-in-multiplicity in the concept of God "prehending" all the manifold activities of the world – evil alone excepted – into his own 'consequent nature', from which his all-embracing love reflects back into the world: and we have pondered upon the thought that what Whitehead calls "the consequent nature of God" *is* what is normally called "heaven".

But the doctrine of the Trinity is not content with this unity-in-multiplicity. It also postulates an essential three-ness both in God's nature and in his self-revelation. It is this essential three-ness that is denied by both Richardson and Wiles: I here mainly follow Maurice Wiles, whose essay has not appeared in book form.* He considers several aspects of God's activity which cannot be attributed specifically to any one of the Persons of the Trinity. I here select three, with my own summary:

1. The inspiration of the Old Testament prophets: this is normally attributed to the Spirit; but by some of the Fathers to the pre-existing Son, as in Paul's "that rock was Christ" (1 Corinthians 10: 4).

2. God's presence in the Christian Church and in the eucharist: again there is confusion as between the presence of Christ and of the Spirit, and each is invoked successively in some eucharistic prayers.

3. God's work as Creator: we today normally attribute this to the Father; St. John and others to the Word or Son; and the final paragraph of the Nicene Creed to "the Holy Ghost, the Lord and giver of life".

The third aspect is the most relevant to the theme of this book, and perhaps the most important. *Creativity* is an activity of God so fundamental that it must apply to every mode or aspect or "Person" of his being. Had St. Augustine not done it for us, we would be forced to postulate some such formula as his *"opera Trinitatis ad extra indivisa sunt"* to show that "the outward activities of the Trinity are indivisible". But it is *only* through his activity that we have *any* knowledge or experience of God; if each of these aspects of his activity does not relate

* When this was written, his book *The Christian Fathers* (Hodder and Stoughton, 1966) had been announced, but not published.

specifically to one or other of three aspects of God's own nature, then how can one insist that either God's nature or his self-revelation has a Trinitarian character? "It seems absurd to claim that we are aware of the Trinitarian nature of God through the threefold character of revelation, and yet to maintain that the threefold character of revelation does not exactly correspond to the three Persons of the Trinity. Yet this dilemma faces us whatever threefold division we choose to make." (Wiles).

Both Richardson and Wiles are scholars whose special field is the history and doctrine of the early Church, and both of them adopt a primarily historical approach to the doctrine of the Trinity. Wiles argues that the assumption that God's revelation was given *in propositional form* played a big part in the formulation of this doctrine, and that if we feel bound to break away from that assumption we are driven to the logical conclusion that the attempt to attribute a Trinitarian character to revelation "is an arbitrary analysis of the activity of God, which though of value in Christian thought and devotion is not of essential significance". Closely parallel to this is Richardson's final description of this doctrine as "an artificial construct".

Both scholars are thus led to a negative conclusion as regards the essential three-ness of God; but in reaching this conclusion they offer positive support, along traditional lines, for the concept of the unity-in-multiplicity of God's nature and self-revelation. It is perhaps significant that this is the one facet of the doctrine of the Trinity to which positive support can also be given along the less traditional lines of process thinking.*

"God is the great companion"

We now return to the positive aspects of the phrases of White-head's with which this chapter began: that God is the chief exemplification of all metaphysical principles; that the divine

---

* Whitehead's thinking has been described as binitarian: (1) God, like all entities, is "dipolar"; (2) "The Holy Spirit might be described as the Consequent Nature of God, as the measure of the creative order achieved in the created world . . . " (Emmet, *Whitehead's Philosophy of Organism*, p. 255). As to (1), Whitehead strongly emphasized that the two "natures" of God are indissoluble: neither can in any sense exist on its own. As to (2), I have described the Risen Christ as also within God's "consequent nature". It is, I submit, the unity-in-multiplicity of God's nature that Whitehead's thinking affirms.

element in the world is to be conceived as a persuasive agency; and that "God is the great companion – the fellow-sufferer who understands".

The suggestion that God is the chief exemplification of principles that underlie the universe must inevitably lead into the whole question of religion and science. Some Christians have sought to overcome the "conflict" between these by maintaining that the two are separate compartments of thought and of truth, which both can and should co-exist amicably side by side. One meets this approach rather less often today, perhaps because its inherent danger has become more apparent: it may show promise of neutralizing any claim advanced in the name of science that the entire religious premiss is false; but it greatly aggravates the charge – more often made today, when abstract notions of truth are sadly at a discount – that this premiss is simply unnecessary. For if thought and truth can be divided into compartments, and if the answers to all our everyday questions can be found within the compartment labelled "science", then it may seem not unreasonable simply to ignore the compartment labelled "religion".

But if God really is the "chief exemplification" of principles that apply throughout the universe, then we must seek, not to departmentalize religion and science, but to set both within a wider unity. Indeed a fundamental reason for commending Whitehead's thinking and seeking to develop its theological implications is precisely that he both postulates a *unity* embracing all truth and all reality and also envisages God as fulfilling *a necessary role* within this unity. Part of this role is his supplying to every entity its "initial conceptual aim". Indeed this is so important that I must here summarize what was said in chapter three. Each entity's "concrescence" or process of becoming must not only start from somewhere – namely from its own past and present environment – but must also have *some* initial aim. Since the entity *is* the growing together of its prehensions it does not exist, and cannot produce its own aim, until its process or growing together has begun: thus its initial conceptual aim cannot derive from itself; nor can this derive from its physical environment, since the entity cannot prehend its environment unless it has some subjective aim with which to do so. Whitehead saw the supplying of this initial aim as a necessary part of the divine activity in the world: Hartshorne and others have developed this into the concept that God supplies a purposive element or "lure" throughout the processes of biological evolution. We have just noted how this ties in with the concept that there is a unity-in-multiplicity both in God and in the world.

Again, if God is the chief exemplification of all metaphysical principles one would not expect his biblical self-revelation to have largely relied upon a series of exceptional and unique acts and disclosures, although one cannot simply rule out the possibility of such acts. But one can, with great profit, see the New Testament as the "chief exemplification" of God's indwelling love and of his willingness to guide and inspire those who truly open themselves to his influence in self-giving prayer: and the Old Testament as a foretaste of this in the life of a nation and its prophets. Here again process thinking is in line with other contemporary thinking: to repeat one phrase of our earlier quotation from Leonard Hodgson, "if God is one and is faithful and true there will be a self-consistency in his self-revelation".*

We now come to Whitehead's statement that the divine element in the world is to be conceived as persuasive and not coercive. The underlying point here is Whitehead's intuition that we "prehend" all other entities, including God, actively and not passively: an entity is entirely dependent on God for its initial conceptual aim, but in all other respects the entity is the subject grasping at its environment. (As we have seen, the great majority of prehensions are not conscious.) Thus God persuades rather than compels.

But there is here a danger of merely juggling with words; persuasion can be pretty compulsive, both in everyday affairs and in our relationsip with God. I earlier† quoted Professor D. D. Williams as suggesting "that Whitehead has underestimated the disclosure of the divine initiative in religious experience" and attributing this to the fact that "Whitehead has reacted so justifiably against [the idea of] the divine Monarch". Williams has also said "there are large coercive aspects in the divine governance of the world".‡ As to our human experience of God, part conscious and part unconscious,

* See the section on the Bible in chapter one.
† See p. 178 above.
‡ In his essay, "How does God act?" in *Process and Divinity*, p. 177.

God's persuasion can come near to compulsion simply because "the radical difference between God and us implies that our influence upon him is slight, while his influence upon us is predominant".*

Analogy with depth psychology suggests that God's influence upon us will be more beneficial to us if we accept the further truth that "God is the great companion – the fellow-sufferer who understands". For psychological therapy can begin only when the patient accepts that his troubles and tensions are not boring the psychologist, but rather that the latter's feelings are *affected*, and affected in some depth, by what is being recounted: only then can the psychologist's judgement and advice have any chance of being effective. In the same way, it may be as we come to accept that God not only cares but is *affected* by our feelings that we are best able to accept his judgement and "advice". It may here be significant that the Christians who have placed the greatest emphasis in their religion on the cross and passion of Christ have often been those who have most nearly equated Jesus with God: whilst intellectually holding to the "impassibility" of God, their emphasis on Christ's sufferings has enabled them to *feel* that God is affected by the world's weal and woe. This same analogy with depth psychology is perhaps reflected in Tillich's "accept that you are accepted by God, although unacceptable" and – in happier vein – in Hartshorne's "We enjoy God's enjoyment of ourselves".†

I have suggested that the twin concepts of God's persuasive influence and of God as "fellow-sufferer" offer a better basis for interpreting the central Christian belief that "God is love" than does much traditional theology. The more God is thought of as absolute and unaffected, the less the resemblance between his feelings for us and love as we know it in our human relationships: for the more one person loves another – be it marriage partner, parent, child or friend – the more he desires to be related to, and is ready to suffer with, that other.

The life of Jesus can be seen as the "chief exemplification" of man's acceptance of God's persuasive influence. The Christian belief that Jesus completely opened himself to God's will is expressed in Whiteheadian terms by saying that Jesus completely "prehended" God's influence, rejecting – that is, "negatively

* Hartshorne, *The Divine Relativity*, p. 141.
† *The Divine Relativity*, p. 141.

prehending" – none of it. Thus powerfully or "completely" prehended by Jesus, God became to a corresponding degree "objectively present in" – or *active through* – Jesus, so that the disciples came to sense the presence and power of God in the words and actions of their master. I have suggested that Jesus "prehended" God and learned his will primarily through deep, self-giving *prayer*, and through meditation upon the beliefs and scriptures of Israel.

If prayer was the main vehicle used by Jesus so closely to unite himself with God, then it is a vehicle of which we both can and should make use. Those who today seek to follow Jesus in the service alike of God and man will, perhaps, find the main practical advantage of process thinking to be the help it offers towards an understanding of prayer and worship as meaningful and intensely valuable activities.

As is well known, the value of these activities is today increasingly questioned both by Christians and by non-Christians. I therefore end this book with what attempts to be no more than an indication of how process thinking can help us to reinstate prayer and worship to their proper place – neither minimized nor exaggerated – within the whole context of the Christian life. A full treatment would involve an analysis in terms of process thinking both of traditional concepts of prayer and worship and of the valuable and increasing literature relating these to various aspects of the fast-growing science of psychology. I believe there to be a very great need for such an analysis, but – as was stated in the preface – any detailed examination of modern psychology needs a book to itself, and is outside our present terms of reference. Without such an examination there would be no value in any prolonged attempt to correlate prayer and process philosophy.

Prayer and worship

Two principal reasons for present doubts as to the efficacy of prayer and worship are the problems raised by psychology and – a largely separate issue – the increasing feeling among Christians that it is in the everyday life of the community, and not in activities involving an element of withdrawal, that they must both serve *and meet* their God. Thus Dr. Robinson says in *Honest to God* that he often finds little meaning in the sort of prayer that starts, so to speak, with God: he prefers to pray *through* the problems of daily life. And many today would join him in thus following the thinking of Dietrich Bonhoeffer.

No Christian would wish to deny that we are called to serve and to meet God in the problems of daily life, but most would also wish to affirm, as I would myself, the value – and the specific value as an aid to tackling our problems – of prayer, in the sense of asking and waiting for the help and guidance of the God whom we find, in one sense, *in* the problems of daily life – and, as process thinking urges, deeply affected by them – yet, in another sense, transcendent to these problems, and waiting to influence and guide us towards those solutions that best accord with his loving purposes.

Now it is integral to Whitehead's theory of prehensions that God and our problems deeply affect each other. In "prehending" God we "prehend" him whose "consequent nature" is affected by our problems, whilst his "primordial nature" is ever supplying just that "initial conceptual aim" which could lead to their best solution. Belief in prayer, in the sense just described, is belief that problems are often best solved tangentially via God, rather than directly: thus we "prehend" God in the context of the problem before we tackle the problem head on. Some would find it difficult to "prehend" or pray to God in the direct context of their problem, suspecting that the result would be a pondering upon the problem, with no more than a formal reference to God. They prefer to start their prayer by concentrating all their thought upon God and trying temporarily to forget themselves and their problems. They may simply "speak" with God, and wait upon him; or they may seek to "be still and know that I am God" by "prehending" God in the context in which his guidance and influence can most easily be observed, and what Tillich calls a "dependent revelation" can most readily be received, namely in the life of Jesus and of the New Testament Church. They would claim that such meditation both increases their sensitivity to God and often leads directly into guidance for the problems confronting them.

Process thinking can help us to find meaning and value in each type of prayer, for both our present problems on the one hand, and Jesus and his disciples on the other, have been "prehended" into God's "consequent nature". Whichever way we prehend or pray to God, we can indeed prehend, grasp at, and receive his guidance. In this context the words "pray" and "prehend" overlap, for whatever prayer is – I do not here seek to define it – "man thinks about God with the same mind as he thinks about, say, gardening":* Whitehead's theory of prehensions applies to prayer, and can make that activity at least slightly less mysterious. But beyond providing a basis for the elucidation of the nature of prayer, process thinking offers us a form of belief in the living God that can make prayer a meaningful activity in a way that seems likely to elude – indeed some sadly admit that it does elude – those who cannot believe in God as in any way transcendent to, or other than, ourselves and our world.

"It would be pointless to pray unless we had some belief in the reality of God and of His effective action in the world, some belief that our prayers could and would be answered. It is of course possible to say prayers without any formulated belief in God. But this is only a form of mental discipline and can scarcely be called prayer. Prayer is meaningless unless it is addressed to someone capable of hearing and of responding. It is an effort to enter into effective relationship with that being. The nature of the relationship we seek will depend upon what prompts us, that is, our particular need, and upon the ideas we hold about the God to whom we pray."

Contemporary doubts about prayer are even greater in the case of corporate worship, partly because the element of withdrawal is here more pronounced and partly, perhaps, because of the alleged misuse of public worship by some churchgoers, who appear to make it a substitute, and not a motivation, for an attempt at Christ-like living.

To say that the difference between *individual* prayer and *corporate* worship is precisely the difference between these adjectives is so obvious that there would be no point in saying it, but for the fact that many people use public worship as perhaps their only occasion for deep individual prayer. I am thinking in particular of the said Holy Communion service in the Church of England, of which it has been suggested that this is the nearest many Anglicans get to meditation. I am far from wishing to decry this practice: in an age when there is little weekday prayer in many Christian homes, acts of worship which are conducive to individual meditation fulfil an important function – but they are not truly *corporate* worship.

* This and the longer quotation that follows are from R. S. Lee, *Psychology and Worship*, (S.C.M. Press, 1955), pp. 25 and 76.

(This point is perhaps of sufficient importance in the present worship of the Church of England to merit a brief digression. I am myself a firm believer in the "parish communion", but I suspect that, in the increasing number of parishes where this is the principal act of Sunday worship, the clergy should always be careful to teach both the individual and the corporate aspects of worship, and should encourage people to come to said celebrations of communion as well as – or occasionally instead of – the parish communion. The worshipper whose weekday prayer is brief is in danger of shallowness in his personal religion if he attends only the parish communion. It is immensely important to meet at the Lord's table together with one's own and other people's children and toddlers – but there is also value in the quiet, meditative approach, with neither toddlers nor hymns).

The distinctive feature of corporate worship is the joining together in a common act of prayer and praise and self-offering. The meaningfulness and value of this derive from the case of individual prayer. The only further insight that process thinking offers in the case of corporate worship is its way of understanding the mutual strengthening that worshippers experience from this common act: I would stress that there are other ways; this mutual strengthening can also be understood in terms of the psychology of the group. The main value of process thinking in this field lies in its interpretation of prayer, rather than in any further insights as to corporate worship.

This thinking emphasizes the fact that every entity affects all other entities: we are all interdependent. Where a number of people are all doing their best to offer themselves to God and to "prehend" God, each will derive added strength from the fact that his neighbours are all doing the same: in prehending each other – which they do all the time, unconsciously perhaps if their attention is focused on the worship in progress – they are aware that the others, like themselves, are all prehending God. Individual prehensions are strengthened by being part of a corporate whole. That simultaneous prehensions strengthen each other can be seen in many fields – for example, an intense political meeting can excite or inspire even those who are not normally deeply concerned about politics; one can feel similarly "carried away" by being part of an enthusiastic audience at the theatre, or even at a sporting event. Such examples serve to underline the power and value that can reside in the mutual strengthening of those taking part in public worship, for our religious feelings are often among the strongest that we possess.

Corporate worship thus gives the worshippers a common focus; but there appears to be great value in having in addition some special focal point. There is often a feeling of great strength and power in the corporate prayer of the congregation at a confirmation or ordination, and at those weddings and baptisms where such prayer exists. In each case the promises that are made mark an important step in the individual's life and constitute – not least in the case of the marriage vows – a significant self-offering: this provides a sharp focal point for the prayer of the whole congregation.

The service of Holy Communion also provides such a focal point. A child will appreciate the fact that it contains movement and action; the instructed Christian will see this as itself focused upon a vital moment in the life of Jesus: his words as he broke the loaf at the Last Supper both demonstrated unmistakably to his reluctant disciples that he was shortly to be put to death and – if we accept St. Paul's version in 1 Corinthians 11 – ordered a continuance of this action as a renewal of their close fellowship together.

The present Anglican communion rite links Jesus' action with bread and wine exclusively with the Last Supper, to which his words "This is my body . . . This is my blood" clearly belong. But it may be that his action of breaking and blessing belongs also to many earlier meals of Jesus and his disciples. There is evidence that Jewish teachers and their followers often met together for regular "fellowship meals", which had both religious and social significance. It seems likely that Jesus and his disciples held similar mealtime meetings, whether formal "fellowship meals" or not, at which the element of close fellowship within their circle will have found strong and natural expression as, led by Jesus, they together turned to God in praise and thanksgiving and self-commitment. I stress this because it provides a valuable supplement to the primary linkage of the Holy Communion with the last supper and with Jesus' self-giving unto death. All down the centuries Christians have found in the Holy Communion both their principal means of receiving divine grace and also the strongest expression of their fellowship with each other. It is helpful to realize that both aspects have strong roots in the ministry of Jesus: at this vital moment in the last evening of his earthly life Jesus may have built upon a combination of prayer and fellowship which had already proved a powerful cohesive force in the life of his band of followers; he also greatly deepened its meaning by linking his words and actions so explicitly with his impending death.

Whatever the precise interpretation that may be given to them, the repeating of these words and actions of Jesus at the Last Supper, and the repeating of them in a setting in some way comparable to the gatherings of Jesus and his disciples, provides an extremely powerful focus for the thoughts and prayers of the worshippers. In the terms used in this book, the worshippers became powerfully aware of the presence of Christ – both crucified and ascended – within the "consequent nature" of God, which is the aspect of God that is available for them to "prehend", and into which God has everlastingly "prehended" what I have earlier called the total event of Jesus. As the worshippers both focus their attention on this key point of Jesus' self-offering to God, and are – or ought to be – especially conscious of belonging together in the corporate body of his disciples, so the total event of the life and self-giving of Jesus becomes very powerfully "alive" for them. Thus in the whole action of the eucharist the mutual strengthening that can occur in any act of public worship extends to include Jesus, so to speak, among and within the congregation. And so the God who was in Christ is powerfully felt and received in this, the central act of Christian worship.

If the worshippers are to derive strength from their awareness that their companions are also "prehending" God and offering themselves to him, this perhaps demands, as a prerequisite, at least *some* common ground of belief. I suggest that this applies to belief in God's *activity* rather than to any particular doctrinal belief about the nature or being of God: a common belief that there *is* a God who in some sense *answers* prayer is perhaps all the substructure that is needed. But I doubt whether Christianity as such will survive unless it also succeeds in maintaining that God is *other than ourselves* as well as within ourselves, for both the Christian understanding of Jesus and the nature of Christian worship depend upon this "otherness". Some who would hesitate to use the phrase "other than ourselves" can and do find meaning and value in Christian worship, but if *all* the worshippers took such a view the character and orientation of their worship would change beyond recognition.

But all prayer and worship is a means to an end, not an end in itself. I have somewhere read that when William Temple gave a series of addresses on the service of Holy Communion he used to end by ascribing maximum importance to the moment when the congregation go out of the church door and back into the workaday world. The Christian is continually seeking God's help in order that, in his own workaday world, he may in some sense follow the example of Jesus Christ. That example is a life of complete self-giving service: it is also, as I read it, a life rooted and grounded in deep prayer to, and communion with, the loving God in whom Jesus had so strong a faith. I greatly doubt whether, either as individuals or as a Church, we can get far in following the example of Jesus' life of service, unless we can also in some degree share in his life of faith and prayer.

The greatly widened panorama of scientific knowledge, combined with the sometimes exaggerated claims of both Christians and atheists, makes such faith and prayer peculiarly difficult for our generation. It is my prayer that this book has faced these difficulties, that it may be of some service in relating the living God both to the world in which we live and to the Master whom Christians strive to follow, and that its thinking may help us to share in his faith and prayer so that we may also share in his life of self-giving service.

"Teach us, good Lord, to serve thee as thou deservest; to give and not to count the cost; to fight and not to heed the wounds; to toil and not to seek for rest; to labour and not to ask for any reward, save that of knowing that we do thy will, through Jesus Christ our Lord.

Amen"

St. Ignatius Loyola

Some Suggestions for Further Reading

A Short List

A. N. Whitehead, *Adventures of Ideas*, Cambridge U.P., 1933 (paperback, 1961). *Process and Reality*, Cambridge U.P., 1929 (approx. 500 pp.; Part IV and some of part II could be omitted on a first reading; see also the Note below.)

Charles Hartshorne, *The Divine Relativity*, Yale U.P., 1948 (paper, 1964). *The Logic of Perfection*, Open Court, La Salle, Ill., 1962.

C. Hartshorne and

W. L. Reese, *Philosophers Speak of God*, U. of Chicago, 1953 (Phoenix Books, paper, 1963) (especially the Introduction, the long chapter seven, and the Epilogue).

L. Charles Birch, *Nature and God*, S.C.M. paperback, London and Westminster P., Philadelphia, 1965.

An Additional List

A. N. Whitehead, *Religion in the Making*, Cambridge U.P., 1926. *Science and the Modern World*, Cambridge U.P., 1926. *Modes of Modern Thought*, Cambridge U.P., 1938.

Ed. P. A. Schilpp, *The Philosophy of Alfred North Whitehead*, Tudor, New York, 1941. (This includes Whitehead's lecture on Immortality.)

J. B. Cobb, *A Christian Natural Theology*, Westminster Press, Philadelphia, 1965 (sub-title: "Based on the Thought of Alfred North Whitehead"); Lutterworth, London, 1966.

Introductions to Whitehead

W. A. Christian, *An Interpretation of Whitehead's Metaphysics*, Yale U.P., 1959.

I. Leclerc, *Whitehead's Metaphysics*, George Allen and Unwin, London; and Macmillan, New York, 1958.

V. Lowe, *Understanding Whitehead*, Johns Hopkins Press, 1963.

Ed. W. L. REESE and
E. FREEMAN, *Process and Divinity*, Open Court, La Salle, Ill.,
  1964 (The Hartshorne *Festschrift*).
Ed. G. L. KLINE, *Alfred North Whitehead: Essays on His Philosophy*,
  Prentice Hall, New Jersey, 1963.
Ed. I. LECLERC, *The Relevance of Whitehead*, George Allen and
  Unwin, London and Macmillan, New York, 1961.

The works of A. N. Whitehead listed above are also
published by Macmillan, New York.

Note

This list has no pretensions of completeness: it simply includes
those writings in the field of process philosophy all or part of
which I have found particularly helpful. I would add the
following, published since my book went to press:
D. W. SHERBURNE, *A Key to Whitehead's "Process and Reality"*,
  Macmillan, New York and London, 1966.

P.N.H.

Index

Entries relating to God or to Jesus are grouped together under these headings.